INFORMATION
SECURITY
IN
FINANCIAL
SERVICES

INFORMATION SECURITY IN FINANCIAL SERVICES

Ken Slater

M
stockton
press

Published in the United States and Canada by
STOCKTON PRESS, 1991
257 Park Avenue South
New York, NY 10010, USA

ISBN 1-56159-021-5

First published in the United Kingdom by
MACMILLAN PUBLISHERS LTD, 1991
Distributed by Globe Book Services Ltd
Brunel Road, Houndmills,
Basingstoke, Hants RG21 2XS

British Library Cataloguing-in-Pubication Data
Information security in financial services.
  I. Slater, Ken
  005.8
ISBN 0 – 333 – 54702 – 0

Typeset and printed in Great Britain

Contents

Acknowledgements

From the many enthusiasts who helped me with advice and encouragement I would like to single out the following:

Peter Ball, Home Counties Safe Co
Geoff Braithwaite, BACS
Bob Cale, Corporation of Lloyd's
Peter Damon, Canadian Imperial Bank of Commerce
Steve Dance, Lloyds Bank
David Davies, Hogg Insurance Brokers
Erik Guldentops, SWIFT
David Hall, Racal Chubb
Bob Holt, Registry of Friendly Societies
Brian Smith, SIB
Peter Sommer, Virtual City Associates
Ian Walden, Tarlo Lyons
Charles Welham, SWIFT

and a multitude of friends and colleagues from Touche Ross in the United Kingdom and DRT International offices around the world, including:

Peter Beale
Steve Daniels
Harry di Miao
Andrew Edwards
Jens Christian Elkjaer-Larsen
Sheila Gillis
Per Rhein Hansen
Siân Jones
Jonathan Killin
David Lang
Chris Loughran
Bill Murray
Eirik Kim Pedersen
Helen Pulm

John Reeve
Suzanne Schiller
Mark Tantam
David Walker

For Chapter 11.4 I am indebted to the following authors: F Hickman, J Killin, L Land, T Mulhall, D Porter, R Taylor, *Analysis for Knowledge-Based Systems: a Practical Introduction to the KADS Methodology* (Ellis Horwood, Chichester 1989) [1]; J Killin, *Combatting Credit Fraud with Knowledge-Based Systems in Compsec International 90: Proceedings of the Compsec 90 Conference* (Elsevier, London 1990) [2]; D Porter and R Taylor, *A Knowledge-Based System for Identifying Credit Card Fraud in Research and Development in Expert Systems VII: Proceedings of the Tenth Annual Technical Conference of the BCS SGES* (Cambridge University Press, 1990) [3].

I would also like to thank my wife, George-Anne, and our children, Loma and Mark, for their unflagging help and encouragement.

1 Introduction

1.1 The Scope of this Book

Over the past few years a number of well-publicised frauds have contributed to a sense of unease in the financial sector about the security of the information on which most of us rely. Most of these frauds have made use of a computer. However the vast majority were computer-assisted rather than direct attacks on a computer system, and were essentially old-fashioned frauds which could have been perpetrated with a similar effect in a non-computer environment. The result of these activities—a questioning of the effectiveness of existing security procedures—can only be seen from a long-term perspective as beneficial.

The defence against fraud lies in the existence and use of appropriate cost-effective security procedures. However, it is unrealistic to consider fraud in isolation from the many other problems which affect the efficient handling of computer systems—problems which can be dealt with by applying the same procedures.

Deliberate crime includes other, less intellectually stimulating, misdeeds. Accidents, errors and sheer sloppiness occur more often and can cost more than the occasional crime. It is logical—and cost effective—to consider all threats to an organisation and implement effective countermeasures.

Although many of these relate specifically to the IT environment it would be a mistake to consider computer security controls as the complete answer to the problem. Security of information demands a close scrutiny of organisational and procedural controls in a wide variety of areas which impact the information-processing functions. Physical security of the computer areas and associated offices must be foolproof, and the organisational structure must ensure an adequate level of supervision and separation of responsibilities. Similarly, controls over hiring and dismissal of staff must take into account the damage which can be caused by dishonest or disgruntled employees. The ideal environment from a security point of view—as well as many others—instils in employees not only an understanding of the necessity for security but also a belief that their personal well-being and satisfaction coincide with that of their employer.

It must also be remembered that all information is not provided by a computer: paper records, or even careless talk, can provide a medium for security breaches. Customers and staff of City wine bars are in a better position to assimilate sensitive information than the brightest of hackers!

This book is the first in a series describing security problems (and some answers to these problems) in specific business sectors. It will focus on the specific threats to security, and the possible results of security breaches, in the activities of the financial sector.

It is appropriate to refer to financial activities rather than financial organisations since definitions are no longer straightforward. Deregulation has meant that banking is not the sole preserve of banks. Many building societies provide a variety of banking services. Similarly, many large organisations whose primary trade is far removed from finance are now active in financial services as a by-product of the massive funds at their disposal. These can be invested or, alternatively, used to provide direct financial services to domestic or corporate customers. As a result the many regulations which have emerged have concentrated on the functions performed rather than the organisations performing them.

The financial sector has for some years been in an extraordinary state of flux primarily caused by two developments:

- changes in legislation;
- changes in the way that financial services are delivered to, and perceived by, customers; caused primarily by the availability of reliable, flexible and comparatively cheap systems.

The essential objective in any financial organisation is the effective management of commercial risk: making money by handling other people's money. In order to achieve this objective, high quality information and efficient transfer systems are needed, as is meticulous attention to customer relationships. It would not be a novel concept to point out that these aspects all depend on people; as in all other aspects of business, the following factors figure largely in ensuring effective security:

- choosing competent staff;
- training them properly;
- managing and supervising them effectively;
- providing them with the correct tools.

In order to safeguard investors and customers there are complex regulations dealing with the behaviour of a financial organisation in all its dealings. Each organisation is expected to be able to demonstrate:

- solvency (through capital adequacy requirements and financial regulation provisions);
- competence and honesty of the firm and each relevant employee. In practice, these comprise controllers and those directly engaged in giving financial advice or selling.

Although safety nets in the form of insurance policies and compensation schemes are available to investors in the event of insolvency, this is not an easy option since the rest of the industry must bear the costs of every failure.

Systems (in the widest sense) have to meet the various needs of the firm to enable it to attract and keep customer business, and to perform efficiently, safely and in accordance with the regulations in force. They also have to meet the needs of customers to transact business quickly, reliably and simply. These two sets of requirements may conflict at times, and need to be balanced. In this scenario security is a central requirement, not an after-thought. It can create a marketing advantage. However, the converse is that a security failure can be a commercial nightmare. Confidence, which is a major ingredient of commercial success (particularly in the financial sector), can be destroyed. Both commercial and regulatory requirements favour good security but need to avoid adding unnecessarily to costs or building in confusing complexity. Striking the right balance is a matter of judgment.

A description of the financial functions considered in this book is given below.

Banking
'The maintenance of adequate records and systems is a statutory criterion for authorisation under the *Banking Act 1987*' according to the *Bank of England Guidance Note* of September 1987 on Accounting and Other Records and Internal Control Systems. 'Records and systems', it notes, 'shall not be regarded as adequate unless they are such as to enable the business of the

Figure 1.1

REGULATION OF THE UK BANKING INDUSTRY

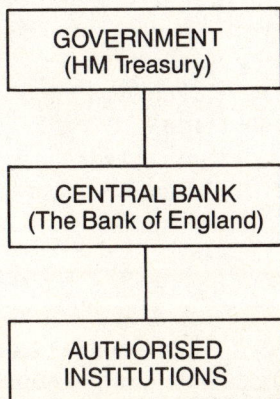

NOTE: An authorised Institution may be a UK Bank, a Licensed Deposit Taker or a Branch of an Overseas Financial Institution.

institution to be prudently managed and the institution to comply with any duties imposed on it by this Act.' From these statements flow wide-ranging requirements for many security-related activities which, if performed conscientiously in the past, could have prevented many of the frauds committed in the last few years.

In order to enable the international banking community to fulfil their main functions (lending, bank operations, financial, treasury), complex IT services are required, supported by a number of communications networks. Each will have an internal network supporting its basic functions and satisfying a number of internal requirements, ranging from word processing and office automation to complex decision support mechanisms. The banks' global operations can be consolidated to ensure effective management of financial risk via their own international networks or using a commercial supplier such as GEIS.

The banks' networks will also make use of a number of specialist external networks and services such as the electronic funds transfer systems which serve specific sectors of the banking community. Examples of these are given later in this chapter.

The use of electronic funds transfer networks and message-switching facilities requires great emphasis to be placed on security, both within the networks and at the sending and receiving banks.

In retail banking the use of ATMs, point of sale banking transactions and cash management services to individual and corporate clients is expanding rapidly, increasing the potential for fraud.

Securities and Investment Services
In the months preceding the passing of the *UK Financial Services Act (1986)* many thousands of man-hours were spent in the City of London in reading the draft rules of the Self Regulatory Organisations (SROs) to be set up by the Act and attempting to interpret the implications of their requirements on information processing systems. Many of these covered security tasks which, although common practice in many installations, were anathema in others. Wide-ranging statements such as The Securities Association (TSA) requirements for systems of internal control, a full audit trail and procedures for preserving the privacy of records forced IT management to consider aspects which many had managed to avoid thinking deeply about in the past. Similar requirements can be found in the regulations of the other SROs, although many are less explicit.

TSA and Association of Futures Brokers and Dealers (AFBD) merged on 1 April 1991 to form The Securities and Futures Association in order to harmonise the ways in which they discharged common regulatory functions. Any avoidance of duplication is welcome and hopefully this co-operation will increase among the SROs.

In addition to the SROs the SIB also supervises the activities of the following bodies:

- Recognised Professional Bodies (RPBs) such as the Law Society and accountancy bodies;
- Recognised Clearing Houses (RCHs);
- Recognised Investment Exchanges (RIEs).

A chart showing these is provided in Figure 1.2.

Figure 1.2

THE UK FINANCIAL SERVICES ACT
STRUCTURE OF THE REGULATORY FRAMEWORK

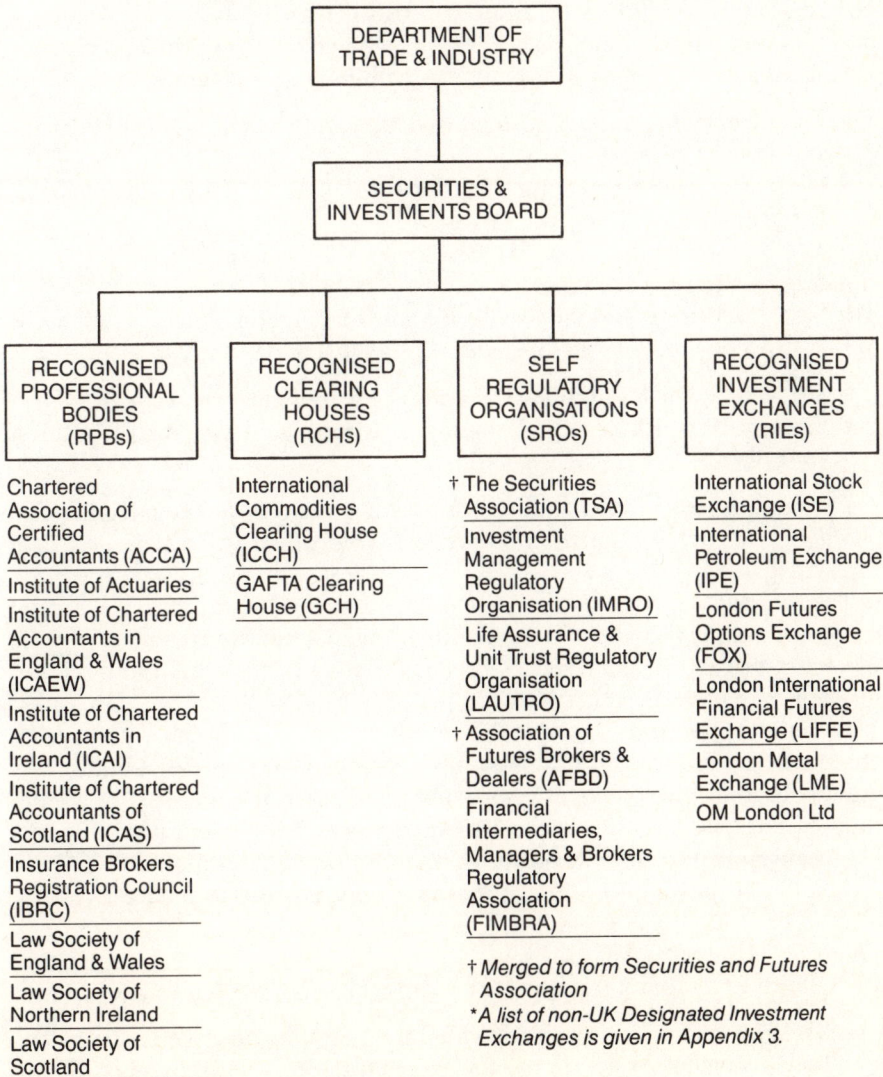

```
            DEPARTMENT OF
            TRADE & INDUSTRY

            SECURITIES &
            INVESTMENTS BOARD
```

RECOGNISED PROFESSIONAL BODIES (RPBs)	RECOGNISED CLEARING HOUSES (RCHs)	SELF REGULATORY ORGANISATIONS (SROs)	RECOGNISED INVESTMENT EXCHANGES (RIEs)
Chartered Association of Certified Accountants (ACCA)	International Commodities Clearing House (ICCH)	† The Securities Association (TSA)	International Stock Exchange (ISE)
Institute of Actuaries	GAFTA Clearing House (GCH)	Investment Management Regulatory Organisation (IMRO)	International Petroleum Exchange (IPE)
Institute of Chartered Accountants in England & Wales (ICAEW)		Life Assurance & Unit Trust Regulatory Organisation (LAUTRO)	London Futures Options Exchange (FOX)
Institute of Chartered Accountants in Ireland (ICAI)		† Association of Futures Brokers & Dealers (AFBD)	London International Financial Futures Exchange (LIFFE)
Institute of Chartered Accountants of Scotland (ICAS)		Financial Intermediaries, Managers & Brokers Regulatory Association (FIMBRA)	London Metal Exchange (LME)
Insurance Brokers Registration Council (IBRC)			OM London Ltd
Law Society of England & Wales			
Law Society of Northern Ireland			
Law Society of Scotland			

† Merged to form Securities and Futures Association
*A list of non-UK Designated Investment Exchanges is given in Appendix 3.

Insurance

In addition to the many regulations imposed on the insurance companies, brokers and underwriters and the Corporation of Lloyd's itself, the business requirement for assurance of confidentiality is paramount.

Details on which premium calculations are based may be extremely personal or sensitive from a business point of view, while information regarding past and present claims could severely affect the reputation of the claimant if it fell into the wrong hands. Equally important is the need for this data to be accurate at all times (retaining its integrity), while loss of system or data availability could severely compromise the insurer's credibility. The insurance industry is founded on 'utmost good faith', a concept which imposes duties not only on the insured but also on the insurer, who would lose business very quickly if believed to be incompetent in any of the above areas.

Insurance companies in the United Kingdom are regulated:

- for solvency by the Department of Trade and Industry (DTI) under the *Insurance Acts*;
- in their marketing activities by the regulators set up by the *Financial Services Act*.

Building societies

The basic security requirements which apply to Building Societies in the UK are covered by the *Building Societies Act (1986)*, particularly:

- Section 45 which describes the criteria for prudent management;
- Section 71 which covers Accounting Records and systems of business control.

The implications of the Act for information systems have been detailed in a *Building Societies Commission Prudential Note* which will be described in Appendix 14.

The societies' activities in giving investment advice, acting as tied agents of insurance companies and transacting investment business are subject to the *Financial Services Act*, the security requirements of which are also discussed in Appendix 14.

As building societies' activities have diversified, other requirements have emerged. Those whose business has expanded into areas traditionally monopolised by the banks are now subject to the relevant banking regulations, while the increasing use of ATM networks has created new potential for technical exposures which in turn require new countermeasures.

A diagram showing the regulatory framework is given in Figure 1.3.

Financial IT Services

In addition to a variety of in-house systems, IT services used might include:

- SWIFT (the Society for Worldwide Interbank Financial Telecommunications), which provides financial message transfer services to more than 80

Figure 1.3

THE UK BUILDING SOCIETIES ACT
STRUCTURE OF THE REGULATORY FRAMEWORK

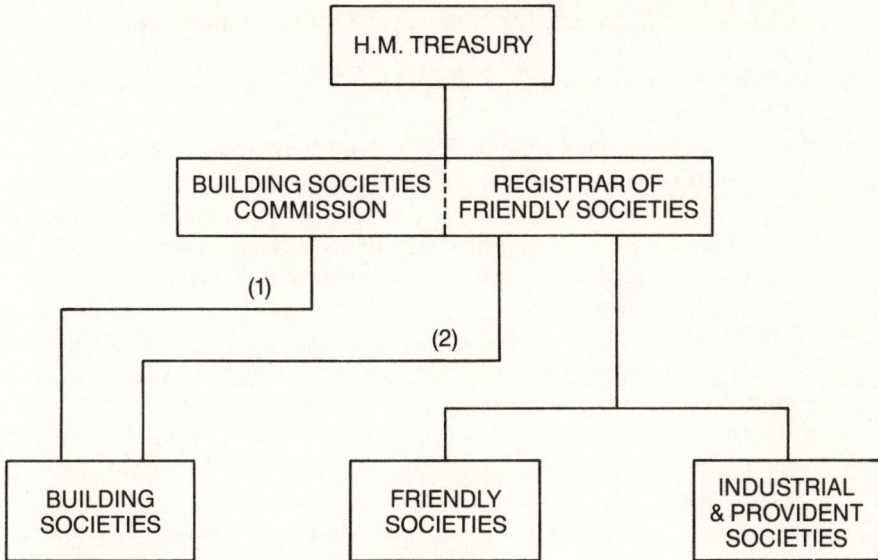

```
                    ┌─────────────────┐
                    │  H.M. TREASURY  │
                    └─────────────────┘
                             │
        ┌───────────────────────┬───────────────────────┐
        │ BUILDING SOCIETIES    ┊   REGISTRAR OF         │
        │     COMMISSION         ┊  FRIENDLY SOCIETIES   │
        └───────────────────────┴───────────────────────┘
              (1)
                              (2)

  ┌──────────────┐      ┌──────────────┐      ┌──────────────────┐
  │  BUILDING    │      │  FRIENDLY    │      │   INDUSTRIAL     │
  │  SOCIETIES   │      │  SOCIETIES   │      │  & PROVIDENT     │
  │              │      │              │      │   SOCIETIES      │
  └──────────────┘      └──────────────┘      └──────────────────┘
```

(1) Responsibilities related to prudential supervision
(2) Responsibility for procedural matters

countries. A description of the security features of SWIFT and its successor, SWIFTII, is given in Appendix 1.

- CHAPS (Clearing House Automated Payment System), the UK electronic interbank system which transmits guaranteed sterling payments for same-day settlement from one settlement bank to another. For a brief description of CHAPS security features readers should refer to Appendix 12.
- CHIPS (Clearing House Interbank Payments System) is a private telecommunications payment service, operated by the New York Clearing House Association, which handles payments in US$ for banks in the New York Area.
- FEDWIRE is a payment service operated by the US Federal Reserve System as a private network for transfers between financial institutions having accounts at the Federal Reserve Bank.
- SAGITTAIRE (Système Automatique de Gestion Integre par Teletransmission de Transaction Avec Imputation de Reglements Etrangers): an electronic interbank payment service operated by the Banque de France within France for SWIFT members and sub-members located in France. The service handles French franc payments only.

- Central Gilts Office (CGO) system, developed jointly by the Bank of England and the Stock Exchange, which handles the daily settlement of gilt-edged (bonds) transactions for market makers, money brokers, discount houses and settlement banks. The Stock Exchange X25 packet-switched network (IDN) is used to transmit data between IBM PCs in the participants' offices and the Tandem TXP mainframes controlling the system.
- the Mint network, which links the ATMs of the Midland Bank, Natwest and TSB.
- home banking systems such as TSB's Speedlink and the Bank of Scotland's HOBS (Home and Office Banking System).
- systems which provide services to businesses. As an example, Lloyds Bank's Lloydslink offers business customers a range of services such as: balance reporting and forecasting; trade finance documentation; international payments facilities.
- EFTPOS (Electronic Funds Transfer at Point of Sale). After the premature conclusion of the EFTPOS UK pilot test in April 1990, the attempt to provide a common national system was abandoned in favour of schemes run by individual, or groups of, financial institutions. Among these are: Switch, set up by Natwest, Midland and the Royal Bank of Scotland, whose users now include the Yorkshire Bank and an increasing number of Building Societies; and the Barclays/Lloyds Visa payment system.

  EFTPOS UK is now concentrating on developing a clearing system for electronic payments, leaving the financial institutions to compete for business. A common backup service is available, which goes some way to support the contention that the national system was technically viable although inappropriate to the commercial requirements of competing financial institutions.
- TAURUS, when implemented, will be operated by the International Stock Exchange, providing electronic share ownership and transfer facilities. Changes of ownership will take place electronically by transfer from the account of the seller to that of the buyer. Taurus will be fully integrated with the Talisman system, by which share transactions are reported, confirmed and settled.
- The French Cartes Bancaires Network, which provides on-line authorisation and total compatibility between financial institutions throughout the country. Nearly all French banks and other institutions, including commercial and savings banks, the Post Office Bank, Crédit Agricole and Crédit Mutuel are subscribers.
- The Link national cash network, formed from the amalgamation of the original Matrix and Link systems is used by an increasing number of UK building societies in addition to banks and other card issuers such as American Express.
- BACS (Bankers Automated Clearing House) was established in 1968 as

an inter-bank clearing facility to process automated payments and direct debits. These were originally submitted on magnetic media but now increasingly via BACSTEL by direct telecommunication channels. For many years BACS has taken a significant role in the British banking system, and it has been estimated that more than 85 per cent of salaries in the UK are now processed through the system. BACS is also used for payment of, among others, the following: insurance premiums; hire purchase and loan instalments; bills from gas, electricity and other utilities; subscription and membership fees; rent, community charge and mortgage repayments; suppliers' invoices, expenses, interest, dividends and annuities. Appendix 13 provides a description of the controls and security measures BACS employs to minimise error, duplication of processing and fraudulent misuse of the system, and some details of the security measures required from the customer.
processing and fraudulent misuse of the system, and some details of the security measures required from the customer.

After spreading a measure of alarm and despondency the following chapters will describe methods of analysing and assessing the potential effects on the victims (organisations and people), and the methods by which the risks can be reduced to a manageable extent. The fact that there is no such thing as perfect security is a truism, although the tendency to use this statement as an excuse for doing nothing must—to put it mildly—be avoided (see Figure 1.4). It is possible to provide a close approximation to complete control, but only by introducing procedures which will severely inhibit business activities at a cost which is, in most cases, unnecessarily high. Experience has shown that in general 80 per cent of a 'perfect' security environment can be provided at around 20 per cent of the cost, and that the Law of Diminishing Returns applies from this point. Since the remaining 20 per cent may consist of security measures over non-sensitive data, or duplicate the effects of existing activities, it is essential to determine the practical security requirements for each system and data type and install only those which are relevant, practical and cost-effective.

Most security measures depend to some extent on the actions of a human being, and human beings (another truism) are fallible. Since risk will never completely disappear the security specialist and the security-conscious manager are engaged in risk reduction. All successful business, particularly in the financial sector, relates primarily to the management of risk, and the installation of the appropriate 'mix' of security measures can be seen as yet another aspect of this.

1.2   A Definition of Information Security

The accepted definition of information security refers to the need to ensure that:

Figure 1.4

A SELECTION OF MANAGEMENT VIEWS

Alibis – spoken and (unspoken)

● No system can be 100% secure (so I won't do anything)

● Security must be cost effective (I won't do it unless it is cheap)

● We shouldn't over-emphasise computer security – there are other aspects (I won't do anything about the other aspects either, thus proving my consistency)

● I can trust my staff one hundred per cent:
   – (I hired them, so my judgment is suspect if they are crooked)
   or
   – (they are all members of my family)
   or
   – (they know where the bodies are buried)

● I have much more important things to think about than security (I've just received an offer of another job and I'm about to resign).

- access to information is restricted to authorised people (confidentiality);
- data is processed completely and accurately (integrity);
- information is available at all required times (availability).

Using this definition we can see information security to be concerned with the following issues, primarily—although not completely—related to computing:

- privacy of confidential data and software;
- protection against unauthorised use of computer systems and equipment;
- assurance that authorised work is correctly processed and transmitted to the intended recipient;
- protection of stored data and software from corruption, loss or deliberate amendment;
- continuation of processing in the event of a hardware or software breakdown.

Most security people can quote examples where one, some or all of the above security aspects were unavailable. Some examples are given below:

a) A fire at the Open University's computer centre destroyed not only the premises and computer equipment, but also—and more importantly— the disks holding the results of years of research. A combination of luck, dedicated work and the use of some previously-untried techniques enabled the engineers at the DEC factory in Germany to recreate the data. However, any number of factors might have rendered this impossible.

Can you suggest ways in which this crisis could have been avoided?

b)   A consultant working in the Data Preparation Department of an American bank learned the password needed to authenticate telephoned transfer instructions. He then requested, by phone, a transfer of over $10 million from a customer's account to an account he had opened under an assumed name in another bank. After transferring the money from this account to another bank he used it to buy diamonds. His problems commenced only when he attempted to sell the diamonds. The potential buyer had never seen him before, assumed he had stolen the diamonds, and contacted the police. If the jeweller had been less suspicious the bank's money would have been lost.

How could the bank have avoided this?

c)   A Data Processing manager read an advertisement in his local newspaper which offered computer-calculated biorhythm charts to applicants who phoned a certain telephone number after 6.30 pm. The number was that of his office telephone. On reflection, he realised that he was well known for leaving the office at 6.00 pm every night.

Security should not depend on a detailed scrutiny of the local newspaper. How could he have avoided the situation?

d)   Every computer user has situations in which output from the computer system is incomplete or incorrect.

This can be caused by, among other things: incorrect input; operator error; system error; machine fault.

How can this be avoided?

Readers who enjoy a good horror story should derive some pleasure from Appendix 11, which describes a number of computer-related frauds in financial organisations—unless they were involved in picking up the pieces!

Although our broad definition of security only takes a few words, the techniques used to achieve security are many and varied. Since security always costs money we must be careful not to over-control. From the many categories of security to be described in this book, it is necessary to select those techniques which together will provide a level which is correct for the data, for the system and for the organisation.

1.3   A Practical Approach to Risk Assessment

Computer security can be big news: a bank fraud, for example, or hackers breaking into a government system. The reality is usually less noteworthy, but just as damaging to those affected.

It is also unpredictable, which makes it difficult to know what risk you run and what you should do about it. What are the chances of a disgruntled employee destroying your accounting files? or of an electrical fire in the computer room? Insurance is available against some losses, but money cannot replace lost business records, or customer confidence and goodwill. The solution is to be protected properly in the first place, but this is not a simple task.

Why Does It Matter?
Think about the role that computers and data communications play in your business. What would happen if:

- you could not use your computer for hours, days or weeks?
- you could not rely on computer output being even approximately correct?
- your competitors could read your files?

No organisation can—or would want to be—completely secure against all threats. The costs would be prohibitive and the benefits minute. Some risks are so unlikely that they can, for all practical purposes, be ignored—provided that the decision to ignore them is based on a genuine assessment. Others may have little effect on the business however many times they occur. It is also necessary to be aware that there are many ways of skinning a cat! The hi-tech, expensive answer may suit the requirement, but the solution may also be achieved by a simple, inexpensive alternative. Cost-effectiveness must always be considered.

Understanding the Risks
No one installs controls or takes security measures for their own sake. In order to assess the level of security required it is necessary to identify the risks which apply to the specific installation and its systems. Once the risks have been identified it is necessary to assess the cost, in financial or other terms, which would be incurred if they took place. This is often performed by a simplistic financial calculation based on two factors:

- the number of times a given risk is likely to occur within a year;
- the cost of one occurrence.

Multiplying the cost by the frequency of the risk creates a figure known as Annual Loss Expectancy (ALE). However valuable this is in some circumstances it cannot be considered infallible. If an installation has never had a fire it will be impossible to provide an accurate assessment of the number of times per year in which a fire can be expected. It is necessary, therefore, to consult statistical tables for the number of occasions per year on which a computer room fire is expected to happen worldwide or within a particular country. However, this is of little value to the specific organisation, which may never have a fire or, on the other hand, may have one tomorrow.

This method can create some odd results. As an example, a data entry error which may take place thousands of times a year at a comparatively low cost per transaction could produce a greater financial risk to an organisation than a fire, which might occur statistically once every 50 years.

Many of the estimates of probability are based on inadequate statistical premises, while the costs are, in many cases, based on unreliable generalisations. The results of such calculations do not generate information of a quality which would be acceptable as the basis of other equally important management decisions.

In some circumstances the ALE calculation, however imprecise, can be useful in assessing the order of priority of each risk to the organisation. If this is considered to be impractical the risks can be allotted a priority level such as:

1. High probability, high cost;
2. Low probability, high cost;
3. High probability, low cost;
4. Low probability, low cost.

A more practical method of allotting priorities, which does not depend on probabilities but uses the judgment of experienced management and staff to identify the dangers to which the organisation may be exposed, is suggested in this book.

Security measures and controls invariably cost money and it is important not to over-control. Since all businesses have different requirements the first stage of a security review must be to consider the type of risk to which the business would be exposed in the event of a security breach. A further level of investigation will identify risks which apply to individual data types and computer systems, since each may have different levels of criticality and exposure.

There are a number of methods—ranging from the highly formal to the extremely informal—of documenting risks and their allied controls. Regardless of the methods used, an essential feature of this process is knowledge of the fundamental threats which face the organisation and the types of loss which will result from inadequate controls in each area.

It will then be necessary to assess the effectiveness of existing security measures, and to identify the need for additions or enhancements. The security measures could be provided by:

- physical devices;
- procedures;
- software packages;
- application or system software coding;
- the organisation of the business.

Even in the most technical environments, security measures are not solely technical. They will typically be found in such varied areas as:

- departmental and business organisation;
- personnel recruitment, training and control procedures;

- physical security over access to premises, and measures which inhibit destruction of equipment;
- logical access control software;
- password control;
- software development and maintenance procedures;
- purchase, use and maintenance of equipment or packaged software;
- operations and network control;
- authorisation, encryption and key management;
- job control and scheduling.

The security requirements of most organisations will require a combination of measures from each of the above categories. The ideal approach to security is one in which the failure of one aspect does not leave data or systems completely unprotected—another security measure should take the strain (see Figure 1.5).

'You should never spend more to decrease a risk than tolerating it would cost you.'
Courtney's Second Law.

Figure 1.5

SECURITY LAYERS
THE 'ONION SKIN' APPROACH TO SECURITY

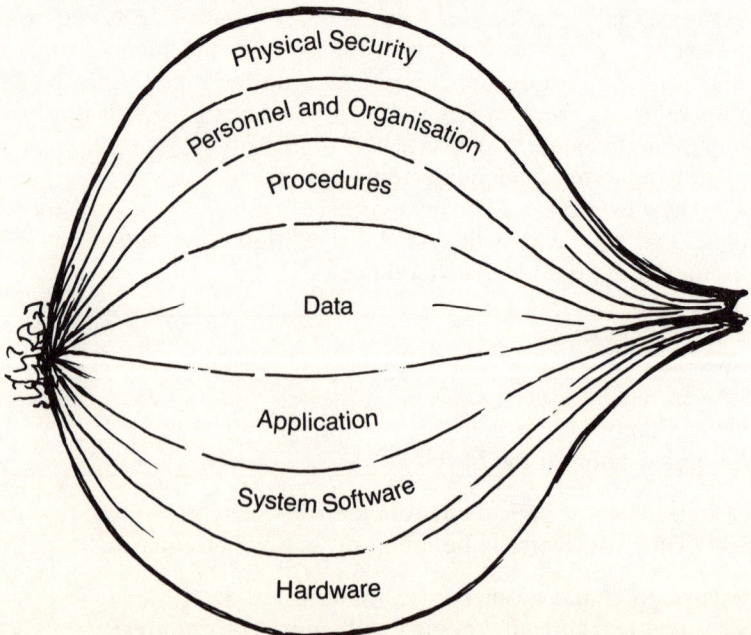

Physical Security

Personnel and Organisation

Procedures

Data

Application

System Software

Hardware

1.4   IT and Security: A Five-Minute Guide

The use of computers has revolutionised the administration of many organisations. Continuing technical innovations have ensured that each year more businesses reach the stage where they are unable to operate effectively without computer technology. In addition costs have decreased, enabling the smallest businesses to consider the benefits they could gain from automating some of their procedures.

However, although there are undoubted benefits from computerisation, new problems have also arisen—and continue to arise! The introduction of large mainframe computers created some new security problems and aggravated many of those which already existed. Among the new problems faced were the following:

- methods of processing changed, creating a series of complex systems which were difficult for non-specialists to understand. This complexity led to the concentration, in the hands of a small group of people, of the knowledge necessary to create and modify systems. Reliance on this group of specialists created a new risk, yet many users gave up the struggle to understand their computer systems.
- physical centralisation of processing power created a risk which would not have occurred previously—complete loss of all processing in the event of an accident in a comparatively small physical area.
- as clerical tasks previously performed by humans were taken over by computer program instructions, the 'common sense' checks performed as part of these tasks disappeared. The programmed controls which replaced them were less easy to understand, and often less effective.
- in many cases, as some managements gave up the struggle to understand their computer systems, supervisory controls faded away.

Gradually many organisations began to understand the changing nature of security and control in the new environment, and to apply commonsense measures to their centralised computer installations and systems. However, once these controls were applied the technology changed again, and it has been changing continually ever since. One of the major irritations suffered by security specialists is the fact that the technology never remains in a static state long enough to identify appropriate countermeasures. As the technology develops, new risks emerge and existing risks change their form and impact. No sooner were security procedures developed for mainframes than new concepts began to appear. Some of these (not necessarily in historical sequence) are:

- timesharing;
- artificial intelligence;
- databases;
- distributed processing;
- microcomputers;

- networks;
- electronic mail and EDI;
- prototyping methods of systems development;
- electronic funds transfer (EFT);
- fourth generation and object-oriented languages;
- information centres.

The introduction of each new concept resulted in new methods of computer abuse as well as increasing the possibility of existing abuse. The security problems could have been anticipated and, in many cases, avoided during development if designers and users had understood the security requirement. In many cases this was the last thing on their minds.

Technical development is not the only reason for change. Most businesses have a need to alter their organisations periodically. A survey undertaken in 1977 attempted to identify the ways in which business computer systems were changing. The conclusion was that 'the present trend is for organisations with centralised systems to decentralise, and for organisations with decentralised systems to centralise.' The same 'trend' still applies, except that some of the organisations which changed in one direction in the 1970s have now reverted.

The following IT trends are typical in most advanced business organisations:

- the increased importance of information as a primary resource;
- recognition of the cost of information as a major business investment (it has been estimated that 67 percent of wage costs now represent information-generating activities);
- threats to the privacy and reliability of information are increasing as computers and telecommunication systems distribute information and provide easy access to data;
- a glut of information threatens our ability to understand and control business activity.

Each of these has increased the importance of achieving a true understanding of the nature of corporate information, the risks posed by the information and the essential security measures.

In many organisations the above developments resulted in an attempt to reduce vulnerability. However, the approach was often haphazard, directed only to those areas where results were visible, such as physical access controls, fire security measures or data backup/storage procedures.

Other organisations have viewed security requirements from:

- a purely 'application' point of view, designing controls into systems operating in an uncontrolled environment; or
- a technical standpoint, ignoring the important organisational, procedural and human aspects.

The view that security can be achieved merely by using technical measures—such as access control packages or encryption devices—is a common misunderstanding. Nothing could be more misleading: controls which are not managed effectively do no more than encourage complacency. Again, the extent of reliance on key technical staff is often not fully appreciated, either in terms of their role in keeping systems running or their ability to alter or delete information.

In many cases a complete lack of management commitment has rendered an expensive security initiative ineffective. In others, management concentration on only one aspect (usually related to the most recent problem) can unbalance the security effort. Budding security officers, or anyone who wishes to address security effectively, must be aware that senior management may only have a limited view of their problems. They will dismiss carefully-constructed, comprehensive security policies, standards and procedures with a comment such as: 'I haven't time to go into that. Will it solve the problem of viruses?' (or whatever the flavour of the month is at that time). It is essential to educate management away from this attitude.

It is far less common for a full and comprehensive review to be undertaken, covering all related areas ranging from policy/managerial aspects to the detailed technical and clerical procedures needed to achieve an acceptable level of security.

In most IT departments a picture postcard can be found on a wall or notice board containing a motto such as 'How can I think of draining the swamp when I'm up to my armpits in alligators?' This book should assist business managers and IT staff in:

  – appreciating the major risks to which they may be exposed ('getting to know the alligators');
while, at the same time;
  – achieving an understanding of necessary security measures and the methods by which they should be implemented ('draining the swamp').

2 Risk and Vulnerability

2.1 What can Happen?

The introduction to this book described information security issues as:

- privacy of confidential data and software;
- protection against unauthorised use of computer systems and equipment;
- assurance that authorised work is correctly processed and transmitted to the intended recipient;
- protection of stored data and software from corruption, loss or amendment;
- continuation of processing in the event of a hardware or software breakdown.

From this statement it is possible to identify the major risks faced at any computer installation:

- unauthorised access to data and programs;
- corruption or loss of stored data and programs;
- unauthorised use of computer systems and equipment;
- incorrect processing or transmission of authorised work;
- breakdown of equipment or unavailability of staff;
- failure to satisfy legal or regulatory requirements.

The major causes are:

- crime;
- accident (often accompanied by its stablemate, indolence);
- the requirements of new or amended legislation.

2.2 Computer Crime

Although this phrase usually brings to mind the more glamorous aspects of computer fraud the more mundane or senseless crimes must still be guarded against.

2.2.1   Theft of Data
Data which is commonly used in an organisation (such as lists of all clients, debtors or those granted special privileges) can be valuable to competitors. The security of 'spoiled' output must also be considered—a printer error in the last page of a report could lead to the entire report being discarded and its disappearance from the waste-bin might go unnoticed, regardless of the importance of the data to a competitor or the media. It should be emphasised that the data stolen may not be printed, micro-fiches, PC disks and cassettes being even easier to hide, while any standard briefcase can hold a 2400' reel of tape.

2.2.2   Theft of Equipment
As hardware becomes smaller and more compact it becomes more attractive to a potential thief. Complete microcomputer configurations can disappear, and the enthusiast who already has a personal computer can defray his costs considerably by 'liberating' his employer's peripherals or consumables.

2.2.3   Service Theft
Although the use of the computer to print pictures (of varying degrees of propriety) might be allowed, employers are less likely to be tolerant of illicit commercial use of the computer centre as a bureau. The DP Manager who was lucky enough to recognise his own office telephone number in a newspaper advertisement was the exception—security procedures must ensure that illicit usage is reported.

2.2.4   Property Crimes
It is possible, by manipulation of stock, purchases or sales systems to misappropriate property—the electronic equivalent of goods 'falling off the back of a lorry.'

2.2.5   Fraud
A narrow definition of the term 'computer fraud' would only include frauds committed using the computer as an accomplice by manipulating programs and data files. This definition is unnecessarily restrictive, since many computer-related frauds simply reflect the increasing use of computers—they would be equally possible in a manual system. Successive Audit Commission reports on computer fraud found that most reported frauds were simple changes to input documents. It is possible to take this at face value or conclude that:

- the more complex frauds were not reported;
- the more complex frauds had not been detected.

2.2.6   Sabotage
Two organisations 'Direct Action Organisation of March 27–28' and 'Comité de Libération Ou de Détournement des Ordinateurs' (CLODO) claimed

credit for a number of bombings and arson attacks on French computer centres in 1980–81. Although no one was hurt over £1 million worth of damage was done.

In the period between May 1976 and December 1978 groups of terrorists attacked nine installations in Italy, causing an average of $1 million worth of damage at each. Different names have been used by the groups but they are all believed to be members of the Red Brigade, an organisation which has declared computer installations and personnel to be primary targets.

In 1972 the Belfast Co-operative Society premises were destroyed by a terrorist bomb causing £10 million of damage. In common with the rest of the building the computer centre was gutted, and equipment and data and program files completely destroyed.

The potential for legitimate industrial action in computer centres is limitless and has already been exploited in the United Kingdom by a number of trade unions. A less legitimate action during a strike was the deliberate sabotaging of an American insurance company's processing by staff who transmitted signals which inhibited its remote terminals from printing details of data processed. No data was lost, but the information flow at 25 offices was blocked for a month.

2.2.7 Mischief

A generation of intelligent, computer-literate 'hackers' is now engaged in attacking the security features of computer and communications systems, accessing—and in some cases changing—data and programs as an intellectual exercise. Some have been caught, others (such as the German Chaos Computer Club) have cheerfully 'claimed credit' for their activities, which they claim are needed in order to expose weaknesses in security.

However, there must be others who are competent enough to avoid capture but act from different motives to those who publicise their activities. Discussion of the numbers involved is irrelevant. The only answer is the incorporation of effective security controls.

2.3 Computer Accidents

Although public attention tends to focus on deliberate crime, unintentional accidents are much more common and, if allowed to occur, can cause as much loss as the activities mentioned above. Accidents, which can cause problems ranging from a major catastrophe to the temporary disruption of a hardware unit, can be categorised as follows.

2.3.1 Hazards

Many natural hazards (such as flooding, earthquake, sand and electrical storms) relate to the geographical position of the computer centre.

Fire is an obvious hazard which is considered, to a greater or lesser extent, in most installations. Explosions or riots directed at neighbouring organisations can create 'accidental' disruption of facilities. Power failure is a common hazard. Less common now is the 'surge' produced by switching off powerful machinery, which could corrupt the contents of a neighbouring computer's memory.

2.3.2   Malfunction

The malfunctioning of computers, peripherals and other essential machinery—such as air conditioning equipment—must be considered and guarded against. Breakdown of communication lines, while not harming the computer(s) directly, can substantially degrade the service provided by a complex network.

Software will break down, usually at the least convenient time. It is essential to be aware of the different categories of software:

- applications systems;
- operating systems;
- database management systems;
- teleprocessing software;
- utilities.

Each are similarly vulnerable to accidental malfunction or deliberate manipulation. However the security measures needed by each may be quite different.

2.3.3   Personnel

The human being is probably the most fallible factor in the system, and steps must be taken to ensure that recovery from all possible operator errors can take place.

The vulnerability of an organisation to industrial action by computer staff has already been referred to. As a general rule the more centralised the processing facility, the simpler it is to disrupt.

In every DP installation there are individuals who are indispensable by virtue of their technical or business knowledge. The increasing dependence of user departments on the 'one man band' responsible for their microcomputer extends the problem. The loss, or even temporary absence, of these key staff can disrupt the organisation's business as effectively as deliberate action.

2.4   The Effects of Legislation

All computer installations are affected by aspects of current legislation which may be expanded and amended as time passes. It is essential to be aware of the changes which affect the organisation. In addition to the relevant sections of the more general regulations relating to employee conditions and security DP management, staff and auditors in the UK must be aware of their responsibilities under the *Data Protection Act (1984)* and the *Computer Misuse Act* (1990). In the financial sector, the security implications of the *Financial Services, Banking and Building Societies Acts* must be considered, as must the penalties for non-performance.

Any of the above could occur in most organisations. However the extent to which each problem can become a tragedy depends to a large extent on its vulnerability which, in turn, is caused by ineffective or non-existent security measures.

A practical, effective security mechanism can only be achieved as the result of a careful analysis of the relevant risks and vulnerabilities, performed by a broad-based group of people with the necessary experience in the business activities, IT and security.

2.5   The Consequences

We have already referred to activities such as fraud, deliberate erasure or corruption of data and obtaining confidential information. The effects of some of these activities on commercial and financial organisations have been copiously documented. The consequences of similar activities on the computers used for health care, research and the nation's defence are also receiving publicity.

Military computer systems and networks have also suffered disruption of service. In some cases these were caused deliberately, while in others (perhaps more frightening) accidental disruption occurred when a hacker overestimated his understanding of the target system.

Evidence given to the Scottish Law Commission during the preparation of its report No. 106 (July 1987) referred to incorrect diagnosis and treatment resulting from amendments to health care information. Other examples included the effects of tampering with the systems controlling the operation of a nuclear reactor. The necessity for foolproof, comprehensive security procedures in such environments is obvious. The corresponding requirements in the financial sector relate to loss of business, goodwill or money—but are just as important to the well-being of the bank, insurance company or securities trader involved.

Every business organisation, while reviewing the risks to its operations, will finally need to ask the paramount question: so what? If any of the security breaches so far explored should, in fact, occur it will be necessary to understand the bottom line. To what extent will any of these occurrences affect the well-being of the organisation? The effects of each on a business may range from the irrelevant to the catastrophic, and an informed opinion must be reached before considering the need for security measures.

The most obvious effect is financial—loss of money or the need to spend more money to replace lost resources, assets or facilities. There are many others which may have indirect financial implications but require other aspects to be considered. Examples are:

- loss of existing or future business;
- loss of reputation, goodwill or public confidence;
- penalties imposed on organisations or individuals in the event of contravention of laws or other regulations. (These range from financial sector legislation—such as the *Financial Services Act*—to more general regulations such as the *Health and Safety Act*);
- even, in extreme circumstances, injury or loss of life.

One example of the loss of confidence which may be caused by knowledge that a system could be breached relates to the use of computer-produced evidence. The *UK Police and Criminal Evidence Act (1984)* will allow a computer-produced document to be accepted as admissible evidence in a criminal case provided that it is certified that there are no reasonable grounds for believing it to be inaccurate because of improper use of the computer. Uncertainty over the system's accessibility would mean that witnesses would lack the confidence needed to confirm the report's accuracy, and the evidence could be rejected.

2.6   Unauthorised Access to Computer Systems

In 1989 the English Law Commission defined the main types of computer misuse as:

- computer fraud;
- unauthorised obtaining of information from a computer;
- unauthorised alteration or destruction of information stored on a computer;
- denying access to an authorised user;
- unauthorised removal of information stored on a computer.

Each of these activities can cause serious harm to computer users; recent examples in the United Kingdom and abroad have seriously affected the activities of commercial and governmental organisations. Attempts have been made to categorise each as a crime using existing laws. However, it should be noted that each can be achieved by hacking into a computer or communications network, an activity which was not a crime in the United Kingdom until 1990.

In the absence of any other crime, hacking can be seen as similar to trespass, while its simplest development is analogous to eavesdropping. Neither of these is a crime *per se* in the United Kingdom, although:

- trespass will often contain an element of criminal damage;
- the *Interception of Communications Act (1985)* and the *Wireless Telegraphy Act (1949)* criminalise many of the means by which eavesdropping is achieved.

A number of public and private sector organisations which had suffered from unauthorised access attempts were surveyed by Touche Ross Management Consultants in 1989.

Although the resulting data can certainly not be seen as a statistically-relevant sample of computer crimes, some valuable information was collected, including the following:

- Large financial losses (attempted thefts of money) were invariably prosecuted. However where costs (even quite high costs) were incurred due to a need to correct data corrupted by employees, victims preferred to deal with the matter internally.
- When evidence of browsing was found, data owners did not contact the police because they knew (at that time) that no crime was involved. The victims almost unanimously shared a sense of unease; in many cases the files read were extremely sensitive, but the victims were unable to quantify the effect of the security breach.
- Costs incurred in recreating corrupt data could be extremely high where data was not regularly copied for backup purposes, or where recovery procedures were inadequate or non-existent.

The survey replies were analysed as follows:

	%
Hacking	49
Employee exceeding access authority	36
Virus	5
Combination of the above	5
Other	5

The police were not informed in three out of every four cases. The following reasons were given:

	%
Victims preferred to deal with the matter in-house	47
Victims believed the police were not capable of dealing with it	32
Culprit's activity was not an offence	18
Other	3

In most cases of hacking, evidence of the breach was found after the event, but very little evidence was found of what had occurred after entry. All systems produced logs of system activities, but they were not always monitored or even retained.

On the limited evidence of the survey, the typical hacker browses, then changes data or programs—sometimes on purpose, sometimes by accident.

3 The Security Policy

3.1 Introduction

The major components of a balanced security programme are:

- existence of a comprehensive security *policy*;
- development and implementation of detailed security *procedures*;
- a method of *monitoring* compliance with, and the results of, such procedures.

The above elements are all essential. The security policy is the foundation of all security activities in an organisation. Procedures which do not relate to an overall security policy will be irrelevant in many cases since the policy is the link between management's business objectives and the day-to-day security objectives. The implementation of individual procedures before a policy is agreed could be counter-productive and dangerous. The activity involved in installing ad hoc procedures over a limited area can sometimes breed over-confidence, generating a short-sightedness which fails to see other risks to the organisation. On the other hand, a policy without well-monitored procedures will be toothless.

The contents of the security policy will develop and evolve throughout the life of the organisation, since any significant change in business or the use of IT will require a review and possible update. Although comparatively short it must cover all aspects of Information Security, albeit at a high level. It will provide a brief, wide-ranging series of statements describing management's view of the security requirements. It must be unambiguous and become the basis of the detailed procedures which will then be installed and monitored in each relevant area.

3.2 Format and Contents

The format of the policy will vary from organisation to organisation, since it must relate specifically to the business priorities of each. It need not be long or detailed—the detail will be provided by the procedures. An information security policy for an organisation in the financial sector will typically include the following:

1) Introduction

- Why security is needed.
- The organisation's overall stance on security.

This section will contain a description in broad terms of the threats to the organisation, with an indication of the possible effects on:

- its owners;
- its employees;
- its customers;
- the community.

It may also be appropriate to provide guidance on the way in which security is viewed at board level. Statements such as: *it is the board's policy to trust its employees unless evidence is received to the contrary*; and *it is the board's policy to dismiss all offenders* are rather extreme attitudes at opposite ends of the range of possibilities. Both have been used in practice (by different organisations!) but there are many alternatives. The choice will obviously depend on the corporate atmosphere as well as the consequences of security breaches.

2) Objectives and Scope of the Policy
A concise high-level statement of the overall security objectives containing, at the most, three sentences. If more words are required this could be a sign that inadequate thought has been given to the subject. The objectives should be unambiguous, memorable and clear.

Considerable thought must be given to the scope of the policy. Although restrictions may appear to be undesirable, the areas in which the policy will be observed must be unequivocally agreed at the outset. Without this agreement detailed procedures cannot be produced or enforced. A total corporate security policy covering data, funds, buildings and other assets would produce an efficient and viable security function. However, this may not be immediately acceptable to the board, who may wish to concentrate initially on IT Security (or information security, which has a broader definition). The policy must ensure that everyone understands the agreed ground rules.

3) Policy Statement
The policy statement should cover briefly the organisation's approach to the security of (among other aspects):

3.1   Operations and custody of IT equipment;
3.2   Systems development and maintenance;

3.3 Telecommunications;
3.4 Acquisition of hardware and software;
3.5 Procedures and documentation;
3.6 Organisation, premises and environment;
3.7 Personnel;
3.8 Third party services: Facilities Management; Bureaux; Development services; Value Added Data services;
3.9 Contractual relationships: with vendors/suppliers; with customers;
3.10 Contingency Planning.

These brief statements will be the raw material from which the detailed procedures will be produced.

4) Allocation of Security Responsibilities
This Section will allocate the responsibilities for the different aspects of security, including those responsible for:

- determining the policy;
- agreeing the procedures;
- reviewing policy and procedures;
- identifying necessary changes to security measures;
- monitoring compliance with policy and procedures.

5) Method of Classifying Security Levels of Data
A method of classifying data must be determined with takes the sensitivity of each item into account. The management responsible for this data will allocate an appropriate classification to each item. Each classification will attract a different level of procedures.
Examples of useful classifications are:

- Confidential;
- Sensitive;
- Restricted;
- Unclassified;

or:

- Client-Sensitive;
- Internal-Sensitive;
- Unclassified.

6) Regulatory Requirements for Data Security
Each of the laws and regulations with security implications which apply to the organisation will be listed here with the name and function of:

- the employee responsible for ensuring compliance;
- the name of the authority responsible for surveillance.

Examples would be:

Regulation	*Surveillance body*
Data Protection Act	Data Protection Registrar
Banking Act	Bank of England
Financial Services Act	SIB, SROs
Building Societies Act	Building Societies Commission
Professional Bodies and Regulatory Organisations' rule books	Various

7) Description of Methods by which Observance of Security Measures will be Monitored

The detailed monitoring mechanism may not yet have been agreed. At policy level it is sufficient to identify the organisational group which will be responsible for policing security, together with an indication of its reporting structure and supervision level.

8) Appendices

These may include:

I.   Description of the assets and functions to be protected;
II. Data owner, custodian and user responsibilities.

4 Personnel Security

4.1 The Extent of the 'Problem'

The major asset of any organisation, as well as the source of many of its potential problems, is the people who work for it. It is necessary, therefore, to:

- provide an environment which will encourage and assist staff to contribute to the well-being of the firm;
- design the necessary controls and sanctions in case they do not.

The people employed by the organisation are the key to all security measures. They must be relied upon to maintain and operate effective security procedures — not only when management are watching them but all day and every day!

Anyone can make a mistake, and the consequences of these must be contained by effective security controls. More worrying — and increasingly frequent — are malicious acts of sabotage or fraud. Both are most likely to occur if a low chance of detection is coupled with a lenient approach after detection.

Psychological studies suggest that the population can be broadly divided into three groups:

- 25 per cent are completely honest;
- 25 per cent are completely dishonest;
- 50 per cent are opportunists — they would commit a crime if they were adequately motivated and felt they could get away with it.

Although this analysis is necessarily simplistic it is sufficient to make the blood of a security-conscious manager run cold — if he is one of the honest 25 per cent! However, the odds can be lessened by reducing the opportunity to commit crimes and increasing the possibility of detection.

The security program must have the support of staff to be effective. Security measures must not alienate them or lose their sympathy. This is largely a matter of presentation and good staff relations, but also requires each security procedure to be relevant and simple to perform.

If the honest 25 per cent can be persuaded of the need for security, their support will be invaluable in providing the peer-group pressure necessary to win the 'hearts and minds' of many of the waverers from the 'opportunist' group. As security procedures are found to be effective, the rest of this group should find that the potential for committing fraud and escaping the consequences rapidly diminishes.

The dishonest 25 per cent will—hopefully—be deterred, prevented or detected by security controls.

Management attitudes to security are crucial. If there is a casual approach (for example, to the use of company resources) at the top, this is sure to filter down.

A clear policy must be established by management to be applied to every detected fraud. It must not be forgotten, however, that the law is a strange animal. No matter how clear the evidence appears to the layman, it may not be sufficient to establish the basis for a prosecution, or to win a verdict if the case goes to court. Many fraud prosecutions result in a failure to convict, and belief that there is only a small chance of conviction may deter the authorities from taking a case to court.

However, consideration of fraud, while extremely interesting, can often divert management from other 'people' aspects of security:

- deliberate sabotage caused by boredom, frustration and even psychotic behaviour;
- errors and carelessness caused by inadequate training, inappropriate staff or general lack of motivation.

An enlightened attitude to staff motivation which ensures that employees continually identify their own best interests with their employers' success, and that all are given tasks appropriate to their abilities and self-esteem, makes sense from a security point of view. It could also mean the difference between commercial success and failure.

To quote one expert: **'Where you have above-average management, above-average security is a logical consequence.'**

4.2 Effective Security Procedures

The security policy and procedures must therefore take into account the dangers of employing IT staff who are dishonest, disgruntled or merely incompetent. Organisations are becoming increasingly dependent on their computing facilities, and the human beings are, as usual, the weakest links. To ignore them, or to trust them blindly, is to invite a disaster of gigantic proportions. Below is a list of some of the aspects to consider.

1) Recruitment procedures should be designed to ensure, as far as possible, that staff are competent and honest. References should be obtained, and always checked.

2) A probation period should be used in appropriate cases to verify competence.

3) Security awareness is a key security measure which must be encouraged. Awareness programmes should be implemented for all employees, included in induction procedures and regularly reinforced by circulars, briefing sessions and workshops. Staff with specific security responsibilities must be carefully trained, with appropriate follow-up when necessary, and their performance monitored.

4) Salary and incentives should be appropriate to the responsibilities of the staff concerned—this should ensure that the interests and objectives of employers and employees coincide!

5) A comprehensive, practical training programme will encourage employees to consider career development within the organisation, and avoid the demoralisation caused by lack of achievement.

6) Staff appraisal and review procedures can, given a certain amount of mutual goodwill, help to ensure that potential difficulties are resolved at an early stage. However, if not properly conducted they have been known to create problems rather than solve them. Great care is essential in this area.

7) Dismissal and resignation procedures must take into account the damage which can be caused by a dishonest or disgruntled employee while serving a period of notice.

8) Staff—particularly those with 'hands-on' responsibilities—should be obliged to take their annual holidays. Failure to take any leave usually displays a need to be continually near the system. It is often when a perpetrator is away that a fraud is detected.

9) Employees should be provided with information on a 'need to know' basis, and dissuaded from giving information to unauthorised personnel.

10) Monitoring and effective supervision is essential.

11) A policy of prosecuting offenders should be enforced.

12) All security responsibilities and activities must be documented in a manual which should be held by, or easily accessible to, all members of staff. The manual should also include the security policy and the name of a person to contact in the event of queries or problems.

13) Job descriptions which unambiguously describe each employee's duties should be provided. These should include his/her security responsibilities and, in order to deter potential breaches of the *Computer Misuse Act (1990)* should define the boundaries of the employee's responsibility and activities.

14) Separation of duties—ensuring that no person has sole responsibility for any activity—should be the accepted policy in every area of corporate work. This principle may be applied, for example:

- in the computer room, where work is scheduled and controlled by separate personnel from those who operate the computer;
- in a data entry section, where sensitive transactions may be set up by an operator, to be initiated after authorisation by a supervisor;
- in a Purchasing Department, where the person who raises an order is not the person who authorises payment of the subsequent invoice;
- separate individuals should specify, program and test changes to computer systems;
- while computer operators will run the software which makes changes to live data, this will only take place on specific documented instructions by users and subject to monitoring by their supervisors.

Rigorous application will assist not only in the prevention of fraud but also in the detection of errors.

15) A related problem is that of the 'one-man band'. IT experts perform a valuable service, often providing long hours of enthusiastic effort to improve their employers' systems, motivated only by interest in the challenge set by their work. Management, who have other pressures and probably do not share their all-consuming interest in IT matters, are usually inclined to leave them to their work, providing a minimum of direction or supervision. They often feel that, since this is not their area of expertise, there is no reason for delaying or restricting the activities of the specialists.

Unfortunately there are major risks in this approach. The 'one man band' is valuable and may very well be potentially indispensable. However, management must be able to answer the following questions:

- How would you know if he/she sabotaged or manipulated computer systems out of a desire to make an illicit profit, or from mere malevolence?
- How would you cope if he/she was dismissed, resigned with a minimum of notice—or even died?

Even staff who are trusted implicitly may receive a better offer from another organisation.

In order to avoid the exposure which would be caused by the activities, or withdrawal, of one talented individual these employees should be identified and given special attention by management. Reserve staff must be trained as soon as practicable in order to reduce the organisation's vulnerability.

Figure 4.1

ORGANISATION AND PERSONNEL CHECKOUT

1. Is the Information Technology Department independent of other functions in the organisation?

2. Is the separation of duties in the IT department sufficient to ensure sound control?

3. Does an up to date organisation chart exist indicating the functions and reporting responsibilities of all IT staff?

4. Are the duties and responsibilities of each member of the IT department detailed in Job Descriptions?

5. Within systems development, are the following segregated:
   (a) application testing from systems design and programming?
   (b) systems software programming from application programming?

6. Are the following functions organisationally separate from any of the above and from each other:
   (a) quality assurance?
   (b) the database administrator?

7. Are the following functions segregated from other operational and control activities:
   (a) the media library?
   (b) software control?

8. Is segregation maintained during sickness, vacations, shift or weekend working?

9. Are the working conditions and terms of employment of computer staff adequate to maintain high morale and staff loyalty?

10. Do recruitment policies ensure so far as they may that the staffing of the IT department is stable?

11. Are references for prospective employees followed up?

12. Are all the years and months of an applicant's career accounted for before offering employment?

13. Do controls ensure that personnel do not work additional hours without authority and effective supervision?

14. Is there a system of employee review, evaluation and development? Is it believed to be productive by both management and staff?

Figure 4.1 cont'd

ORGANISATION AND PERSONNEL CHECKOUT (cont'd)

15. Do staff training procedures ensure that satisfactory efforts are made to develop staff out of their known weaknesses?

16. Are staffing levels adequate for the tasks to be performed?

17. Is annual leave monitored to ensure that operations and development staff take their entitlements?

18. Are dismissed personnel required to leave immediately?

19. Is consideration given to ensuring that a member of staff who resigns should also be required to leave immediately?

20. Are there standby staff for key positions?

21. Are access badges and other materials returned by staff who leave the organisation?

22. Are passwords held by staff who leave immediately cancelled?

23. Is a conscious effort made to maintain good staff relations?

24. Are employees sufficiently qualified and trained to perform their tasks effectively?

All security procedures must apply not only to permanent employees but also to temporary staff, contractors and employees of other firms (such as maintenance engineers, catering staff and cleaners) while on the premises.

5 Physical Security

5.1 Introduction

An expensive selection from the variety of technical security measures can be ineffective if the elementary principles of physical security are ignored. This statement appears to be self-evident, and yet many organisations fail to heed it. The reasons for this lapse are many and varied, but stem mainly from the well-known ITSEJ ('It's Somebody Else's Job') syndrome. Office and building safety and security responsibilities were allocated, in many cases, to the officials responsible for building management many years before the introduction of electronic methods of data processing. The gradual introduction of IT, and the need for appropriate levels of security over the storage and processing of electronic data, have been seen as unconnected to the day-to-day problems of building safety, physical access control and surveillance. In many cases a division of responsibilities developed, where control over the central computer room and areas housing its ancillary equipment was delegated to an IT Security Officer while control over the rest of the building and the environment remained the responsibility of others. In itself this was not a problem, but, combined with a lack of formal liaison between the two functions and—in many cases—a lack of understanding of each other's priorities, it provided the basis for many of the security breaches which have occurred. Misunderstandings over the limits of each official's responsibilities created the potential for mischief, and in many cases the opportunity was eagerly grasped—to the disadvantage of the organisation.

The potential for causing damage to information systems if physical security is inadequate has increased recently. Even if an organisation has a central computer installation, microcomputers now hold large amounts of sensitive data in widely-dispersed parts of the building. The computer suite can rarely be seen as the only part of the building where critical processing is taking place. In some organisations there is no central computer room, processing taking place at a number of widely-dispersed sites linked to each other by communications networks which are themselves considerable sources of risk.

The enhanced levels of physical security required originally for the central computer room need to be applied in many cases to the entire building. The risk of potential exposure in the financial sector means that suspension or dilution of security measures in any part of any building needs to be fully justified, and its impact on the rest of the organisation formally analysed. The onus must be placed firmly on those who wish to diminish security.

Ideally all security should be the responsibility of a single group. If this is not possible, detailed objectives, duties and procedures must be agreed for the separate functions, and effective liaison mechanisms set up. Security must be seamless, with no gaps or misunderstandings which can be exploited by fraudsters, saboteurs or careless employees.

Many of the security measures described in this chapter are expensive, and none should be incorporated until a comprehensive Risk Analysis has identified an appropriate requirement. Many organisations have no need to install security measures which would be essential at Fort Knox. On some critical sites the full range of security measures—a brick-walled fortress without windows, but with all the trimmings—would be found to be essential; while more frequently, at the lower end of the scale, basic access control and fire resistant cabinets would be satisfactory. Reaching the correct decision needs information—and this will be provided by the Risk Analysis.

5.2 Building Location and Design

If the building has not yet been designed, a number of factors related to its location and construction need to be considered. The extra comfort provided by the features described below will be considerable. Some of these can be incorporated after construction is complete, although the cost and effort will, of course, be greater.

When considering the location of the building its vulnerability to a number of potential exposures should be considered. These can be caused by:

- natural hazards, such as flooding caused by rivers, faulty sewers or inadequate drainage;
- the neighbours; check on the existence in the vicinity of:
  - dangerous sites such as fuel stores, chemical plant or timber yards;
  - gas mains or other pipelines;
  - electricity pylons, radar establishments or other producers of emissions which may interfere with processing or transmission;
  - public footpaths or rights of way, which may allow curious or malevolent passers-by access to the premises;
  - flight paths;
  - high profile, contentious organisations such as research or military establishments which might attract demonstrations or saboteurs;
  - high levels of vandalism;
- inadequate or easily-interrupted power, telecommunications, water or other supplies.

The location of police, ambulance and fire services should be confirmed, and an assessment obtained of their capacity, experience and ability to deal with the emergencies which could occur in the proposed building.

A central computer installation should, if possible, be surrounded by buildings owned by the same company. A 'sterile' perimeter should be created around the building and car parking should be forbidden within a reasonable distance. CCTV cameras will enable the activities of anyone entering this space to be monitored.

The nature of the building may be disguised by omitting its function from signs and directories. A continuous secure wall around the perimeter will provide a deterrent and this should be enhanced by security cameras and/or alarms.

Good external lighting will help to deter attacks on staff or buildings at night in addition to alerting guards or outsiders of potential attacks.

The need for standby communications, power and other facilities must be considered when designing the building. The site may require two (or more) independent communication lines to the local telephone exchange. The possibility of accidents, industrial action and load shedding at peak periods may need an evaluation of methods for providing standby power. A UPS (uninterruptible power supply) unit—which will guarantee a constant, precise voltage, irrespective of fluctuations in the mains supply—could be incorporated. This will take over if the main power supply fails, and in a severe emergency allow the system to close down in a controlled manner.

The alternative power supply should be sufficient to provide power not only for the computer but also any necessary air conditioning, lighting and associated equipment.

The construction of the areas containing computer and ancillary equipment, and those used to store data should be of sound construction, using fire-resistant materials. Precautions against fire and other natural disruptions should be incorporated, including alarm systems and automatic extinguishing systems.

Computer and communications equipment should not be sited below the ground, since they would be vulnerable in the event of flooding.

Automatic fire detection equipment should be installed in any space where a fire could develop or spread undetected, such as communications cable housing.

If the computer installation is not in a separate building the offices should be structured in such a way that all stairways, lift and entrances can be monitored.

There should be as few entrances and exits as possible, provided that safety regulations are complied with. The building should be segregated into zones on a 'need to access' basis which will provide a basis for the access control methods described in section 5.6.

The computer room should ideally have no windows, and this must be taken into account when considering the level of lighting required. If windows

Figure 5.1

SITE CHECKOUT

1. Is the site of the installation away from such public hazards as:
   - (a) gas mains and other pipelines?
   - (b) national grid pylons?
   - (c) rivers or low lying areas subject to flooding?
   - (d) other hazards, e.g. oil storage tanks, volatile chemicals, timber yards, etc?
   - (e) a location vulnerable to terrorist attack (e.g. above a car park, on display from the street)?
   - (f) location on a flight path?

2. Is the computer centre building physically remote from the other activities of the organisation?

3. Is the computer centre sited away from the areas of public access such as main roads, footpaths, car parks, etc?

4. If the installation is not in a separate building are the offices so structured that all stairways, lifts, and entrances can be monitored?

5. Has an assessment been conducted of the locations of emergency services, and their ability to deal with the types of emergency which may be expected?

---

are required, care should be taken to ensure that they are not overlooked by casual passers-by and that they are constructed using strong, opaque glass and secure, resilient frames.

Toughened glass can withstand a normal amount of wear and tear. However, a sharp blow by a hard object travelling at a reasonable velocity can shatter it, while a second similar blow will empty the shattered glass from the frame, causing possible damage to anyone trapped on the other side. Wired glass will delay the process. Laminated glass, although not totally attack-proof, will take some time to penetrate.

In an 'open' environment (such as a bank or building society branch) consideration may be given to a 'fast rising' screen in which heavy telescopic steel screens rise quickly from a counter recess to the ceiling.

Power and communication cables and underground services such as gas and water must be protected as carefully as the facilities inside the building.

5.3 Precautions against Fire, Flooding and other Hazards

When assessing the fire risk, one must consider three aspects; the types of media to be stored, the severity of fire that may be suffered and the likelihood of building collapse.

Paper is the least vulnerable of the media, beginning to char at 170°C and usually becoming unreadable after 200°C. Computer tapes, Winchester and other hard disks are much more vulnerable, their safe temperature being no more than 60°C. The most sensitive items are computer diskettes which can distort and become unreadable at as low a temperature as 50°C.

The severity of the fire will depend on the type of building and its contents. For example, the protection needed in an office over a furniture showroom will need to be of a much higher standard than one in a concrete and steel industrial environment.

If storage is to be in a part of the building that is liable to collapse, then the protecting cabinet must be strong enough to withstand the damage. It should also protect against the sudden increase in heat that could arise if the cabinet falls into an established fire—a potentially explosive situation.

Precautions against Fire

1) Fire precautions in the computer area should include:

   a) heat and smoke detectors in all appropriate locations (including floor spaces, where the greatest combination of wiring is to be found);
   b) fireproof doors and fireproof partitioning;
   c) a regularly tested, satisfactory alarm system;
   d) a regularly practised, satisfactory fire drill;
   e) fire fighting equipment, such as: fire blankets; automatic fire extinguishing systems; hand extinguishers.

2) Heat and smoke detectors should be connected to internal security and the fire authorities premises.

3) All fire prevention and fire fighting equipment must be regularly serviced and checked by the manufacturers.

4) Electrical power must be automatically isolated before the fire extinguishing system operates.

5) All areas must be kept free of combustible material and 'No Smoking' rules rigorously applied.

6) Detailed fire instructions must be displayed prominently and understood by all staff.

7) Rehearsals of all emergency procedures must take place on a frequent, but irregular, basis. Any inadequacies during these drills must be taken seriously, and the necessary steps taken to ensure improvement.

Once started, a fire can be made worse by combustible elements in the environment. The space under the raised floor of a computer room may

Figure 5.2

FIRE CHECKOUT

1. Are there adequate fire precautions in the computer area including:
   - (a) Heat and smoke detectors?
   - (b) Fireproof doors and fireproof partitioning?
   - (c) A regularly tested, satisfactory alarm system?
   - (d) A regularly practised, satisfactory fire drill?
   - (e) Fire fighting equipment, such as:
     - (i) fire blankets?
     - (ii) automatic fire extinguishing system?
     - (iii) hand extinguishers?

2. Are heat and smoke detectors linked to security and fire services?

3. Is all fire prevention and fire fighting equipment regularly serviced and checked by the manufacturers?

4. Is electrical power automatically isolated before the fire extinguishing system operates?

5. Are all areas kept free of combustible material?

6. Are detailed fire instructions displayed and understood by all staff?

---

collect the paper discarded from stationery during printing, and this ignites readily. Examples such as this illustrate the apparently self-evident fact that cleanliness and good housekeeping procedures are potent security measures.

The materials used in ceiling fittings such as ventilation grills and light diffusers should be made of material which is not easily combustible, since a fire in the void above a suspended ceiling may not be detected for some time.

Advice should be sought from the fire authorities on the stock of hand-held fire extinguishers required, their disposal and maintenance.

The smoke and heat detectors should, unless cancelled in a short time, activate a fire suppression system. These are usually of three types—water, CO_2 or Halon, although a new development produces a fine mist of water droplets which seems to combine the advantages of all types. A description of the features of the gases used for fire suppression is provided in Appendix 4.

Health and Safety requirements when gas flooding systems are installed include:

a) suitable warning notices at all entrances;

b) provision for manual operation from outside the area;
c) discharge system to be switched to automatic on leaving the area.
d) where human beings are present mechanisms are required which inhibit automatic discharge.

However the last requirement can be circumvented; automatic systems are usually allowed in occupied areas if there is a time delay after the alarm is sounded to allow employees to leave.

Other Natural Hazards
In an earlier section the need to allow for natural hazards in the design of the building was introduced. If the building already exists it is important to identify, assess and control any risks which cannot be avoided. Consideration must be given to the risks of flooding from:

- rivers or other external sources, such as water mains or blocked drains;
- burst waterpipes, washroom overflows and other internal accidents;

A 24-hour call-out contract with a plumber could also be useful.

Figure 5.3

NATURAL DISASTER CHECKOUT

1. Have all flood risks been allowed for in the development of the computer centre? If not, what are the risks and how are they being tackled?

2. Have appropriate safeguards been incorporated in the procedures to cover potential damage from fire protection efforts?

3. Has consideration been given to the possibility of flooding from burst waterpipes, washroom overflows etc?

4. Has the risk, if any, from storm been evaluated and catered for?

5. List the other natural disasters to which your environment could be exposed. Have the necessary safeguards been adopted?

5.4 Media Storage

A wide variety of robust storage methods are available for safe storage of operational, backup and archive tapes and disks. They must, of course, be fireproof, but must also provide protection from other hazards, such as:

- water (including the damage produced by fire-fighting procedures);
- dust;
- humidity;
- magnetic fields;
- electrostatic damage;
- burglary.

As a general rule, tapes or disks holding critical data or software must be as safe while being stored as they are when being processed.

All aspects of the fire risk are reflected in the major international fire tests to which reputable cabinets are subjected. The most severe of these are the Underwriter's Laboratories Test (UL) in the USA and the VDMA test from Germany. In these tests, the cabinet is loaded into a furnace at room temperature and tested for periods of one and two hours.

The cabinet is held in the furnace for one or two hours, depending on the test chosen, and the internal temperatures measured by thermo-couples. The cabinet is removed and dropped nine metres onto a bed of rubble to simulate a fall through two or three floors of a collapsing building. It is then replaced in the furnace for a further period of heating.

In the VDMA and UL tests, the cabinet is not then immediately removed from the furnace. This simulates the condition where, in an actual fire, it may have to lie in the hot rubble for some hours. It is left in the furnace, with the heating turned off, until the temperatures inside the cabinet reach their maxima and stabilise.

As a contrast, Swedish and Japanese tests specify that the cabinet should be removed and cooled down immediately the test period is completed; a significantly less severe exposure.

To simulate the explosive effect of sudden heat rise that could result in a building collapsing, the cabinet (in a separate test) is placed cold in an already preheated oven, and the effect of rapidly expanding gases observed.

The effect of fire-fighting efforts on equipment and stored data must also be taken into account. Computer equipment can suffer more from the water or chemicals in fire extinguishers than from the fire itself, although pure water will not permanently damage major hardware components. In addition, the contents of fireproof safes have often been spoiled by the methods used to fight a fire.

In the past, heavy metal safes incorporating two aspects have been used to deter the twin threats of burglary and fire. Because the outer lining must be made of heavy, thick steel to resist physical attacks, while fire resistance requires the steel to be as thin as possible to prevent conduction of heat to the inside, the traditional method is to build a fire resisting safe inside a burglar resisting outer cabinet. The result, in many cases, was a safe so heavy that only specially-strengthened floors could take the weight. Recent developments in modern engineering plastics have been used to produce lighter safes which are almost as hard as diamond (to withstand cutting implements) while providing a high level of resistance to fire. Although these safes cannot at present be used for computer media, they can be extremely useful where sensitive or valuable paper records are held.

5.5   Equipment failure

There are two major safeguards against equipment or supply failure:

- *preventive:* effective maintenance and support;
- *corrective:* alternative facilities.

The performance of all equipment must be monitored in order to pre-empt failures. Legible records must be kept to identify intermittent or gradual faults. Any problems which cannot be dealt with by routine maintenance must be escalated to a higher level in the supplier's organisation. Equipment must be tested regularly by suppliers, installation staff and the appropriate authorities.

The backup facilities must be appropriate to the risk of exposure and the type of processing. Many systems may not require UPS equipment — many may find it essential. The decisions on acquisition of each item of standby equipment or supplies (hardware, power generators, air conditioning etc) must be based on realistic business requirements and any necessary equipment must be maintained and tested as rigorously as the main equipment.

Figure 5.4

EQUIPMENT CHECKOUT

1. Does a backup power supply exist which is capable of operating the computer, air conditioning, heating and lighting?

2. Is switch-over to backup electrical supply automatic without loss of power?

3. Have backup electrical arrangements been tested regularly?

4. Is electrical equipment adequate to avoid voltage fluctuations?

5. Are there comprehensive instructions on procedures to be followed in the event of power interruption?

5.6 Physical Access Control

Although physical access controls can never be a complete solution to an organisation's security problems they play an important part in the overall security framework. Effective access control, in addition to fulfilling its required function:

- helps to engender a security-conscious attitude among employees;
- provides the first exposure of most visitors to the firm; creating a valuable, positive first impression;
- will deter the 'opportunist' criminal.

Restricting access to computer equipment calls for stringent controls. However, they must be taken seriously; token controls are, in many cases, less safe than no controls since they can provide a false sense of security. IT staff are often the worst offenders in violating their own access controls. Even where access to equipment in the computer centre is well controlled it is quite usual to find that on-line terminals in outlying offices, building sites or factories can be accessed in a completely uncontrolled fashion.

The major access security features include:

- control of access to all entrances and exit points from the building;
- staff identification methods, such as passes, badges, photocards, radio tokens and methods of biometric identification;
- more stringent access control methods for the computer suite, terminal rooms and other sensitive areas (air conditioning, power supplies and communications);
- use of security staff and surveillance equipment (such as CCTV and movement detectors).

The control mechanisms will, of course, be an added expense to an already overstretched budget, and it is economic and sensible to evaluate the risks of a security breach in each area rather than flooding the building with expensive security devices. This may lead to a system of zoning, in which specific areas with particular levels of sensitivity will be given greater—and possibly more expensive—protection.

Identification usually depends on the user demonstrating one, or a combination, of three things:

- something he knows, such as passwords or keypad/keycard numbers;
- something he possesses, such as a keycard, badge or radio token;
- less frequently, something unique to the person ('biometric' controls).

A number of biometric methods have been researched recently, and a small number are actually being used in practice. More frequently it has been found that considerations such as perceived discomfort, threat to civil liberties or invasion of privacy have restricted the potential for anything approaching a commercially-viable market for some techniques in this category. Biometric techniques include:

- signature recognition;
- fingerprint checking;
- retina scanning;
- voice recognition;
- hand or face recognition.

There has been no word recently from the team researching the Body Odour recognition device, which was claimed to identify the unique odour of any individual. It was said that neither the use of the strongest of perfumes nor the consumption of copious quantities of alcohol could fool the delicate sensing equipment, but this invention appears to have sunk without trace.

Readers will note that the philosophy and many of the techniques of physical access control also apply to access to computer systems. Another related technique is that of logging physical access—in many installations micro-computer software will log all users of cards, passes or doors, providing an audit trail of each person's activities and ensuring that security staff are aware at any time of the presence and location of employees. An example of these combined access and security management systems is Racal-Chubb's SPECTRUM which, using an IBM XT or compatible PC, can control the use of up to 30 doors and 2000 access cards. The software package restricts access to cardholders and produces comprehensive reports on access and movements in the building.

Guard Services
Ultimately every control mechanism depends on people. The most sophisticated electronic access control mechanisms can probably be bypassed in an emergency by a human being, while most organisations without access control of any sophistication rely solely on the professionalism and common sense of a guard or receptionist. In the absence of formal identification methods the guard has a heavy responsibility to recognise everyone and, except in the smallest of organisations, badges or identity cards are essential. The major problem here is that guards, particularly those who have performed the same job for some time, begin to recognise staff and frequent visitors, and may wave them through without asking for their passes. Ex-employees and well-known visitors who may not be authorised to return can be cheerfully invited to enter and do their worst by guards who merely wish to be helpful, friendly and to avoid accusations of autocratic behaviour.

Routine inspection of passes or badges must be enforced, and this will only be possible if a good example is shown by senior management. Many security officers have agreed comprehensive access control procedures throughout the organisation which on the first day were found to conflict with the demands of the chief executive's ego. Once an exception is made for the most senior, permission to avoid producing a pass will become a mark of high status and, since most employees are convinced of the importance of their jobs, the carefully-designed security procedures will degenerate into another aspect of office politics.

It may be appropriate to consider the use of contractors, rather than employees, to provide security services. The major advantage, of course, is their independence. They do not know the staff (particularly if security personnel are changed regularly) and are more likely to insist on full observance of procedures. In addition, collusion is less likely. The contract with the security firm will ensure that holiday and sickness cover is provided, which may be difficult in a small in-house security team. However the loyalty of in-house staff must not be underestimated.

Whoever performs the security duties, they must be protected and assisted to act decisively. Methods of protecting them from harm, such as security screens, must be considered and there should be regular reviews of such methods of controlling further access as:

- door locks controlled by the guards;
- alarm buttons and methods of summoning help;
- CCTV monitoring from within the building.

Security staff must have convenient access to telephones, and have an up-to-date list of telephone numbers of responsible managers and public services for use in an emergency.

Patrols of the building should take place on a frequent but irregular basis to ensure that unauthorised access has not taken place.

Off-site Equipment

The security of terminals and PCs at sites far away from the main computer centre must be treated with equal seriousness. Critical data and systems can be as vulnerable from these outposts as from the centre itself and in many cases the comparatively lax approach fostered by lack of proximity to Head Office may allow potential malefactors a greater opportunity. The main system should be designed to discourage access attempts, but good office security and a thoughtful approach to password control at the outlying sites are essential.

Figure 5.5 lists some of the questions which should be asked during a review of physical access controls.

5.7   Electronic Eavesdropping

It is possible to monitor, pick up and display radiation from computer and word processing equipment up to one kilometre away, extending the 'orthodox' bugging targets (telephones, rooms, people) into the electronic arena. VDUs, printer cables and power supply lines create significant exposures:

Figure 5.5

PHYSICAL ACCESS CHECKOUT

1. Is there outer perimeter control against unauthorised access, and is this regularly tested?

2. Is there access control to all entry points to the computer area, and is this effective?

3. Is the computer centre secure against penetration by intruder, bomb, gun, missile or arson attack from outside?

4. Are programs, data, media and documentation in secure storage?

5. Is access to the computer area restricted to only those who should have access?

6. Is there a satisfactory system in operation for controlling the access of authorised visitors to the computer area? Are visitors always accompanied?

7. Where on line terminals are in use is unauthorised use of terminals possible?

8. Are staff encouraged to challenge unaccompanied strangers?

9. Do the security measures apply equally at all times?

- *visual display units* (VDUs) owing to the high energy levels involved and the relative ease with which the signal can be recovered;
- *printers* as a result of the large electrical impulses required to operate most types of printhead;
- *cables* which carry serial data streams because they act as antennae.

The equipment needed to pick up this radiation is not always expensive, and relies on the type of technology used in a television detector van.

Close-range interception can be achieved at a cost of around £500, although detection at greater distances would require extremely sophisticated equipment and techniques with a steep escalation of costs.

The phenomenon has been well-known in military circles for some time, and demonstrations have been provided recently in commercial environments. It should be stressed however that the fact that this is possible does not mean that it can be easily applied in a profitable way. The signals can be picked up and stored. However, in a typical automated office, it would be extremely difficult to select and analyse the important information from the 'clouds' of data produced by different equipment. Once again, it is necessary to evaluate the risk posed by this threat before determining the level of countermeasure—or whether a countermeasure is even required.

It is possible to use cryptographic equipment to protect communication circuits which pass outside a controlled area, but this will obviously not protect data which is displayed on a screen. However, a similar technique can be used by which data is presented to the VDU in a pseudorandom manner which is then decrypted for display by special circuitry. The person viewing the display sees the plaintext version but the infiltrator will capture a seemingly random collection of data. Alternatively, extra lines of data can be added which will be radiated (although inhibited on the host screen), or 'white noise' can be generated to disguise the signal.

A number of methods of protection are available, and 'sensitive' government installations purchasing computer and communications equipment will require proof of adequate protection before agreeing to purchase hardware.

Protection against detection of this radiation can be provided by taking simple precautions, such as careful siting of vulnerable equipment close to the centre of the building to take advantage of the natural shielding provided by the building materials. Wherever possible, the VDU should be kept away from telephone lines or metal items, both of which can aid transmission.

The use of plasma screens, fibre optic cables and the provision of a filtered power supply should also reduce the vulnerability.

If, after taking the above precautions, further measures are believed to be necessary, a variety of source suppression mechanisms are available. These use radio frequency filtering and shielding techniques which, if properly installed and used, will almost completely reduce the possibility of compromising radiation being captured. They consist of a copper-based shield which can be installed around the entire computer room or, more usually, only around the items carrying particularly sensitive data.

The expense involved in shielding equipment (a shielded VDU can treble the price) should ensure that this solution is only used if essential.

6   Security of Computer Operations

6.1   Introduction

As computer operations become more diverse, distributed and complex the varieties of threats have increased. Although the more technical security breaches may now often be generated many miles from the main computer installation, using communications technology, they are still likely to be directed at data or software held and processed in the centre, and their chance of success will depend on the level of control over the computer installation.

In addition, every computer centre has the potential for the less sophisticated exposures—misuse of computer facilities, internal sabotage, errors and slipshod work—which have taken place in the past and continue to imperil our attempts to achieve the required level of confidentiality, integrity and availability.

It is necessary to identify the correct mix of deterrent, preventive and corrective controls which need to be applied in each installation. This chapter discusses the major control requirements. It is important to realise that these controls are a 'shopping bag' or 'tool kit' from which the correct mix of controls should be selected. This can only be done after a risk analysis has been performed, since controls which are not related to actual risks are, in most cases, a waste of money.

6.2   Controlling Operators

The objective of security in this area is to optimise productive computer time, lessen the risk of error and fraud, eliminate unauthorised work and secure the confidentiality of information.

Every activity performed by a computer operator should be scheduled and properly authorised. Operating instructions should be available in an understandable form for each application.

The organisation of the Operations Department should allow for proper division of duties to ensure that the potential for unauthorised operation and fraud is minimised.

The System Log should be analysed to provide management with detailed information on all normal and abnormal occurrences during each processing period. The availability of the log is extremely valuable but it is of no use whatsoever unless management read it and act on the information provided. Effective security demands that this happens and that evidence of their resulting activities is documented. Management supervision is one of the most important, although least effectively used, mechanisms for controlling operators.

The Computer Operations Checkout in Figure 6.1 provides examples of the detailed questions to be asked.

Within the Operations Department a number of activities are performed by staff who are organisationally segregated from the operators, providing valuable controls over day-to-day processing. These may include:

- the Media Library, whose staff are responsible for storage, release and ensuring the safe return of all data held on tapes and, where relevant, movable disks.
- the Data Control Group, which is responsible for ensuring that all input is correctly and completely processed.

Checkouts for these are provided in Figures 6.2 and 6.3.

6.3 System Use and Availability

Hardware and systems will occasionally suffer minor breakdowns. In addition, operators—even in the most efficient installations—occasionally make mistakes. It is important to ensure that sufficient resilience is built into the equipment, software and communications network to prevent minor problems from turning into major disasters.

In order to ensure that system availability is maximised, the utilisation of all hardware should be monitored on a regular basis.

Equipment failure records should be analysed to confirm that the failure level conforms with industry experience, and is acceptable to management. The adequacy of repair and maintenance procedures should be assessed on a continuing basis and the use of fault-tolerant hardware investigated.

A detailed programme of preventive maintenance by computer operators and engineers should be documented and enforced.

Statistics should be produced on hardware utilisation. These should be carefully monitored so that performance can be improved and any necessary enhancements planned well in advance.

Statistics should also be available on the utilisation of the central processor and main storage by application programs and operating systems.

An analysis of usage by user system should be prepared regularly. In addition to details of normal operations all 'out of the way' occurrences—such as unscheduled operator intervention—should be reported. Details of all

Figure 6.1

COMPUTER OPERATIONS CHECKOUT

1. Do service agreements exist between DP Operations and the user?

2. Do documented procedures exist covering the responsibilities of, and relationships between, IT staff and users?

3. Is machine usage analysis used as a basis for evaluating EDP performance and, where applicable, determining charges to users?

4. Does computer usage analysis differentiate between:
   (a) 'down-time' and 'up-time'?
   (b) application development and production work?

5. Are the following identified for subsequent investigation:
   (a) re-runs?
   (b) computer time lost through operator error?
   (c) development wrongly treated as production and vice versa?
   (d) unauthorised work?

6. Is there evidence of management review of system use?

7. Do operating instructions exist in an understandable form for each application?

8. Are only operators permitted to operate the equipment?

9. Are operators prohibited from working on their own?

10. Do operators only operate the computer:
    (a) with the relevant instructions in front of them?
    (a) on receipt of signed and authorised run instruction sheets?

11. Is it standard practice that operators do not restart programs that have failed without supervisor intervention?

12. Is a log automatically produced which records all normal and abnormal occurrences during each processing period? Is it possible to bypass production of this log?

13. Is it a laid down procedure that any printed version of the log shall only be removed by the Operations Manager, and that all paper breaks shall be initialled by two people?

14. Is the log examined on a frequent but random basis, and does evidence of this exist?

Figure 6.1 cont'd

COMPUTER OPERATIONS CHECKOUT (cont'd)

15. Are there written instructions specifying when generations of files may be released for each application?

16. Are there procedures which determine which files should be copied for retention in a remote store?

17. Are all 'sensitive' jobs run under appropriate supervision?

18. Is computer waste paper and carbon destroyed in a secure manner?

19. Are operators aware of, and do they understand the basic principles of, the Data Protection Act?

20. Does the IT department have any standards or guidelines by which they measure/control the work of operators? Are staff tested for dyslexia and numeracy problems?

21. What controls/restrictions exist over temporary operators? Do they carry out the same tasks as the permanent operator they are replacing?

22. Is there a system of preventive maintenance (e.g. peripheral cleaning) by computer operators? Is it adequately documented and enforced?

23. Is a machine maintenance program (by engineers) in operation? Is it adequate? When was it last reviewed?

24. Has consideration been given to awarding the maintenance contract to a third party, and was the maintenance contract subject to the organisation's normal tendering requirements?

25. Is a measurable minimum level of machine performance guaranteed by the maintenance contract?

26. Are statistics available on the breakdown of each item of hardware?
    (a) Where is this recorded?
    (b) What action is taken?
    (c) Are there instructions available on what to do following breakdown?

27. Does management evaluate the performance of hardware and take the necessary action?

28. Does management evaluate the quality of the maintenance service?

29. Are statistics available on hardware and system utilisation?

30. Is the utilisation of all equipment carefully monitored, so that performance can be improved and necessary enhancements planned well in advance?

Figure 6.2

MEDIA LIBRARY CHECKOUT

1. Are all tapes and, where relevant, exchangeable disks held in a separate media library when not in use?

2. Is it separated by walls from the rest of the computer centre?

3. Is access to the media library strictly controlled and is the library secure from unauthorised entry?

4. Is there satisfactory environmental control of the media library?

5. Are confidential files kept in locked racks and cabinets, and is a list held of those persons authorised to access confidential files?

6. Are procedures in force to ensure that no one person is left alone in the library?

7. Are operators excluded from the library?

8. Is the library permanently manned by a designated librarian who is responsible for issues and recording of returns?

9. Is tight control kept over the quantity of disks and programs out of the library at any one time?

10. Is there an automated file management system?

11. Is it linked to a security system which checks access authorisations?

12. Does it record and verify physical tape and disk numbers?

13. Is an up to date register kept in a safe place?

14. Do external labels and records correspond to the actual files held?

15. Are tapes and disks only issued to persons with the proper authority.

16. Are library records adequate to ensure that tapes/disks can be accounted for at all times?

17. Are there adequate procedures to ensure prompt return of media?

18. Are there controls over overdue tapes/disks to ensure they are:
    (a) identified?
    (b) investigated?
    (c) cleared?

19. Is magnetic media handled correctly and in accordance with the manufacturer's specifications?

Figure 6.2 cont'd

MEDIA LIBRARY CHECKOUT (cont'd)

20. Are there controls to prevent accidental overwriting?

21. Are all tapes/disks classified according to:
    (a) confidentiality?
    (b) commercial sensitivity?
    (c) value?

22. Is there a regular independent check on the accuracy of library records?

23. Are there controls to ensure that the level of supply of tapes and disks is adequate to meet demand?

24. Is there adequate control over the maintenance of media?

25. Is there adequate control over the disposal of media?

26. Are the contents of out of date files erased before re-use?

---

re-runs should be highlighted for discussion between operations management and the users.

6.4   Backup Procedures

From time to time disruptions will occur and it is necessary for procedures to be available which will allow a trouble-free recovery. To ensure continuity of processing, backup procedures are needed.

At the simplest level, backup consists of a set of clerical procedures which will come into operation to replace the computer system. More usually, a varying amount of redundancy is built into the system; that is, extra features are provided which would not be required if the system were crash-proof. This means that continuity of essential services can be guaranteed by such means as:

- the availability of an alternative power source;
- an instruction that in, say, a six disk-drive installation no procedure should use more than four, allowing processing to continue even if two disk drives were unavailable.

Since redundancy means that money will be spent on equipment or processes which will never—or hardly ever—be used, the level must be determined by management after carefully evaluating risk against cost.

Figure 6.3

DATA CONTROL CHECKOUT

1. Is input reconciled with output by an independent 'control group' to establish the accuracy of processing?

2. Is this activity, and its results, documented?

3. Are there written instructions for each job and are these instructions updated regularly?

4. Is the physical security of all input and output ensured while in the custody of the control group?

5. Is a record maintained of the receipt, processing and despatch of all documentation to avoid loss or delay?

6. Is this record monitored and supervised?

7. Is the control over the security of data received by remote entry and over the return of such data to remote locations adequate?

8. Is a record maintained of all errors and complaints?

9. Is this record monitored and does evidence of supervisory checks exist?

10. Is investigative action taken over abnormally high error rates, and in response to complaints?

11. Is there a control to ensure that all corrections are processed?

12. Is there satisfactory supervisory control over:
    (a) the group
    (b) all records
    (c) documentation

    and all checks evidenced?

In order to recover in the event of data or software being corrupted or destroyed, copies of this information must be held in off-site premises. These should have the same level of security as the 'live' versions. In practice this is not always the case, and the off-site store is often the weakest link in the security framework. In many cases files have been stolen from off-site premises, avoiding any need to breach the complex security procedures in place at the computer centre. In some cases, owing to inadequate documentation and checking, their absence was not noticed until the live files were accidentally destroyed, upon which a minor emergency rapidly inflated into a catastrophe!

A responsible person should be designated as the administrator of the off-site store, whose duties must include ensuring that copies of all files are received according to the agreed schedule. The administrator will also be responsible for ensuring the security of the premises, including the level of protection against fire and other hazards. Periodic checks of the contents of the files should be made to ensure that they contain the expected data. Any changes to the computer installation (hardware, systems software etc) must be accompanied by a review of the stored data to ensure that it can still be read and processed after the change.

In the absence of a suitable in-company remote location, organisations can use commercial facilities. The best of these offers, in addition to secure storage in an acceptable environment:

- regular collection and delivery of material;
- assurance of delivery to the regular, or an emergency, processing centre within agreed timescales.

6.5   Waste Disposal

Many effective 'low-tech' crimes have been initiated by a simple trawl through wastepaper baskets for sensitive or profitable material, an activity which can be very successful in a computer room or in the office housing a remote terminal. It is often difficult for an operator to understand that a print-out which has been 'spoilt' by a printer malfunction on one page is valuable to outsiders and should be disposed of as carefully as any other report.

The following rules should help to avoid placing temptation in the path of upwardly-mobile employees. They should apply not only to printed reports but also to tapes, disks, printer ribbons, carbon paper, log print-outs and data and program dumps.

1) Sensitive waste must be made unreadable by shredding or other methods of destruction.
2) Destruction must take place as close as possible to the point at which the item was generated.
3) Sensitive work should be destroyed as soon as possible after its generation. Destruction by IT staff should be supervised by an appropriate official of the user department and the material should be stored under secure conditions until this takes place.
4) Closed containers should be used for all such waste on site and while being transported.

7 Communications Security

7.1 Network Security

The term Network Security can be misleading. It implies a seamless overcoat which is placed over the entire network regardless of the use made of individual nodes. However, in common with all security matters, it is essential to concentrate on genuine business risks, which vary according to the applications and business served by the communications facilities.

There are three basic types of network, and a brief description of each is given below.

Dial-Up

This is the simplest form of network, based on dial-up telephone connections, using the Public Switched Telephone Network (PSTN). Typically this is used by simple teletype terminals to access a central minicomputer or mainframe. Dial-up lines are also used to backup private circuits in case of failure. The cost depends only on the duration of the connection.

The main advantage of dial-up is that, since the PSTN reaches practically every building in the country, it is possible to use it from any location. It is inexpensive for small volumes of data, while no backup is required since it is always possible to redial a connection.

The main disadvantage is that dial-up circuits operate at relatively low speed. While sufficient for an interactive VDU the speed does not usually allow for the transfer of data files. For prolonged use of more than an hour or two per day, dial-up techniques are uneconomic. For sites with multiple terminals one dial-up link is required for each—with a private circuit it would be possible for several terminals to share a link. In addition, dial-up circuits must be connected each time access is required, which can be inconvenient for high-activity terminals.

Private Circuits

PTTs can provide private circuits, which are telephone links dedicated to an organisation and are of higher quality than dial-up circuits. They can therefore operate at higher speeds. The costs are a fixed annual charge, independent of usage. Typically, multiplexing equipment will be attached to a private circuit, allowing several users to share the link.

Initially private circuits were of the same type as voice circuits, commonly called 'analogue'. Now many PTTs have introduced digital services. This removes the need for modems as the computer data remains in digital format throughout. Digital circuits can operate at far higher speeds than analogue lines.

The disadvantages include:

- high initial costs;
- lack of flexibility—only fixed sites can be interlinked;
- lack of resilience—an alternative connection is required if the line fails.

Public Data Networks
The PSTN and analogue private circuits were designed in the late nineteenth century to carry voice traffic and are not ideally suited to data networks. Even the newer digital links are only available on a point-to-point basis; i.e. it is only possible to link two fixed locations. The PTTs now provide public data networks (PDN), in most cases based on the X.25 standard. X.25 is a standard-based technique using 'packet switching' which differs from conventional techniques using 'circuit switching'. In the UK this service is called Global Network Services (GNS).

In circuit switching a path is set up between the two intercommunicating parties for the duration of the session. All data inserted at one end appears at the other end, and there is no destination information in the data transmitted. The telephone system works in this way. In packet switching it is possible to establish dialogues with several different destinations simultaneously. This is made possible by sending the data through the network in small messages ('packets'). Each packet is individually addressed and passes through the network as a separate unit. Connection to the PDN can either be via dial-up or private circuit. Charges are based on the amount of data sent.

The advantages of public networks are:

- it is possible to communicate with many locations via a single link;
- for dial-up access it is only necessary to call the nearest access point, usually a local call;
- it is possible to communicate with other organisations;
- the PTT manages the network;
- the PTT has many alternative circuits, automatically providing backup when a line fails.

The disadvantages are:

- for high volumes of data the service is expensive;
- network performance and control are outside the user's control.

The Integrated Services Digital Network (ISDN) provides a system in which the same digital switches and paths are used for different services, including voice, fax, data and videotext. This approach should produce increased efficiency, providing the customer with a wide range of communication services via a single interface.

The use of increasingly complex networks carries the promise of more effective business use of IT facilities. However, a number of new or increased security implications lurk among the inevitable problems caused by any new development, and the potential risks must be understood in order to install the necessary countermeasures.

IT networks have increased dramatically in size and complexity, and many varied services are available. One communications system can carry applications data, Funds Transfer messages, electronic mail, Telex and Fax data; while access to a complex variety of information databases and Value Added Data Services (VADS) is available to businesses and individuals. User workstations may be connected using a Local Area Network (LAN), which may in turn be linked to large national or international corporate facilities.

A variety of users now have access to information over public communications networks. Massive databases provide fast access to text services, financial data and quickly-changing information such as Stock Market prices. Individuals and the business community can transfer money and financial messages using such systems as SWIFT, CHAPS, CHIPS or Link. The use of ATMs or EFTPOS facilities is increasing, and the ordering of goods or services via Prestel and Minitel terminals is expected to develop rapidly.

Developments in communications techniques, and the associated expansion of services, have been accompanied by a change in the nature of the data transmitted through networks. The data may include information which would result in substantial losses to the organisation if it were revealed to another, lost or amended in transit, or merely delayed by a few minutes. The transmissions may constitute contractual commitments. The development of such powerful networks has considerable social and economic implications, and national legislation will affect both the nature of the traffic and the consequences of poor security. It has been estimated that, using electronic funds transfer, the entire financial reserves of the UK government could be transferred out of the country in a matter of minutes.

In order to provide assurance that the service will retain an adequate level of confidentiality, integrity and availability, security measures are required. In the communications environment, as in all other IT areas, these must be seen to be practical and helpful, rather than bureaucratic and negative.

The data travelling through networks must be protected from criminal activity, network disruptions and accidents. This is most effectively achieved using a combination of hardware, software and communications control techniques and management procedures. A variety of measures will be needed since network security covers all types of communications, including telephones, facsimile units, telex, satellite and other radiated services such as microwave communications links.

The security requirements of a network will be determined by a number of factors, including:

- the type of data transmitted;
- the services available to, and used by, the network;
- the complexity of the network;
- national and international standards;
- the volume of network traffic.

The level of security achieved will also depend on a variety of factors. These will include:

- the type of cable used;
- the physical security of terminals, nodes, cable and cabinets;
- access control software;
- password procedures;
- encryption and authentication techniques;

and, of course,

- the honesty and ability of employees.

Planning for network security should take place at the same time as that for network development and enhancement. Not only will costly mistakes be avoided but cost savings may occur as security is integrated into network components from the outset. At a physical level, fire and water protection for all cables is vitally important and must be incorporated at an early stage. The protection and location of the main telecommunications inter-connection cabinets is also vital, since they guard the communications lifeline between the organisation and the outside world.

However, it should be noted that many of the more technical methods employed to enhance the security of a network could have an impact on its efficiency and traffic throughput. This must be taken into consideration during network planning since it could have a major effect on the network's ability to satisfy the business requirements.

Telecommunication is essential, widespread, expanding, competitive and can be very profitable. Any tricks to obtain, manipulate or disrupt the information under transmission can be worth vast sums of money. Where that sort of force is at play the most respectable people can develop criminal characteristics, making defensive measures not only desirable but essential.

Security and Open Systems
After a period of unstructured network development a need was identified for an architecture which would provide 'Open Systems Interconnection', enabling different manufacturers' systems to work together. The model developed for Open Systems is known as the OSI Basic Reference Model, and is based upon the concept of layers. Each layer relies upon the services of the lower layers and delivers services to the upper layers.

The OSI Model was a major breakthrough in the move towards Open Systems and the principle has gained substantial political momentum. Most computer manufacturers and vendors are committed to delivering products which conform to the OSI Model and many European Government administrations have developed procurement policies based on the OSI principle.

Following the development of the OSI Basic Reference Model, the same group developed and published an associated OSI Security Architecture. In doing so, the group set out to answer the following questions:

- What security services are appropriate to OSI?
- What mechanisms should be used to provide such services? (The model clearly distinguishes between services which upper layers can use and the mechanisms by which such services are provided.)
- Where in the Reference Model should the various services and mechanisms be located?
- How should each of the services be invoked?

The details of the OSI Security Architecture are provided in Appendix 5.

The challenge to network providers, especially those who wish to support a wide range of application systems, is to offer selectable security protection.

Such networks must be able selectively to provide the security features and services as required by individual applications since, in those cases where the data being carried is less sensitive, comprehensive security features will be an unnecessary and costly overhead.

7.2   Security Techniques

The security problems of a computer centre are usually containable, since the necessary techniques and countermeasures are applied in a discrete and (usually) controllable area. The difficulties are compounded in network systems by the fact that the communications links are not within the organisation's control. They are leased from PTTs or commercial organisations and pass through many locations where it is impossible to impose the precautions which could be applied internally.

There are four main ways in which network security breaches can occur:

- disclosure of confidential information;
- messages being changed, deleted, added or rerouted;
- an unauthorised person pretending to be authorised;
- disruption of service.

Hacking, unauthorised interception and modification of messages, introduction of bogus messages, viruses and illicit program changes are included in this group.

A *spoofing attack* is performed by connecting an illicit terminal to the network and masquerading as a legitimate terminal to the host system, or as the host system to other users.

Interceptors could record message traffic on the network, possibly combined with details of associated parameters such as dates and times of transmission or location of circuit. This may be followed by the introduction of spurious messages to be delivered to users, host computers etc. The spurious message may be created by the attacker or it may take the form of a replay of a previous valid message.

Disruption of service can be disastrous to an organisation which is highly dependent upon the timely communication of data. The disruption may take the form of a selective loss or delay of legitimate messages, or a complete breakdown of communications. The attack may be achieved by simply occupying a communications line at the expense of a legitimate user, even though the attacker may be incapable of creating legitimate transactions. Another form of disruption is the deliberate modification of legitimate messages, either for the benefit of the attacker, or for purely malicious purposes.

However, while considering the more exotic forms of crime the security-conscious manager must not forget that accidental disruption occurs much more frequently, and plans must be in place to deal with this aspect.

There are a large number of countermeasures available, whch may be technical, organisational or procedural in nature.

Dial back: this procedure allows the host system to restrict dial-in facilities to only those users and locations with the necessary permission. After receiving a dial-up call the system hangs up and calls a previously agreed number. This is not suitable for people who need access from several locations, and the fact that calls can be diverted reduces its effectiveness in many circumstances. In general, dial back should only be used in association with supervised terminals.

Encryption techniques: these take different forms, but all allow data to be transferred with a reduced likelihood of confidentiality being breached. The methods are:

- link-by-link encryption;
- node-by-node encryption;
- end-to-end encryption.

With *link-by-link encryption*, data is encrypted on each communication link connecting two nodes in the network. Each link on the network requires two data encryption/decryption units in this mode of operation; large complex networks may thus require the installation of hundreds, or even thousands, of encryption units. This approach may be too expensive and difficult to administer in large networks.

Node-by-node encryption provides a more cost-effective solution for large networks. In this mode incoming data to a node is decrypted, with a cryptographic key corresponding to that used in the previous source node, and re-encrypted with a different key, prior to onward transmission. The cryptographic functions, and the storage of the keys, are performed by security modules, and not in the node computer.

Figure 7.1

CONVENTIONAL CRYPTOGRAPHY

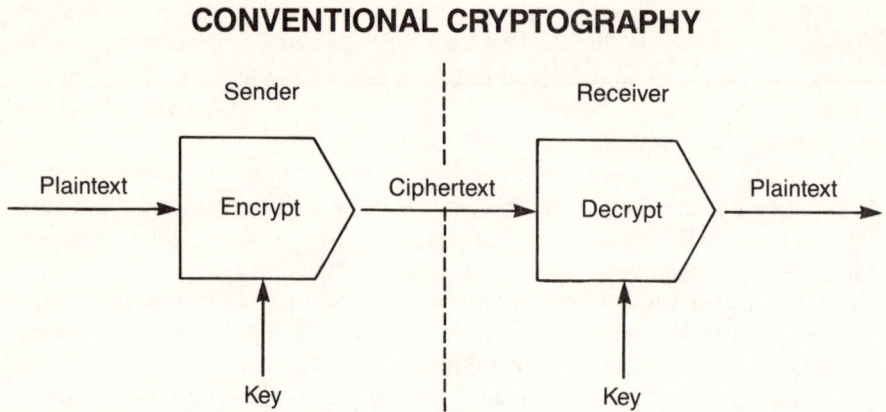

Both link-by-link and node-by-node techniques are vulnerable to attack by line-tapping between the terminal and the encryption equipment, since the traffic is in plaintext over these links. Such illicit access may be achieved with data monitor probes in a front-end communications processor of a mainframe computer, so physical access controls are required for such areas.

With *end-to-end encryption*, the data is encrypted by the sender and decrypted by the receiver. Thus it is never revealed in plaintext form at any intermediate node. In this mode of operation the encryption equipment is a component of the terminal and host computer.

The three techniques have their individual advantages and disadvantages. In some cases a combination may be used.

End-to-end encryption probably presents the safest and lowest-cost solution and is likely to be the predominant mode employed in the 1990s. It is inherent in the application layer security services specified for the Open Systems Interconnection (OSI) model (see Appendix 5). The number of points where encryption and decryption must take place is minimised, with resulting savings in the number of encryption devices or sub-systems. The overheads imposed by the encryption process will have minimum effect on the overall performance of the network—an important consideration whenever encryption is considered. However, there are key management implications caused by the fact that link encryption requires only one key, while end-to-end encryption needs a separate key for each system user.

Message authentication techniques are used to confirm the accuracy of message contents and the sender's authority to transmit the message. A code is calculated from the contents of the message, and passed with the message to the receiver. By recalculating and comparing the code the receiver can confirm that the message's integrity has not been breached.

In order to perform the calculation a key must be used which is known to both sender and receiver.

Authentication protects messages from being altered deliberately or accidentally. It also protects against messages coming from an unauthorised source, since valid messages can only be generated by someone with the correct secret keyword. However it does not protect against a criminal intercepting a message and replaying it again later, since it will still be valid.

The use of secret keys constitutes a problem. Where a simple link exists between two buildings a secret key can be placed in the encryption machines at each end and changed at regular intervals as a further precaution. However this becomes impossible for major networks with thousands of locations—such as the cash dispenser and EFTPOS networks.

A particular problem is that the longer a key is used the easier it is to 'crack' it. To avoid any key being used too long a hierarchy of keys can be used. A single 'master key' is entered in a terminal which is used once per day to transfer another secret key to the machine. This is used to encrypt messages for the day and is replaced by a new key each day. The use of public keys may simplify the key management problems inherent in this approach.

More recently, techniques have been evolved which effectively bypass this key management problem by automatically changing the key after every transaction in a way that is unpredictable to criminals, but can be calculated by both the terminal and the central computer.

The machines used for encryption and authentication are made 'tamper proof'; that is, they are designed so that all information in them is erased if anyone attempts to tamper with the equipment.

Other security methods are:

- *Resilience:* duplication of network features to ensure uninterrupted network service;
- *Closed user groups:* will restrict access to authorised users on a public switched data network.

Physical security methods are equally important. Every computer security manager must be able to inspect and obtain full information on the following:

- location of all internal data and telecommunications cabling;
- location and accessibility of the main telecommunications interconnection box, usually installed by the PTT or public network company;
- type and nature of all connections to the network cabling.

This requirement extends to the cable connecting the network to a mainframe's front-end data communications computer systems. When eavesdropping on data cables the same techniques apply as for any simple voice-level tapping operation. Probes may be inserted into the cable at numerous points, but certain areas, which include the main telecommunications centre for the building, are especially risk-prone. This is the principal point of connection of the internal data network within a building to the external, wide area public data network and contains the main junction points for connection.

All data links must be available for inspection.

Equipment which can be used to eavesdrop on transmitted data, such as datascopes, must be securely stored and procedures should exist for its custody and use. All employees who use this equipment must be aware of their responsibilities, must not misuse it and must ensure that others are unable to do so.

A short Communications Checkout is provided in Figure 7.2.

Figure 7.2

COMMUNICATIONS CHECKOUT

1. Has the risk of falsification, re-routing, corruption or illegal access to data under transmission been investigated?

2. Do all messages carry identifiers showing source:
   (a) user identifier?
   (b) physical terminal?

3. Are all messages checked for completeness and accuracy at input and output stages?

4. Is the network subject to physical risks or terrorist attacks?

5. Is the network physically secure?

6. Does the overall contingency plan include activities in the event of loss of communications facilities?

7. Are encryption/authentication techniques used for relevant transmitted data?

8. Where appropriate, are the following safeguards used:
   – dialback?
   – membership of a Closed User Group?

8. Are sufficient network features duplicated to provide an acceptable level of resilience?

9. Is all use of network resources accounted for and reconciled to expected use?

7.3 Digital Signatures

Message authentication is primarily a method of preserving the integrity of data by allowing a receiver to verify that no material changes have been made to the message during transmission. It fulfils the basic control requirements of:

- determining a sender's authority to make the commitment represented by the message;
- assuring the receiver that the message received is the message that was originally sent.

However, authentication cannot assist in the resolution of disputes. Since the same key is used to calculate and subsequently prove the message authenticator, an authenticated message could be subject to either of the following disputes:

- The sender of the message could claim that he did not send the message and that the receiver forged it;
- The receiver could forge a message and claim an authenticated message was actually sent.

The problem here is caused by the fact that either party has the facility to create an authenticator. Since both parties use the same key to construct an authenticator and subsequently verify the message, there is no true basis of repudiation should either party be dishonest. In either of the above situations it would be impossible for a third party to exercise judgment if a dispute occurred.

Where this situation is considered to pose a risk, a much stronger form of message authorisation and verification is required. To obtain the necessary levels of confidence and to support meaningful arbitration by a third party, a system is required which allows a sender to authorise a message restricting the receiver to the ability to verify that authority, rather than recreating it.

Public key ciphers operate on the basis of two different keys—a public key and a private key—and employ a sophisticated algorithm which can create a value with one key and verify the results with another.

The process is best understood by example; where data security is maintained by a public key cipher process, the issuer of the message generates two keys—a public (enciphering) key and a private (deciphering) key. The public key is sent to the intended recipient of the message while the private key is retained by the sender. The underlying mathematical concepts and the algorithm used provide a basis for the sender of the message to authorise the message using the private key and the receiver to verify the authorisation via the public key. However, since the receiver is not in possession of the private key, he is never in a position to create, or be accused of creating, a message.

It is not difficult to see why the term 'digital signature' has been applied to this process. If we consider the private key as a means of generating a unique signature and the public key as a method of verifying the signature, the similarity between this and signing, say, a cheque becomes apparent. The person signing the cheque puts his/her unique signature on the cheque; the receiver of the cheque (for example a bank teller) has the facility, via signature records, to validate the signature. Conceptually, at least, whilst the bank teller is able to verify the signature (and thus cash the cheque) he does not have the facility to recreate it.

Some digital signature systems ensure that a unique 'signature', based on the contents of the message, is calculated for each individual message by using a randomising value to ensure that each signature is different from the previous one. This can be achieved by designing the hardware and software which perform the signature process to accept a constantly changing value, such as time of day, into the signature-producing algorithm.

Creation and Use of a Digital Signature System
Figure 7.3 shows the overall operation of a digital signature system and the functions performed by each component.

1) Random Number Generator
This is usually a hardware-based function and provides the initial starting point in the process. The generator produces a starting number, or seed, via a randomising process which is fed into the key-generating function.

2) Key Generation
The key-generating function accepts the previously-created random number and feeds it into two algorithms. Though different, the algorithms are mathematically related, ensuring that the keys generated from each, though different in value, are also related ('key pairs'). The original

Figure 7.3

PRINCIPLES OF OPERATION
OF A DIGITAL SIGNATURE SYSTEM

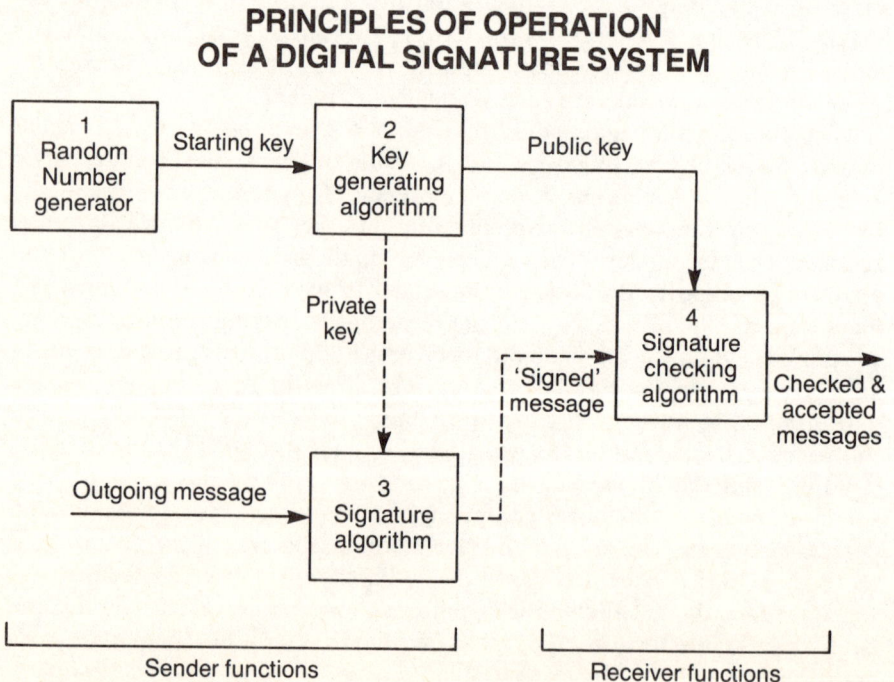

Sender functions   Receiver functions

random number which was used to originate the calculation has no further use and is discarded.

The key-pair are now resident in the key-generating module of the system. One key is transmitted to the intended receiver of the message — this is the public key. The second key (the private key) is passed to the signature process. The receiver now has the basis for determining the authenticity and authorisation attached to the message from the sender, but is not able to reproduce the 'signature' which will be derived via the private key.

3) Signature Process

The message to be transmitted is now 'signed' by passing the private key and the message text through an algorithm which processes all the values to generate a signature. The resulting signature is attached to the body of the message and is then transmitted to the receiver.

4) Signature Checking

The signature check is applied by the receiver on receipt of the signed message. This is done by applying the resident algorithm to the message text with the public key which was transmitted earlier. The public key, though different from the private key, returns a value that enables the receiver to assure himself of the validity of the signature attached to the message.

As with any control scenario (particularly those based on a hardware/software solution) an awareness is needed of the potential threats which could compromise the overall process. A security solution resident in an inadequately-controlled environment is little better than no solution at all. The following issues should always be considered when evaluating digital signature sub-systems.

1) Digital signature sub-systems are normally provided as a 'black-box'; that is, a purpose-built hardware/software environment. Unauthorised physical access should be restricted at least by audible alarms and preferably by a tamper-proof mechanism which clears all memory locations if the 'box' is disturbed.

2) The resident software should be based on Read Only Memory (ROM) to guard against unauthorised amendment. It should preferably be stored in encrypted form in order to deter browsing using, say, diagnostic equipment.

3) The key generation process should be conducted in complete privacy, with no visual displays of the operation. There should also be facilities to prevent 'eavesdropping' over this process, since it could be stored and 'replayed'.

4) Confidentiality of the private key is of particular importance, especially if the key is to be maintained for a long period of time. Where the same

key is maintained for some time, it should be stored in an encrypted form.

The unique properties of a digital signature system enable a high degree of reliance to be placed on the integrity of electronic messages. Using this approach a wide range of trade documentation, payments, orders and legally-binding documents can be processed and exchanged automatically. The comparatively cheap hardware and low level of user interaction with the hardware and software components of the system pose few implementation problems, enabling many small businesses to participate in large data interchange networks regardless of the limited technical skills of their employees.

The biggest barrier to the digital signature being considered a binding obligation will be its acceptance by the legal community. With the growing number of government initiatives to encourage Electronic Data Interchange in all areas of industry and commerce, such an acceptance must surely be only a matter of time.

7.4   Micro-Mainframe Links

The improved cost-effectiveness of using a microcomputer to perform some processing while allowing speedy access to vast quantities of information on the host mainframe makes this technique very attractive. However, the downloading of potentially sensitive data from a secure mainframe database to a possibly less secure micro environment produces a major risk, and great emphasis is needed on security in this area.

In addition to adequate mainframe and network security features, the following would be expected:

- adequate physical access control;
- an effective level of management and supervision;
- monitoring of all processing and associated clerical procedures;
- sufficient staff to be trained in the use of the micros to ensure that 'one man bands' do not develop;
- standard procedures for the purchase and use of micros and packaged software.

Since application processing may take place on two or three systems the overall application is not visible to, and cannot be logged by, the host mainframe. Although the mainframe will log its perception of processing, it will be unaware of the microcomputer activities, which may generate no audit trail. Even if the audit trails exist, combining and analysing these will be extremely complicated.

Data transferred to a micro is only valid at that point in time. Any update taking place after the transfer will not be notified to the micro user, who must take this into account when using the information received. If this is not allowed for, far-reaching business decisions may be made on the basis of currently invalid, inconsistent data.

7.5   Local Area Networks (LANs)

A local area network allows shared facilities—such as processing, storage, printing, information retrieval and electronic mail—to micros within a comparatively small geographic area. Three network topologies (star, bus and ring) are commonly used—not always exclusively—and an understanding of the vulnerabilities of each is needed to assess the need for security measures. For example, since ring and bus networks do not have a controller, it may be possible for an attacker to tap a node wire and establish an apparently authorised session without being detected.

Figure 7.4

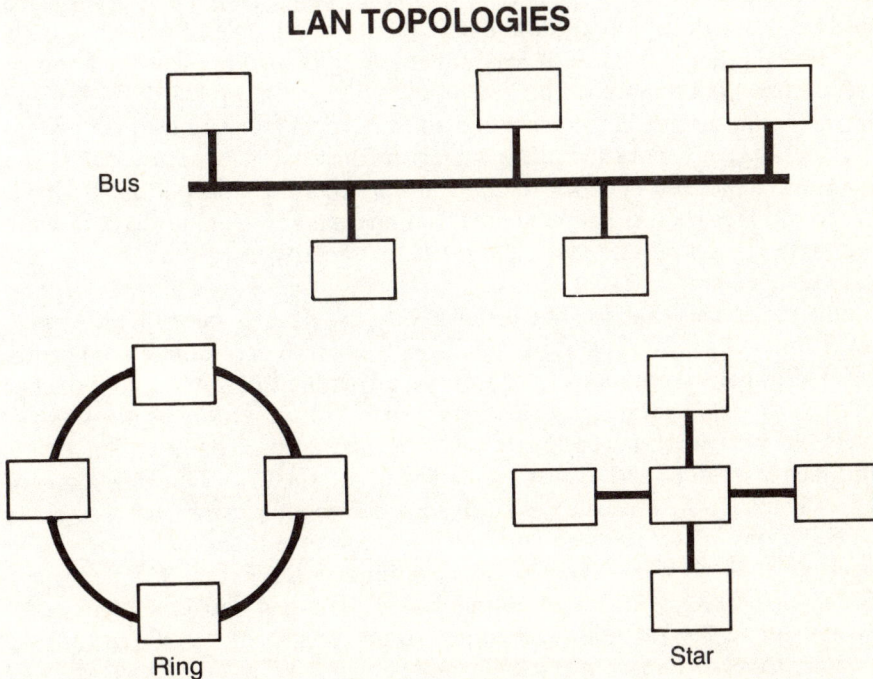

LAN TOPOLOGIES

Bus

Ring

Star

Risks to a LAN are, to a large extent, the same as to the wider data communications network, although the level of technology required by an attacker for full penetration of a LAN may be somewhat higher. The threats associated with LANs are similar to those applying to other networks, and include:

- introduction of false messages into the LAN;
- eavesdropping, made easier by the fact that data in a LAN is available to all users;
- disruption of service;
- attaching an illicit terminal or node to the LAN;
- rerouting of messages to fraudulent terminals or nodes;
- illegal access via gateways.

Most of the above are made easier by the absence of any method of checking for unauthorised connections to the LAN.

Information related to cabling, and physical access to cables, is not normally available in the case of telecommunications services supplied by the national carrier. However, with LANs the introduction of false messages, eavesdropping and disruption to services are made easier by the fact that staff have ready access to the cabling and to its details, such as type and location. Thus LAN co-axial copper cable may be tapped, both actively and passively, either on the cable directly or at termination and connector points. LAN cable must therefore be physically protected (for example, by using steel cable ducts with keylocks), although it should be capable of being regularly inspected. Fibre optic cable is less vulnerable (although not entirely immune from attack) but the initial purchase price is higher. It also has the advantage of not being susceptible to magnetic and electrical interference from within the building, nor does it radiate signals to the eavesdropper except at the point of connection between the optical fibre and the workstation. If LANs are to be extensively used in the organisation, management must consider the purchase of appropriate test equipment for security as well as backup and maintenance purposes.

Illicit terminals can easily be connected to most LANs since simple, office-level connectors are usually employed: indeed, such ease of interconnection for additional workstations is one of the advantages of LANs. An attacker may cause LAN messages to be replayed by the insertion of illicit driver software at a workstation. Such software may also contain Trojan Horse routines to monitor and record selected traffic on the LAN. The development of such illicit software is simpler if personal computers are used as LAN workstations, since attackers are likely to have extensive knowledge of the operation of the network, its workstations and servers. Cryptographic systems, located at the workstation and server, can provide a degree of protection against unauthorised access to, and misuse of, LAN data.

If the LAN is connected to a wide area network (WAN) through a gateway then management should be vigilant over the operation of the gateway: it may provide an entry into the LAN to hackers, and grant opportunities for expensive, unauthorised use of WAN facilities by employees.

Aspects of LAN operations which should be included in a security review include:

- the methods by which data is packaged during transportation;

- the possibility of electronic eavesdropping on cable;
- the security devices which protect the network from illegal access. These can be:
  - network access control methods such as dial back, authentication and password generators;
  - data encryption methods which could use node, link or end-to-end encryption;
  - modem security devices, which are particularly important for LANs which interact with wide area networks;
  - the use of diskless PCs.

The adequacy of the network security features should be reviewed regularly in the light of the security needs of the application systems and data.

The Network Administrator is, in many respects, the key to the effective and secure operation of the LAN, and his/her procedures, records and activities must be effectively supervised and monitored.

All terminal activity must be reviewed regularly and instances of attempts at unauthorised activity and apparent misuse of authorised functions investigated. All resulting actions must be documented to confirm that monitoring has taken place and any questions have been resolved.

As with all systems, the adequacy and control of all passwords should be reviewed regularly.

7.6   VADs and VANs

Value Added Network Services (VANS) and their successors, Value Added Data Services (VADS), are networks set up by independent organisations to supply services to third parties, and are prime targets for a variety of attacks ranging from large-scale fraud to pure mischief. Many of the systems used by financial organisations, such as those described in Chapter One, fall into this category.

The user-friendliness demanded by legitimate users provides a major benefit to the attacker. Since attacks on dial-up communications networks can be launched from remote locations, the perpetrators can be extremely difficult to catch. Even leased-lines are not completely secure. The major security risks derive from the fact that users belong to a different organisation to the service-provider. Aspects of this problem include the following:

- the service provider has little control over the correct operation of user procedures;
- terminals may be located in insecure premises such as shops, or even the users' homes;
- it can be difficult to determine responsibility when something goes wrong.

The potential damage to the service-provider falls into three categories:

- loss of service revenue;
- claims from users or third parties;
- loss of public confidence, leading to loss of business as the service loses credibility.

Security aspects of a VAD system will include:

- the control of passwords and access privileges in the service-providers' DP Operations and Systems Development organisation;
- physical access security over premises housing parts of the system where sensitive data is held in clear, or which may be a target for malicious damage;
- control of service operations and maintenance;
- use of remote diagnostics, which should take place only under controlled circumstances;
- backup and resilience procedures;
- disaster recovery plans;
- clarity and comprehensiveness of the contract between the user and the service-provider;
- encryption and key management.

7.7   Telex and Facsimile Transmission

Telex is still the most common method of transferring critical information in many organisations, owing to its universal acceptability and the fact that in some countries telex messages have legal status. The process is becoming more complex—in some cases combinations of telex with data communications and voice networks are taking place. In these new environments the risks of using telex need to be re-evaluated on a regular basis, taking all new developments and interfaces into account.

Typical security requirements include:

- central management of the telex functions which should include development and implementation of the procedures for:
  - receipt of messages;
  - filing and ultimate disposal of hard copy;
  - distribution of messages;
- the addition of an authentication code to each message, to be confirmed on receipt;
- where appropriate, encryption of messages.

The use of facsimile transmission (known variously as 'Fax' 'Dex' and other derivations) is spreading rapidly. As with the photocopier, it is now difficult to remember how businesses managed to operate successfully without it. The decreasing cost of not only the standard office terminal, but also the portable unit, has guaranteed a continuing increase in the use of this facility.

In the more recent machines, the security aspects are being addressed by features such as the following:

- the 'personal mailbox' facility which will store incoming messages, only printing them after entry of an authorisation code;
- messages may include the date and time of transmission and the addresses of the source and destination machines;
- logging of, for example:
  - number of pages;
  - time of transmission;
  - addresses.

In order to reduce the opportunity to transmit fraudulent documents, the cover sheet should include the firm's logo and a sequence number which can be confirmed by telephone.

Since the coding scheme for facsimile transmission is a publicly-known standard, it is possible to obtain information from fax messages by wire tapping. There are encryption devices which can be added to fax units, but these will not, of course, prevent unauthorised persons from reading the printed message. Essentials are such simple physical controls as:

- siting the terminals in a secure area;
- placing messages on receipt in a locked box;
- secure distribution procedures.

7.8 Electronic Mail and Voice Messaging

Electronic mail (E-mail) services are provided by special-purpose software in workstations and host computer systems, together with similar software in the telephone switching computers of the PTT, to exchange messages between widely dispersed users. User 'mailboxes', protected with a user password, hold data files within the computer-based store and forward communications switching system supplied by the common carrier.

A number of different E-mail systems exist worldwide with widely-varying security features, although these systems are expected eventually to interconnect with systems conforming to ISO X.400 standards and the associated X.500 directory services standards (the 'telephone directory' of E-mail). This set of international standards details the techniques and formats to be used for the interconnection of message systems worldwide. Other E-mail services include those based on videotex systems such as Prestel. In addition, companies and other enterprises may set up their own proprietary E-mail services which in turn interface with those provided by the national carrier.

From a management viewpoint it would be wise to create a checklist of security concerns to discuss with the providers of a network service. This checklist may involve addressing such issues as:

- Are there any coding restrictions which could have an impact on the use of cryptography to protect messages? (Some E-mail systems only accept the printable ASCII characters; an encryption system such as DES produces all values of a 7- or 8-bit field.)
- If the data is sensitive, password control is critical, and the use of additional techniques (for example hand-held tokens) may be appropriate.
- Application to the system and the mailboxes of logging and audit trail facilities.
- Methods in the E-mail service to ensure prevention, or at least reporting, of attempts to delete, reroute, modify or corrupt messages.

Although maintenance of the system and liaison with the supplier may be the responsibility of a specific individual, office managers should beware of the 'one man band' syndrome mentioned elsewhere in this book. They must be aware of the type and cost of messages transmitted by the system, and have strict control over the list of authorised users. They must also understand the system as well as their staff, and constantly guard against the installation or development of software which can transmit files held in workstations to other parts of the network.

Voice mail, or voice messaging, systems operate in a similar fashion to electronic mail, except that the individual messages comprise digitised audio data. These are transmitted to user mailboxes, retrieved, and played to the recipient. From a confidentiality viewpoint, they share the security characteristics of E-mail systems. However, since the voice characteristics of the speaker are retained in the message, an attacker may have rather more difficulty in modifying messages or inserting false messages.

7.9   Electronic Data Interchange (EDI)

The benefits of EDI have become apparent in a variety of commercial and industrial environments during the last few years. The improvements in workflow and accuracy which accompany the process have helped to increase efficiency in many organisations during a period in which full utilisation of resources and speedy cashflow have been the keys to continued economic survival.

As an example, for a machine manufacturer supplied with many components by a variety of organisations, EDI will:

- eliminate paperwork;
- enable suppliers to respond more quickly to requirements;
- reduce re-input of data, eliminating transcription errors.

Electronic transmission of invoice details will enable customers to be notified of their indebtedness more quickly, leading (hopefully) to prompter payment.

Another example is the exchange of product design information in graphical form. Many automotive component suppliers are beginning to work more closely with their customers—the car manufacturers—in the design of components. Typically, the car manufacturer will decide on the broad characteristics of the component, draft a design on his CAD system and transmit the result to the supplier. The supplier's design team will then add detail to the design before passing the drawing back—electronically—to the car manufacturer. The process is interactive, designs being repeatedly modified by both parties until they arrive at an acceptable result.

The effects of disclosure of:

- in the first case, details of competitive prices, discounts and settlement terms;
- in the second, details of research results which could have cost a great deal of time and money

could be catastrophic, although it must be admitted that disclosure in each case could be more economically achieved by bribery of key employees.

In the finance sector the banks, in particular, are increasingly involved in the application of EDI. Customers who use EDI for invoicing and ordering often prefer to complete the payment cycle electronically. Third-party EDI networks are enthusiastically volunteering to extend their range by carrying banking transactions. SWIFT is currently investigating the feasibility of carrying EDI messages. However, the major banks—themselves the owners of large telecommunications networks—have also seen the possibilities inherent in providing EDI services direct to their customers.

Banks running trials in the UK at present include Citibank, Lloyds, Natwest and Barclays.

The Security Challenges of EDI
Close-coupling. In contrast to electronic mail, EDI involves the transfer of structured data from computer to computer. It is fundamental to EDI that the structured nature of the data transferred permits the receiving application to process the data with little or no human intervention.

Since, therefore, we are in the arena of application-to-application communications, not only must the security of the transmitting application and the network be assured, but so also must that of the receiving application. As discussed elsewhere in this book, important features in secure applications include:

- appropriate logical access controls;
- effective procedures for authorising the release of transactions for onward communication;
- controls to ensure that outgoing messages have not been sent more than once;

- controls to ensure that incoming messages have not been sent more than once.

This close-coupling, or dependence upon the application systems of a supplier, has been recognised by the most successful exponents of electronic trading. One major motor manufacturer has included, as part of its supplier quality assurance program, a review of the supplier's application systems. Failure to meet the requirements of the customer can result in a supplier losing future work.

Absence of Human Intervention. A second change brought about by EDI is the absence of human intervention or interpretation. This is often viewed as an advantage since computers tend to perform repetitive tasks more consistently and speedily than humans. On the other hand, removing humans from the process also removes a degree of security protection since computers are incapable of applying curiosity or commonsense to instructions.

Paperless Trading. The absence of paper from the electronic trading transaction brings with it its own set of advantages—and disadvantages. The advantages are obvious.

However, the absence of hardcopy evidence in support of these business transactions has serious implications both from a legal standpoint and from the auditor's perspective. Many current users of EDI in the commercial sector have chosen the easy option and print out transactions for archiving purposes. A more forward-looking response would be to archive the data on magnetic media together with third-party notarisation by means of a digital signature.

Determining the Security Requirements. The threats are similar to those in any network environment, and include:

- masquerade (spoofing), where an unauthorised user pretends to be an authorised user;
- modification, where message data is actually altered;
- the insertion or deletion of false messages;
- the repetition of a message or part of a message;
- the use of a 'trapdoor'. One example of a 'trapdoor' is the use of a rogue piece of validation code to allow an attacker to produce an unauthorised effect;
- 'Trojan Horse', where something is added to the system which produces an unauthorised effect. Trojan Horses, as their name suggests, are often difficult to trace because the system's authorised functions are, typically, unaffected.

This list of potential threats is by no means exhaustive, but serves as an example of the sort of issues which need to be considered when assessing the possible threats to which a particular application could be exposed.

EDI and Open Systems. Many organisations and third-party network providers use proprietary protocols with which to transfer EDI packets or interchanges. It is generally accepted that for the use of EDI in the international arena to grow and prosper, the policy of Open Systems must be adopted. When the United Nations Joint EDI or JEDI committee was established in 1985 it was the aim of that committee to establish an International Open Standard for EDI message syntax. The fruits of its endeavours can be seen in the EDIFACT standard (ISO 9735).

A description of the current status of Open Systems security standards is given in Section 7.1.

Packet-encryption Devices. The majority of EDI software and hardware products on offer use a packet-switch interface designed to connect to the national carriers' packet-switched public data networks (PSPDNs). The only security which common carriers are currently able to offer users is a Closed User Group based on validation of the network user identity and network user address.

Encryption of a packet is somewhat problematical since, for the packet to be correctly delivered, the network user identity and network user address fields of the packet must not be encrypted.

Some companies have, nevertheless, developed and launched packet-encrypting devices which operate by filtering the addressing and user identification portions of the packet and then encrypting the message part before recombining the two.

Use of such packet encryptors in the international arena is, however, dependent on the proprietary interfaces with which national PSPDNs are connected. Unfortunately, a number of factors have combined to produce a variety of levels of conformance to CCITT and CEPT recommendations. Owing to the evolution of X.25 standards, the different timetables for implementation amongst national carriers and the different manufacturers' implementations of the X.25 recommendations; a lower level of service quality is available to the international user than that experienced at national level. For example, the Closed User Group facility described earlier is not available in the international arena.

The resulting proprietary interfaces not only impair the service quality but also result in a reduction of the line speeds available at the international level.

EDI and X.400. There has been some debate recently regarding the suitability of the CCITT X.400 recommendations for Message Handling Systems as a transfer mechanism for EDI.

Although they are both concerned with application-level communications, standards for EDI and X.400 have evolved separately and with little apparent co-ordination.

In 1988, Vanguard, the DTI's VADS initiative, commissioned a study to examine the relationship between EDI and X.400. The report from this study concluded that X.400 provides a very close match with the functional requirements for handling EDI messages. It is likely that an EDI Messaging System protocol—equivalent to the existing Interpersonal Messaging System protocol but directed towards computer-to-computer messaging—will be available in the near future.

By far the biggest advantage to be gained from using X.400 as the primary EDI transfer mechanism is its potential for universal connectivity. X.400 services have already been established in most Western European countries as well as in North America and Japan. All the major computer manufacturers support, or have made commitments to support, X.400. It has even been suggested that X.400 could one day provide the same connectivity as has been achieved by the telephone service.

As the size and interconnection of networks increases, the ability to implement security facilities independently of the internal security of the networks being used will become increasingly important. X.400 would appear to offer this ability and it is to be hoped that products conforming to the 1988 recommendations will soon appear.

8 Controlling the System

8.1 Introduction

A computer system is made up of a mixture of software:

- the application programs written in-house to fulfil the business requirements;
- application packages purchased from outside suppliers;
- utilities carrying out standard routines which may be used many times by the system;

and last, but certainly not least:

- the systems software:
  - operating system;
  - teleprocessing software;
  - database management systems;
  - compilers etc;

without which the application could not run.

This complex combination of software—some written in-house, some provided by hardware manufacturers and software suppliers—needs to be controlled in order to ensure that data is processed:

- securely;
- accurately;
- completely;
- only once;
- in the correct timescale.

8.2 Application Controls

Within the application programs or packages a combination of manual and programmed controls is needed, some components of which are described below. It should be remembered that not all controls are required by all systems—risk analysis should identify the items in the following 'toolkit' which are required by each.

8.2.1   Security of Input

Background controls. Sound techniques and procedures which should assist in the avoidance of errors include:

- good form design;
- avoidance of superfluous input forms and transcription;
- effective training and instruction manuals;
- orderly working methods.

Overall reconciliation. Control totals are established prior to the input of the data to the computer, to be reconciled with totals produced at the end of the computer run.

Batch controls. These collect data into easily-manageable quantities, using counts and totals calculated from each batch as control totals. Each batch is input and processed together, enabling the system to reconcile at regular intervals, confirming that data has not been lost or corrupted. The approach can be applied effectively to all batch systems, including those being operated from multiple terminals, ATMs etc. The philosophy can be adapted to real-time systems, using totals produced at the end of a set time period.

Sequence checking. If the documents holding input data are pre-numbered (for example invoices), the computer system can incorporate a sequence check. A problem with sequence checking occurs when recovery is required after an error has been identified. Since the system depends on the comparison of a number with a previous number, one error could upset the basis of future comparisons, and the recovery process will need to take this into account.

Check digit. The calculation of a check digit from the digits of an important reference number (for example an account number) provides a valuable control over that number, no matter how many times it is transcribed or transferred. The check digit, once calculated, becomes part of the number, and is recalculated and checked whenever the number is referred to. It should be pointed out that this process only confirms that the check digit is applicable to the number with which it is associated—not that it is the correct number. No check digit system is 100 per cent foolproof.

Validation checks. Data validation involves the review of input data by a program to ensure that it falls within predetermined parameters and is as free from error as possible. Relying on the data input operator's ability to spot errors displayed on the screen is not an adequate data entry control. Where direct input takes place, controls can be programmed to highlight the errors on the screen. Errors can be rejected by the system and shown on the screen with a meaningful error message describing the reason for rejection.

There are a number of different types of validation check. These include:

- *data format checks* which ascertain that the item contains the correct number of digits and that these are the correct combination of alphabetic and numeric characters;
- *presence verification* where the program automatically checks that all mandatory fields in the input record are present, and rejects the record if this is not the case. Another version of this check is where the program automatically confirms the presence of the record the transaction is trying to update;
- *range checking* which ensures that the input data falls within certain predetermined limits. The amount of protection provided by such a check will depend upon how it is applied. One weakness of this category lies in the fact that usually the range must be set wide enough to accept all possible valid data. This check does not test the correctness of data but only ensures that figures are within acceptable boundaries.

Range checks can be absolute, setting an overall value such as a maximum chargeable rate per hour. This is an insensitive method which can be improved by setting up a table linking a limit with some other factor such as a department or grade and applying the check more selectively.

It is not always necessary to specify values when setting limits. A value can be considered in ratio to another item.

The use of range checks will be affected by the action taken when items outside the range are found. If data failing the check is to be rejected then the limits tend to be fairly wide, which may allow some erroneous data through. If failure to pass the check results only in a report, with the data continuing to be used, tighter limits can be applied if necessary.

Crosscasting checks. These mean that the computer automatically validates arithmetic and in doing so confirms the underlying data.

Data authorisation procedures. Critical data should be authorised prior to being input to the computer system. There are a number of possible alternatives, such as:

- the checking of a document by a senior member of staff who signs or initials it to signify authorisation;
- the checking of batches of documents by a senior member of staff, who signs or initials a summary document to signify authorisation of the batch;
- scrutiny of on-line input to the system by a supervisor who progresses the transaction using an authorising code.

8.2.2   Security over Processing
Header and trailer records. Tape files have electronic 'labels':

- header labels which contain information which identifies the data held on the tape;
- trailer labels which contain control information.

Checks against the information held on these labels can be incorporated into application program controls.

Run to run controls. These are created by the accumulation by a program of control totals. As records are added, deleted or amended the control totals are amended accordingly and a reconciliation (b/f plus or minus amendments = c/f) is performed either by program or manually at the completion of processing. Even if the reconciliation is performed by the system, a printed report should be produced.

Audit or management trail. A facility must be available to identify individual transactions at all critical stages of processing. It is the duty of an organisation's external auditors to make such tests and enquiries as are necessary to form an opinion on the reliability of the records. The use of the computer is irrelevant to this statutory responsibility and an audit trail should be established which will obtain the details behind the summarised totals and analysis. An auditor, having found a discrepancy in a total, would want to investigate the detail causing the discrepancy and the audit trail must be capable of being followed through the system from source data to final output. It must also provide readable evidence at each stage if required.

The internal auditor, with wide-ranging responsibilities for monitoring internal controls, will also require the facility to access individual transactions in this way. However, this feature should not be seen as an audit requirement only, and this is recognised in many organisations by the use of the term 'management trail'.

File security. Although the file security arrangements operating in the tape/disk library are part of the general security measures required in the Computer Operations Department (see Chapter Six), some procedures may be specific to particular applications.

Tape-based systems may use the 'Grandfather-father-son' procedure in which the tape master file input to each process is stored after processing, together with the transactions which were used to update it. The output tape is, in turn, input to the next processing run and, on its conclusion, is also stored with the relevant transactions. In this way loss or corruption of a current master file need not be a tragedy since it can be recreated by repeating the previous processing run.

Controls over disk files. These need to be more complex. The process of updating non-sequential disk files differs from that of tape files in that:

- new disk files are not created during every update;
- the complete file does not need to be read;

So the reconciliation of control totals cannot take place as a by-product of the application.

Control totals need to be produced as a separate activity, but this can be part of the security 'dumping' process (when data is copied to tapes which are then stored at remote sites). Control totals must be produced and reconciled before the tapes are released to storage.

Standing data. This needs special treatment. The term covers:

- reference data on master files, such as addresses, account numbers or descriptions of customer status;
- data held on tables, in specific files or in programs, which is constantly referred to and used as the basis for further processing, but only infrequently changed. Examples are:
  - pay rates;
  - prices;
  - interest rates.

All amendments to standing data should be printed and checked for accuracy and proper authorisation. These files must be periodically checked by the user department.

Checkpointing. This entails the periodic copying to tape of the contents of a file being processed. In the event of a breakdown the contents of the most recent tape can be read back into the computer, saving the time which would otherwise be needed to start from scratch.

Frequent checkpoints save work at restart but they require more overhead. When calculating the ideal checkpoint interval for any system it is necessary to compare the cost of taking checkpoints with the cost of delay.

8.2.3 *Security of Output*

Output reconciliation. This completes the chain of control which commenced with the creation of batch totals or counts, and produced run-to-run controls. A final report will be produced which provides evidence of reconciliation through all stages of the system, thus verifying the accuracy of the output.

Stationery control. Special controls should apply to all 'sensitive' stationery such as cheques.

Exception and suspense reports. There must be adequate procedures (which must be followed) for investigation and any necessary resubmission of rejected or 'suspended' transactions. Resubmission itself must be carefully controlled.

Report continuity. The user must be satisfied that all pages of a report are received. Programs should:

- sequentially number the pages of all reports;
- ensure that the first and last pages are identified as such.

Microfiche. Use of this and other output media must be controlled in a manner appropriate to the sensitivity of the data held. This may seem to be unexceptional and obvious, but in practice many organisations' view of security of output is restricted to paper and the more exotic electronic media.

8.3   Systems Software

All applications software depends on the correctness and secure operation of systems software, which creates the environment in which the hardware obeys the application program's instructions. Each program instruction, for instance:

- is converted to a machine-understandable instruction by a compiler;
- is acted upon according to instructions provided by the operating system;
- sees only the data in a database which the DBMS (Database Management System) will allow it to see.

Errors in systems software can cause the entire system to collapse. Fraudulent code could cause significant losses to the organisation without being picked up by the controls which regulate the applications system.

Many IT staff often depend on utilities without thinking of the effects of their manipulation or erroneous operation.

Most computer installations have experienced systems collapse or degradation because of the failure of some component of systems software. Despite the vast amounts of testing undertaken before the best examples are marketed, unexpected situations do arise and, if not catered for, can have extensive—and expensive—repercussions.

In order to ensure that the system maintains its expected level of service, and to reduce the possibility of abuse, it is important that each organisation takes steps to secure its systems software. Control over the experts who use it is also a critical aspect, and this is dealt with in Chapter Nine of this book.

Security personnel and auditors should take an interest in operating systems and associated software. The systems software itself often provides facilities which help to control computer users, such as those provided by many operating systems to protect users' files and to record accesses to them.

The operating system should provide software features which will enable control to be exercised over all applications and systems software. They should include:

- access control features (this will be covered in more detail in Chapter Ten);
- the facility to log all changes to programs;

- a version number, which should be automatically incremented each time a change takes place;
- a recorded time and date for each execution of all programs;
- a method of cross-referencing the 'object' or 'executable' version with the source code of the same version;
- backup and restore features which will apply to:
  - the entire library;
  - individual items.

The physical files holding programs should be held in a secure media library and maintained and issued under the controls described in Figure 6.2.

All files should be 'dumped' periodically, providing security copies to be held under controlled circumstances in offsite premises (see 6.4).

The activities of most reasonably-sophisticated computer systems include the simultaneous processing of several programs. The Operating System and related systems software must combine with hardware integrity checks to ensure that this takes place without the occurrence, or possibility of, security conflicts. The following must be achieved if any trust is to be placed in the results of processing:

- All attempts by application or systems software to access system resources must be checked for the correct level of access authorisation.
- All conflicting requests for the use of resources must be resolved in a way which is transparent to the user, although reported for future analysis.
- The software which provides these features must itself be secure from unauthorised access.

8.4 Database Security

IT staff are often quick to adopt a new term and slow to respect its meaning. This has certainly been true of the word 'database', which had scarcely been invented before it was being applied to any simple computer file or even to a sheaf of papers. Many installations found the change to database was simple—merely changing their terminology.

Many businesses first invested in computers in the 1960s and installed one system—usually the payroll. When this was done they went on to another system, usually on the basis of 'Buggin's Turn' or 'Who Shouts Loudest Wins'. After a few years of haphazard development the computer installation found itself with a heap of unrelated and redundant data. Each new application created its own separate files and linking these with anything else was complicated, if not impossible. The database was invented to address these, and other problems.

The usual definition of a database is: 'A collection of interrelated data stored together without harmful or unnecessary redundancy to serve multiple applications.'

The data is stored so as to achieve independence from the programs that use the data, and the structure of the data allows for future applications developments. Data is entered once only and is available to whoever wants it, subject to security restrictions. It will also be available to future applications, if they need it.

In systems which use conventional 'non-database' technology, data items are grouped together as records and contained within files.

Programs must specify the characteristics of these files and records in some detail and, during processing, may read through a great deal of information not required for the task in progress. A payroll program, for instance, may access the personnel files to extract basic rates of pay, but it will also have to read and disregard details of addresses, date of employment, etc.

The same item of data may be held several times within one computer system.

The results of this method of holding data are:

- Changes are complicated and expensive: one file may be used by numerous programs and one program may use numerous files, so amendments to files and programs have a chain effect—one small change requiring a series of changes through the system.
- Data access times can be lengthy—particularly for 'enquiry' type processing. Whole files or large sections of files may need to be read to retrieve small amounts of data.
- Storage requirements are large and expensive with the same item of data being recorded several times.
- Updates to files can be lengthy and lead to inconsistencies unless procedures ensure that all versions of a data item are updated together.

In a database system each individual field (data element) is a separate entity. The Database Management System (DBMS) keeps a map of every element, noting its relationship to other elements and its physical position in the database. This is called the database 'schema'.

The concept of records and files, in the conventional sense, does not apply in a database environment. Instead, the individual data elements required by each program are collectively called a 'sub-schema'.

The DBMS maintains a record of which programs use which sub-schemas. When a program is running the DBMS uses its sub-schema to identify the individual elements of data required and uses the overall picture provided by the schema to retrieve them from the database.

Thus it can be seen that the data and the program are independent of each other, but linked by the DBMS.

The advantages of this method in an ideal environment are that:

- data and programs can be changed without one affecting the other (data independence);

- access is usually faster since only the required data is extracted;
- updates are more accurate as each data element is stored only once (no redundant data) and inconsistencies cannot arise.
- storage requirements are less.

In practice there may be some data redundancy and data independence is not absolute.

This approach to database design imposes a rigid structure on the database and can lead to very complex indexing arrangements. The relational database method introduced by EF Codd revolutionised database concepts and removed the demand for complex indexes.

The relational database is based upon the simplest possible data structure (ie, tables or flat files). These tables, referred to as relations, can be manipulated to provide a view of the data appropriate to the particular application. The users can be effectively provided with an individual database—which is a subset of the total database—geared to their particular requirements. This individual database does not involve any physical partitioning or re-arrangement of the stored data. It does not therefore introduce the dangers of duplication or inconsistency inherent in the production of multiple 'private' databases. The provision of local views also simplifies security procedures since individual users are only provided with a sub-schema consistent with their security grading.

The modern trend is to employ relational databases accessed interactively with simple query languages or processed by fourth-generation languages. Whereas earlier databases were primarily processed by application programs in batch mode, current systems are designed to support both this mode and on-line access, for ad hoc queries and updates by a large and diffuse user population.

Data Dictionary

With the huge volumes of data associated with a database, it is essential to maintain a central index, or dictionary, of all the data items or elements within the database.

This index is often called a data dictionary and consists of a list of all the data items and their relationships to each other, their location in the storage media, and which programs or sub-schemas use them.

The dictionary may also be extended to include a human-readable definition of each term and an indication of the ownership of each data item.

Clearly, such a dictionary is necessary before changes can be made to the data structures if chaos is to be avoided. The dictionary could theoretically be maintained manually, but practical considerations dictate the use of software packages.

Administration

The overall responsibility for the database is in the hands of the Database Administrator (DBA).

The DBA (in practice often a department) must be responsible from the outset for defining the database and subsequently for maintaining, running and reorganising it. This responsibility extends to maintenance of the data dictionary.

No changes may be made without DBA authority and all access to the data must be controlled by the DBA.

This role of central control and organisation is of paramount importance if the database is to operate satisfactorily.

Among the activities of the DBA are the following:

- designing the physical aspect of the database;
- balancing conflicting user demands;
- supporting application programmers in their use of the DBMS;
- organising security measures and use of utilities;
- investigating and correcting faults.

Maintenance

By their nature, databases attract large volumes of data, a certain amount of which becomes redundant after a time. Athough it may be deleted from the users' point of view it still remains physically within the data structure and can slow down access times considerably.

Consequently, the database is reorganised periodically to remove this 'dead' data and, if necessary, rearrange the links between existing data items. These 'house-keeping' activities contribute significantly to the effectiveness of database systems and can also, as described later in this chapter, assist in their control.

There is also a process known as 'tuning' which is applied when the pattern of use of the database has been established: by 'tuning' the database (rearranging the way in which the data is stored), technical staff can often significantly increase the efficiency of the systems.

Database Management System (DBMS)

The DBMS, by making a distinction between the 'physical' (schema) and 'logical' (sub-schema) views of data, creates an extra level at which security features must be considered, since interference at both levels is possible.

The DBMS performs the following functions:

- handling of multiple concurrent usage, avoiding contention and inconsistency if two or more users access the database at the same time;
- providing an access control mechanism which allows the DBA to limit reading or updating functions to specific users;
- providing a mechanism for recovery from hardware and software

failures. Apart from traditional dumping of data, logs can be written of the 'before' and 'after' image of each record when it is changed;
- providing a toolkit of utilities, with features such as:
  - loading;
  - reorganisation;
  - debugging;
  - performance monitoring.

Included in these utilities will usually be software which allows the DBA to 'patch' data by simply overwriting it at the physical level. This utility, if used, must always be controlled;
- offering an interface to a programming language: this allows a program to 'call' the DBMS.

A query language interface is provided, usually as an 'extra', although programmers may build in similar programs for specific users.

Security and Control
The security arrangements for a database should meet the requirements listed below:

- No person, or groups of persons, should be able to access, modify, add or delete the data illegally.
- No unauthorised person or group of persons should be able to infer the value of a confidential item by manipulating queries or performing computations on released data.
- The security arrangements should be flexible and users provided with privileges appropriate to their function and needs.
- The security mechanisms should not significantly degrade the performance of the database management system (DBMS).
- The accessibility of the system should not be reduced for legitimate users.
- The cost of the security arrangements should not be incompatible with the function of the database.
- Use of any software which is capable of altering data at schema level must be restricted.

On-line access in a multi-user environment demands both a simple user interface and a sophisticated database management system which guarantees security and integrity under all operating conditions. The database must be protected against aborted transactions which could leave it in an inconsistent state; for example, an accounting transaction which credits one account but does not debit the corresponding account. It must also be possible to reconstruct the database in the case of system failure. Concurrent users must be protected against mutual interference, particularly if both are updating the same record.

The total population of database users is expanding rapidly. At one end of the spectrum there are massive databases designed for corporate bodies, and public databases serving national and international users. At the other, there are a variety of microcomputer database management systems designed for small businesses and professional users.

In non-database systems it was usually possible to identify a user for each file. They could be held to be primarily responsible for the control of the systems using their files.

Since a database usually only holds an item of data once, and this can be used by a number of 'users', there is no natural way of assigning responsibility for each item. Partly as a result of this problem, the role of Database Administrator described earlier was established and formal responsibility for the control and integrity of the data is assigned to the DBA.

Although the complexity of database management systems has made it necessary to vest control in a DP specialist, it is unfortunate from a security point of view that the user is deprived, to a certain extent, of his opportunity to satisfy himself of the proper functioning of his operation.

The organisation's dependence on the DBA is almost total. He has both the knowledge and the opportunity to cause chaos to—or fraudulently manipulate—the database. In order to do his job of optimising the storage of data he:

- needs access to the database, in order to enquire and to amend data;
- has access to all system documentation;
- has access to the DBMS software;
- knows the restrictions on access to data;
- knows how the application programs process the data;
- has authority to initiate computer runs.

The only thing he may not fully understand is the application system. With the above facilities available he does not need this knowledge since it would be possible to circumvent the application controls.

To control the actions of the DBA, evidence of his activities must be printed by the system and independently checked. It may be possible to identify a 'primary user' for each system who should be responsible for this. However the technical nature of his activities may necessitate delegation of much of this work, perhaps to a senior member of the team responsible for development of applications systems. In addition, the DBA should never be allowed to be a 'one man band'.

- He should be effectively supervised;
- Fall-back staff should be trained to man the DBA function in an emergency;
- A contingency plan should exist for use if the database was rendered inoperable.

Restrictions to Database Usage
Users should be restricted in what they are able to do to the database. Each program, preferably under the control of one authorised user, will be allowed access for one of the following purposes, and be blocked by software from any other action:

- read only;
- read and add new data;
- read and amend;
- read and delete.

Validation of Input
The ideal time to validate data is at the stage at which it is input to the system, and this is usual with conventional systems. With a database, different elements of the data to be validated may be input at different times. It is essential that users and systems designers specify necessary validation tests and authorisation requirements as a formal design procedure.

If it is impractical to authorise input prior to submission, 'after-the-event' authorisation would be acceptable in some systems. The data will enter the system and be held on the database, but a listing or display will be provided for the 'authoriser' and no action will take place until he signifies his agreement.

Database Control Totals
Run-to-run control totals are easily produced when a tape file is read sequentially from start to finish. It is not so easy with databases, since the system has no compulsion to read the entire database every time a run takes place. Only selected records are read and control totals are only produced when the disk goes through a 'housekeeping' (reorganisation) process, or when 'dumped' to tape for security purposes.

Since control totals are necessary to confirm the integrity of the database, a special 'control run' must take place, either as part of security dumping, housekeeping or, if the frequency of these runs is not sufficient, as a separate run.

Database Recovery
In addition to the security copy of the database, all transactions processed should be logged, together with the 'before' and 'after' images of the records in order to provide easy recovery.

8.5 Comparing the Risk Factors in IT Systems

While planning security reviews of individual computer systems it is necessary to identify the more critical systems and create a prioritised list. The risks associated with each system may need to be assessed on a number of occa-

Figure 8.1

RISK ASSESSMENT SCORE SHEET

Scoring Criteria		*Score Factor*
Development	– formal systems development procedures	1.0
	– no formal systems development	2.0
	– orthodox development	1.0
	– prototyping	1.6
Language	– high level	1.0
	– 4GL	1.2
	– low level	1.6
Estimated number	– 1–5	1.0
of modules	– 6–10	1.2
	– 11–20	1.4
	– 20–35	1.6
	– 35 +	1.8
Systems users	– 1 user	1.0
	– multiple users	1.5
Organisation	– no re-organisation	1.0
	– re-organisation	1.5
Type of project	– maintenance	1.0
	– enhancement	1.2
	– development	1.6
	– major development	2.0
System type	– stand alone	1.0
	– integrates with other systems	1.4
Complexity	– batch (not on line)	1.0
	– on line batch	1.2
	– real time	2.0
Data Structure	– master files	1.0
	– databases	1.6
	– non-sensitive system	1.0
	– financial system	1.5
	– sensitive non-financial system	1.5
Development	– estimated cost: – £10K	1.0
	– £10K – £50K	1.2
	– £50K – £100K	1.5
	– £100K – £250K	1.8
	– £250K +	2.0
	– estimated time – 3 months	1.0
	– 3–12 months	1.2
	– 12–24 months	1.6
	– 24 + months	2.0

To arrive at a total score for the system, multiply the score for each section (eg: 1.6 × 1.4 × 2.0 etc)

sions throughout its life. There are several possible techniques, but perhaps the simplest is the use of a score sheet. One such score sheet is shown as an example (Figure 8.1). It will not be suitable for all organisations and will need to be modified to suit the particular circumstances of each. Scoring criteria and score factors may be removed, added or changed; but once decided on and used, the score sheet must remain in that form for future assessments. In this way the risk factors between systems of different sizes and types become comparable.

The example compares the criteria which would be considered when comparing systems under development. However the same principles—and many of the same criteria—will also apply when constructing a score sheet for comparing 'live' systems.

The method does not use probabilities. It uses objective data for each criterion and then applies a factor to each. The absolute accuracy of the score factor is not critical provided that the factors used remain the same for each system being assessed. In this way comparison between the systems remains valid and objective.

In the same way, the total score should not be taken as the sole selection criterion. The individual scores are more meaningful and need to be considered, one system with another.

9 Secure Systems Development and Maintenance

9.1 Introduction

A project: **'An indeterminate number of unknown activities conducted to variable standards by different people, all of whom have their own objectives, perceptions and misapprehensions.'** (Anon.)

This definition applies to many types of project, but IT specialists and managers will find no difficulty in recalling many systems development projects which incorporated most of the features described.

As the cost of hardware decreases, the proportion of expenditure involved in the development of systems becomes greater and the proper control of development becomes more important.

An uncontrolled systems development will automatically produce a system which is uncontrollable. 'Bugs' and other accidental errors will proliferate while these systems are a fertile breeding ground for attempts at fraud. Viruses, Trojan Horses and simple errors are generated in different ways and for different reasons, but they reach live systems via the same weaknesses— lack of effective development and implementation procedures.

It is essential that all security aspects of a system under development be considered as early as is practicable. These will include not only the application controls and logical access rules but also the variety of requirements which may relate to:

- any hardware or systems software changes;
- use of new or unfamiliar techniques;
- procedural changes, especially those which affect employee activities;
- social aspects, such as changes in terms of employment, working hours or staff location;
- any necessary environmental changes.

IT strategy studies must include consideration of security at strategy level, and security development should accompany all stages of the development life cycle. In this way, additional or enhanced security features can be planned and incorporated as a natural component of the development process, avoiding the extra cost and stress which invariably accompanies the 'retrofitting' of security.

Initial planning must produce:

- realistic business and technical objectives;
- achievable milestones;
- deliverables;
- an agreed project organisation;
- a detailed list of activities;
- details of all resources required to achieve the objectives, including:
    - people
    - finance
    - equipment and services.

It must also include 'defensive' planning ('what will we do if . . .').

A systems development methodology such as that shown in Figure 9.1 should be used by every organisation. This enables development to take place in a controlled fashion, allowing for proper supervision and reviews at agreed checkpoints. Users should be involved at all stages of the development since this is the only way in which they can be sure that the system they receive will be the system that they require. The organisational structure of the programming and systems design departments should ensure that it is impossible to include program instructions or modules which are not authorised. Detailed testing for implementation should ensure that the system which finally 'goes live' is exactly the system required by the user—no more and no less!

9.2 Control of Systems Programmers

Systems software (see Chapter 8.3) is usually purchased from commercial vendors and is sometimes modified to fit a particular organisation's needs. The software is selected, installed, and maintained by systems programmers, who are usually highly skilled and have access to the most sensitive elements of the computer system.

In many organisations, systems programmers are isolated from the conduct of the organisation's primary business and, as a result, are outside the usual patterns of control—even those applied to applications programmers and designers. Their activities are often unsupervised, while the systems they handle do not undergo managerial review to ensure that they support the organisation's business objectives, as is usually the case with application systems.

In the absence of other controls, their expertise and knowledge give them the power to:

- manipulate elements of system software;
- use systems software and utilities to amend applications programs and data files.

Figure 9.1

STRUCTURED SYSTEMS DEVELOPMENT

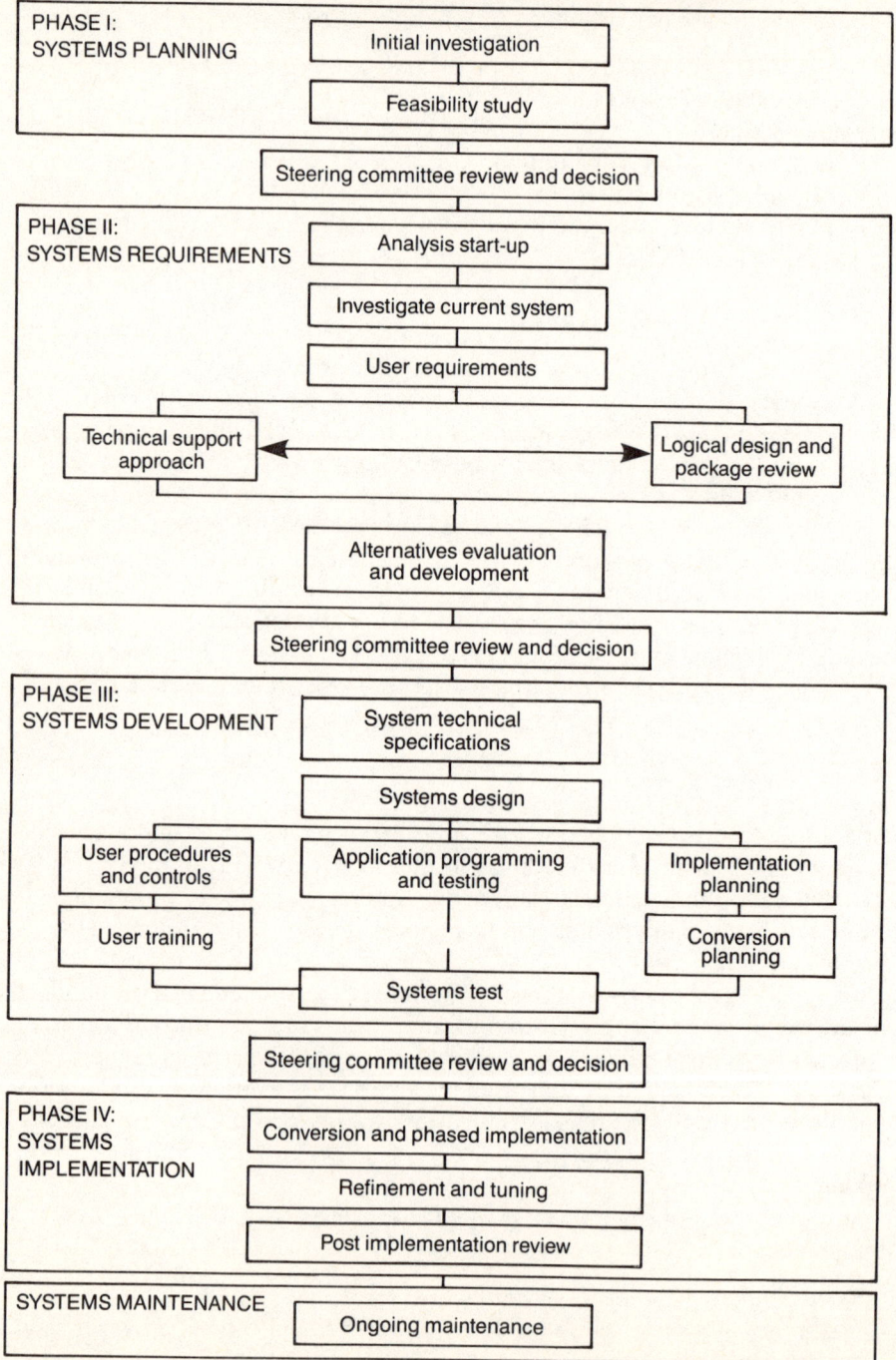

PHASE I:
SYSTEMS PLANNING

- Initial investigation
- Feasibility study

Steering committee review and decision

PHASE II:
SYSTEMS REQUIREMENTS

- Analysis start-up
- Investigate current system
- User requirements

Technical support approach ⟷ Logical design and package review

- Alternatives evaluation and development

Steering committee review and decision

PHASE III:
SYSTEMS DEVELOPMENT

- System technical specifications
- Systems design

User procedures and controls | Application programming and testing | Implementation planning

User training | | Conversion planning

Systems test

Steering committee review and decision

PHASE IV:
SYSTEMS
IMPLEMENTATION

- Conversion and phased implementation
- Refinement and tuning
- Post implementation review

SYSTEMS MAINTENANCE

- Ongoing maintenance

The most common security weaknesses in a systems programming environment include:

- lack of adequate physical or logical access controls;
- lack of comprehensive and easy-to-use documentation of the systems environment, causing over-reliance on the few employees who understand the details;
- lack of fundamental controls over modifications to systems software;
- lack of periodic comprehensive testing of disaster recovery procedures.

In addition to the possibility of deliberate manipulation referred to above, this can lead to problems such as:

- loss of data integrity;
- errors during updating of files;
- software not operating according to specification.

Management can minimise these risks by:

- managing systems programming in the same way as it manages other vital departments;
- bringing systems programming under the standard patterns of controls associated with other vital departments;
- defining business requirements in terms that will guide the systems programming group.

Systems programmers must be subject to relevant organisational controls, such as:

- restricted access to computer facilities;
- restricted access to live software and data;
- segregation of duties.

Their activities should be supervised and subject to frequent peer review. Since controls of this type are frequently allowed to lapse under pressure, their use must be monitored.

Security measures are needed in the following areas:

- software;
- procedures;
- organisation;
- supervision.

Examples are given below.

Software
- Installation of security software supporting multi-level password protection for program and data libraries.
- Incorporation of security and file access features into the systems software to support restrictions over systems programmers.

- Installation of an authorised program facility to restrict use of authorised programs.
- Use of job accounting software to monitor use of systems resources.
- Use of software such as System Management Facility (SMF) to provide detailed audit trails of jobs processed by the operating system.
- The facility to log all changes to programs.
- Version control.
- Installation of encryption software where appropriate.
- Installation of software to monitor and measure the performance of teleprocessing software.

Procedures
- Standard procedures for loading and running all software.
- Standard procedures for applying program fixes and installing system upgrades.
- Standard backup and retention procedures for vital program records and files.
- Standard procedures to control the issue and return of physical access devices such as keys, magnetic cards, and identification badges.
- Standard procedures prescribing retention periods for console logs and job accounting systems records.
- Standard procedures to govern system generation activities.
- Establishing and periodically testing disaster recovery procedures such as fire precautions, backup electrical power and standby processing.
- Procedures which control the issue and use of a password.

Organisation
- Segregation of duties within the systems programming function to ensure that responsibilities are assigned in a way that enhances control and limits opportunities for unmonitored or unrecorded activities.
- Training staff to provide a 'reserve team' for all specialists.
- Participation of the systems programmers in the development of contingency plans and the recovery process.
- Clearly-defined reporting and supervising responsibilities.

Documentation
- Maintenance of on-line documentation of operating system configuration tables, written procedures, guidelines, etc.
- Up-to-date and comprehensive documentation of the contingency plan and recovery process.
- Documentation of output from the system monitoring and network logging software.

Supervision
- Management review of the systems logs which record use of the computer, programs, and data files.
- Attendance by appropriate supervisory staff during all shifts.
- Routines for regularly assuring management that controls are maintained; such as exception reports, initials evidencing review activities, logbooks of review activities, written reports and checklists.

9.3 Control of Dangerous Utilities

Utilities are available which can amend specific storage areas containing data, or applications or systems software, without leaving any traces or being identified by application controls. The use of these 'patching' utilities should, if not banned outright, be carefully monitored. Examples of these utilities are SUPERZAP, ALTADATA and PFIX. Other software packages, such as Data Query, include an 'Update' feature which should be similarly restricted.

Other utilities, such as file copiers, listing programs, interrogation software and report generators are capable of fraudulent use and must be similarly controlled.

9.4 Remote Maintenance

There is an increasing trend for computer manufacturers to maintain and investigate faults in computer systems by 'remote diagnosis'.

The manufacturer's systems engineers use facilities which allow them to dial into the customer's computer system, using special software to collect details of faults in the hardware or systems software. The systems engineer can then often apply a correction directly, saving the time involved in a visit. In this way system faults can be identified and rectified more quickly.

Before agreeing to remote maintenance, management should make enquiries about the types of security procedures which have been instituted by the manufacturer. Password checks and hard-coded terminal identifiers in the systems engineer's terminal help to ensure that the system cannot be accessed by unauthorised people. The manufacturer will be expected to accept liability for abuse of the system by his employees and, where possible, connection should only take place after dial-back by the customer. Sensitive files should not be present on the system, or access to them should be disabled, during remote maintenance.

Installations which require a very high level of security should reload their systems software from backup after remote maintenance has taken place, in case elements of the systems software have been changed. If remote maintenance activities involve making legitimate changes to elements of the systems software, the updated piece of systems software should be isolated, checked by the installation's systems programmer, then loaded with the backup copy of the rest of the systems software.

9.5 Security of Associated Documentation

The least regarded activity in systems and software development is the production of the documentation which:

- describes the system;
- records the steps by which it was developed.

Since this documentation may be the only way of confirming the processing, it must be kept securely.

The documentation must be accurate and up to date, and updates must take place at the same time as the relevant software changes. A document register should be maintained with details of all changes, and this should be frequently compared with the register holding details of software upgrades.

Decisions will be needed on the method and location of storage, and the responsibility for the documents must be allocated unambiguously to the appropriate members of staff.

A regular review must take place of the adequacy of storage.

9.6 Quality Assurance (QA) in IT Projects

The responsibility for compliance with an organisation's IT development standards lies unequivocally with project management. However, detailed monitoring of an IT development project is often delegated to a QA team reporting to the project manager or the IT manager. Both project management and QA can be seen as security features.

An effective QA function will initially assist the IT department and project teams to define an acceptable level of quality in terms of both IT standards and the requirements of the potential users of the system. Subsequent monitoring of project results and supporting documentation will check for:

- accuracy, reliability and consistency;
- conformity with specified user requirements;
- conformity with agreed standards of security and control;
- conformity with technical specifications and corporate development standards;
- adequacy of documentation;
- technical weaknesses or errors.

9.7   Control of System Maintenance and Enhancement (Change Control)

The development process is not complete when the system is implemented. Throughout the life of the system, changes and enhancements will be generated by:

- 'bugs' identified during live running;
- new user requirements;
- new technology.

Each of these carries the same potential for error or deliberate insertion of unauthorised programs as the original development, and must be controlled accordingly.

The essential control over changes to live systems is that they should be treated in the same way as systems development projects and be subject to the same checks. An effective change control system must document all stages of development, testing and implementation. Although this mechanism may sometimes appear to be heavy-handed and to endanger the prompt delivery of changes, there are also considerable benefits. The documentation produced will provide evidence that each change has been accomplished correctly and undergone the necessary supervisory checks and testing procedures before being applied to the live system, producing some assurance that unauthorised amendments have not been included.

All requests for changes must be accurately and unambiguously described in a formal Change Request document which must be authorised at an appropriate level of user management. There should also be a procedure which ensures that all valid requests for changes are accounted for and dealt with promptly. All change request forms should be serially-numbered and entered in a register which will be updated with details of each stage the change goes through.

The register can be valuable, not only in providing 'after the event' evidence of correct change procedures but also as a means of progress chasing. Change Requests should be regularly reviewed by a responsible person.

There must be adequate supervision of all stages of the change and no amendments to the live system—however small—should be performed and tested by the same person. Testing must be thorough and comprehensive, covering all possible combinations of 'spin-off' effects on other parts of the system, and should be performed by a person or group independent from the team responsible for the enhancement. Controls must ensure that only authorised changes are incorporated in the live system, and that only one version of each program exists in the production library. It is, naturally, essential that the software needed for the 'cataloguing' process (which promotes the change to the 'live' system) is held and used under secure conditions.

Although program change procedures must be strictly enforced they must be flexible enough to cope with urgent amendments. In some cases 'fixes' are needed—typically at night—when the personnel needed to authorise changes are unavailable. Although all changes must be properly authorised, approved and checked, these procedures may need to be applied—in exceptional cases—after the event. All staff must be aware that the retrospective nature of these controls does not mean that they can be ignored.

Change in Real-Time Systems
Although changes to real-time systems can cause many problems, they differ from those experienced in batch systems in degree rather than type. It is important to control the timing of changes, which should be made after the end of the day's real-time processing. In order to allow for reversion to the original system in the event of an emergency, the modified program should be placed in a 'pseudo-production' library until the end of a specified quarantine period.

Frequent backup copies of on-line program libraries should be made in order to ensure the protection of the latest versions of all programs.

Security Aspects of Change Control
An uncontrolled program change system provides unlimited scope for fraud or mischief. It is often in this environment, rather than the more controlled development process, that many Trojan Horses, time bombs and viruses have been introduced.

The installation of an effective series of change control procedures is essential for security purposes, although any well-managed IT department will need this for many other reasons. Once the procedures have been installed they must be reviewed frequently, confirming that all changes are:

• properly authorised;
• dealt with promptly and correctly;
• adequately documented and reviewed by IT management.

Systems which have experienced an abnormally high level of changes should be investigated by management.

The potential for disaster inherent in the emergency overnight 'fix' must be recognised, and these activities should be reviewed even more frequently than the more formal changes.

9.8 Fourth-Generation Languages

Systems development staff are under continuing pressure to increase speed of production and decrease costs. During the past few years, many organisations have moved towards the use of a different approach to systems development, which may produce tangible benefits but also produces extra security considerations. Using this 'prototyping' approach, users and programmers work together to design and build software applications, using simple but powerful fourth-generation languages (4GLs). Lead time on projects has been considerably reduced by providing users, as quickly as possible, with a 'rough draft' of the required system which can then be further developed until the final product has been accepted. The introduction of 4GLs has led to the adoption in many installations of a speedy, user-friendly method of development. 4GLs are comparatively simple to learn, and users are finding them valuable in accessing a database, selecting information and producing meaningful reports.

This approach has, in many cases, significantly increased:

- productivity in developing software;
- the speed at which systems are developed;
- user involvement in developing systems.

Prototyping techniques using 4GLs have created opportunities. However, as usual, there are attendant risks which must concern security staff and management.

Since systems are more dynamic, more easily changed and more responsive to users, they could be seen — in a poorly-controlled environment — to be less stable. Because systems action is dispersed among the users, control activities cannot be centralised and depend on the security-consciousness of widely-distributed groups, many of which may not understand the need for strict adherence to laid-down procedures.

There is a danger that this technique used by inexperienced staff could result in little attention being paid to review and testing. As programmers back out of their traditional isolation and begin to work with dispersed users it becomes more difficult to ensure that their work is being reviewed. Users may adopt the prototype and declare that it is the system they want before it can be properly tested. If so the relieved programmer may accept this decision too readily, without confirming the user's understanding of the system's limitations.

Frequently, the security and reliability requirements are omitted in an attempt to produce 'quick and dirty' programs which work. Often there is an intention to add these features later, but if a working set of programs has already been shown to the customer it becomes difficult to justify the extra time and cost. All too often, these essential features are, under pressure, ignored.

The problems can be far worse if end-user programming is introduced in an uncontrolled fashion. Users may generate untested programs without documentation. Quality will be very variable unless proper standards are introduced. However, the existence of standards is not enough. Users must be educated to understand the need for standards, and management convinced that they must control their staff without detracting from the benefits of this creative initiative.

End-user programming can become very dangerous if the following principles are not applied:

Figure 9.2

THE PROTOTYPING SYSTEMS DEVELOPMENT APPROACH

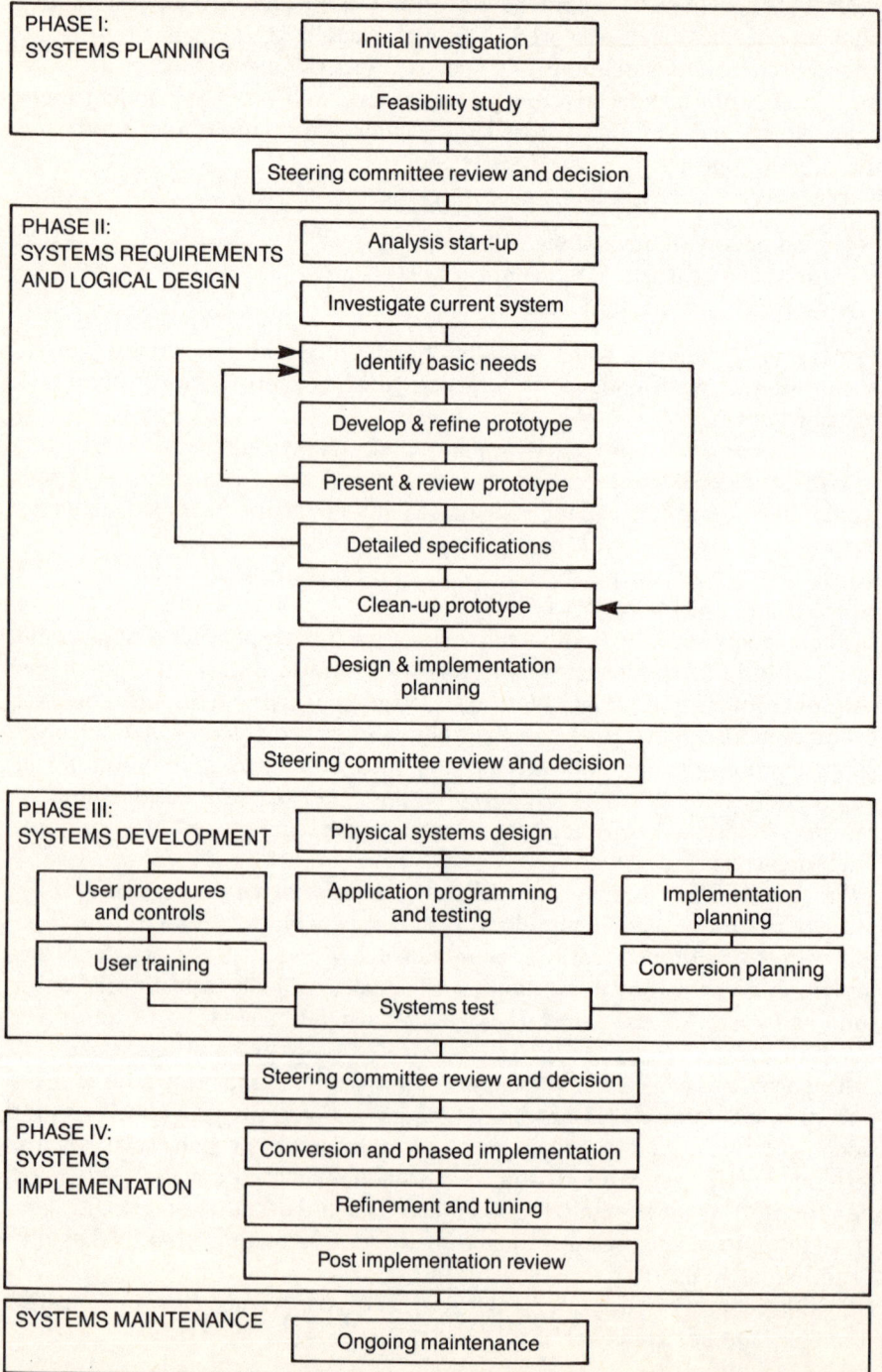

PHASE I:
SYSTEMS PLANNING

Initial investigation

Feasibility study

Steering committee review and decision

PHASE II:
SYSTEMS REQUIREMENTS
AND LOGICAL DESIGN

Analysis start-up

Investigate current system

Identify basic needs

Develop & refine prototype

Present & review prototype

Detailed specifications

Clean-up prototype

Design & implementation planning

Steering committee review and decision

PHASE III:
SYSTEMS DEVELOPMENT

Physical systems design

User procedures and controls

Application programming and testing

Implementation planning

User training

Conversion planning

Systems test

Steering committee review and decision

PHASE IV:
SYSTEMS
IMPLEMENTATION

Conversion and phased implementation

Refinement and tuning

Post implementation review

SYSTEMS MAINTENANCE

Ongoing maintenance

- the users' programs should not be permitted to alter the corporate database;
- the output from each end-user's program should identify itself as such.

If end-users are allowed to update the corporate database of information which is used to produce reports for other users, or is further processed by corporate systems, the integrity of corporate information cannot be assured. Errors made by users may affect the vital information on which the business depends, which is patently not acceptable. In order to protect the corporate database from corruption, all input and updates must be subject to appropriate validation procedures. Since it is impractical to police validation procedures in user-produced programs, the most effective recourse is to prohibit user programs from updating corporate files.

Since formal testing procedures cannot be effectively enforced in an end-user programming environment, all reports from end-user programs should be treated as having the authority of handwritten or manually typed documents. For example, if a report produced by the marketing department has a column heading 'Profit', then a member of the Finance Department when reading it must ask himself 'What do Marketing mean by profit?' and not assume that the term is being used in the same way as it is by the corporate information system. Identification of end-users' reports will assist this process.

Identification of end-user reports should not be left entirely to the users, but be tackled on a corporate basis. A variety of methods can be used. Reports which are part of the corporate information system can be clearly identified, thus identifying all other reports, by default, as end-user reports. This can be achieved by using special paper, or a special house style in heading or footing corporate reports. While this option is simple if printers controlled by users are attached to the system, it may be impractical to enforce without restricting the production of corporate information to centrally-controlled printers.

Some 4GLs allow interfaces to be incorporated to produce standard headings as a default. It is also possible for the IT department to write their own front-end program to do this. If this is done, control can be increased further by forcing the system to print out the end-user program which generated a report immediately before printing the report. In this way, any user familiar with the 4GL can read the logic of the program, enabling him to understand the basis of the report.

Even those end-user programs which do not update the database may still be used for inappropriate purposes, resulting in a corruption of corporate information. For example, end-user programming might be used to value a company's inventory, the corporate database only keeping records of the number of items and a history of purchases. From one month to another, the end-user's program may, for instance, alter the basis for stock valuation (for example, from FIFO to LIFO or average) in an uncontrolled way, corrupting management information and causing incorrect business decisions to be made.

The answers to these problems lie in standards and procedures which determine the information which should be provided by end-user programs. Where reports from these programs are used as the basis for important business decisions, the programs producing them should be subject to an

Figure 9.3

SYSTEMS DEVELOPMENT AND MAINTENANCE CHECKOUT

1. Are acceptable development and maintenance standards in force, and are these regularly reviewed to take advantage of new methodologies and techniques?

2. Are development staff adequately supervised and procedures for their activities clearly defined and documented?

3. Are programs 'desk checked' by independent programmers after they have been coded?

4. Are staff given sufficient training to ensure that they can take advantage of new techniques and methodologies?

5. Is system documentation complete, up to date and of high quality?

6. Are sufficient generations of software retained, are they secure and are sufficient copies held?

7. Is there a code comparison facility to enable program changes to be identified?

8. Before amended programs are promoted to 'live' status are they tested, checked and authorised by an independent person with this specified responsibility?

9. Do secure change control procedures ensure that only authorised programs are transferred to the operational program library?

10. If urgent changes to live programs are required is access to the programs only allowed on the authority of a responsible officer? Does 'post-event' authorisation of all such changes take place at the earliest possible time?

11. What are the procedures for granting access to programs and data?

12. Is there an effective Quality Assurance team?

13. Are all key employees and 'one man bands' appropriately monitored?

14. Is the custody and use of 'patching' and other dangerous utilities under adequate control?

15. Are end-user programming activities adequately controlled and do the users understand the risks involved?

appropriate level of review and testing. Identifying reports as the product of end-user programming acts as a warning, but this must be backed up by procedures and education enabling management to understand the need to confirm that the information on which they base their decisions has been properly prepared.

9.9 EC Harmonisation of Security Requirements

An increasing quantity of software is purchased in package form rather than being developed in-house.

During the last few years a number of national and professional bodies have attempted to identify a series of objective criteria by which the security features in purchased software can be assessed. Owing to their differing objectives the results have varied in content and format. The most significant of these are:

- the US Department of Defense *Orange Book*
- the UK Department of Trade and Industry *Green Book* for commercial IT security products
- the German Information Security Agency 'ZSIEC' criteria
- the French *Blue-White-Red Books*.

More recently France, the Netherlands, Germany and the United Kingdom have combined to introduce a harmonisation method which will:

- provide standard criteria;
- allow each nation to gain from the experience of the others.

The draft first version of this document—the *Information Technology Security Evaluation Criteria (ITSEC)*—was published in May 1990. Evaluation based on the criteria is now being performed in the United Kingdom by organisations appointed as Commercial Licensed Evaluation Facilities (CLEFs) under the UK IT Security Evaluation and Certification Scheme.

10 Logical Access Security

10.1 Introduction

Access controls depend on software features, some of which may be found to a greater or lesser extent in the operating systems provided by computer manufacturers.

Where the required level of security does not exist in the operating system, proprietary packages may provide it. However, no matter how advanced the software is, its effectiveness depends on the implementation and enforcement of good password procedures. This statement may seem self-evident—in practice it is often the weakest link in the system.

Unless data files are on line 24 hours a day they must be stored securely. Even if the main database is permanently on line, other valuable data which is not required on a continuous basis will be transferred to 'archive' or other files which will spend most of their time waiting for occasional use. The libraries in which they are held must be effectively controlled; some of the worst disasters have been caused by the accidental or deliberate unavailability of such data when needed for processing.

10.2 On-Line Access

In conventional batch processing systems the control over programs' access to data files was exercised by DP staff. Usually referred to as the 'job control' or 'scheduling' section, it was their responsibility to ensure that files would not be released to the operators unless a signed authorisation certificate was produced. This depended on human actions and as a result was often ignored. However, in installations where it was enforced it usually operated effectively. Most operating environments are now very different. Files are held on permanently-mounted disks and cannot be controlled in the manner described above. The development, commencing in the 1970s, of massive systems using hundreds—or even thousands—of files, and the use of databases holding data in common for a number of users, means that the simple, human-based controls are now impracticable.

Requirements vary depending on the nature of the data. However, a basic level of control is required for all data. Even non-critical files must be protected against unauthorised activities, such as deletion or amendment.

In answer to the wide-ranging requirements for access security in highly-complex, sophisticated processing environments, software was designed to provide a wide range of control facilities in a variety of installations. It has now been recognised that these facilities may be required not only in large organisations using vast computer power, but also in smaller organisations using only microcomputers; suitably-priced software controls are now being sold to fulfil some of these requirements at the lower end of the market.

Many manufacturers now include access control features as part of their operating systems or telecommunications software. In addition, add-on security software packages, which provide a much higher level of security than the standard operating system, are available for some systems.

Facilities which are required in a large-scale access control system include control of passwords which:

- identify and authorise users to the system;
- authorise access to specific data;
- specify the functions which can be performed by each user, for example read only, add, update or delete.

Other software features which should be available are as follows:

- The password should not be displayed on the terminal screen when it is being input, or on any output produced from the screen. There should be no facility to view or print a list of passwords and related user identities.
- The central computer should retain a record of the identifiers of all authorised terminals or other connected devices in a table, and should refuse access to the system to devices which are not on this table.
- The system should be capable of disconnecting devices which attempt to access the system illegally, or after an incorrect password has been inserted a specified number of times.
- A limit should be set on the length of time that a terminal can be 'open' and inactive. This will avoid the situation where a terminal is signed-on by an authorised individual, then left unattended and accessible to unauthorised people.
- Logging facilities should provide records of authorised and unauthorised accesses to the systems or specific files. Any apparent breach should be notified to the system controller immediately, and all records of access should be reviewed regularly.

All these features use computer time and resources, and a great deal of current work is directed at increasing economy and efficiency by minimising the processing overhead.

There is an increasing trend for users to be considered as the owners of the data relating to their applications, with the responsibility for controlling access to their files. Systems are therefore designed to allow the user to change his password when required. Some systems will encrypt the user's password, using one-way encryption techniques which render it unreadable to anyone gaining access to the file. If the user loses his password, it must be changed by a password controller who is allowed to change, but not read, passwords.

However, one point (already mentioned) should be emphasised. No matter how technically sophisticated the access control facilities are, the system itself is completely ineffective unless it is operated properly. Good clerical procedures are essential to ensure that the access rules are kept up-to-date, as is a commitment to security among the users of the system which translates into enthusiasm for maintaining the integrity of their passwords.

Some well-known software packages which provide access control facilities for mainframe systems are:

Packages	*Supplier*
CA-ACF2	Computer Associates
RACF	IBM
CA-Top Secret	Computer Associates
Infoguard	Unisys
Safeguard	Tandem

There are many similar packages available for use on PCs. A description of the relevant features of these is contained in Appendix 8. Extra security features are being built into new generations of manufacturers' operating systems, and in some cases an even higher level of security is offered as an add-on extra. An example of this is ICL's High Security Option (HSO) for its VME Operating System.

10.3   Password Security

No matter how sophisticated the system of access control, its success depends on passwords, which in turn depend on two aspects of the humans responsible for them:

- the imagination they bring to the problem of password determination;
- the self-discipline they are prepared to adopt when using them.

As mentioned earlier, the most flexible systems allow the user to determine his own password, and to change it when required.

Ideally, a password should be completely nonsensical, and as long as possible. However, if this is taken to the extreme the user will be incapable of remembering it. The user's ideal password would be short and easy to remember, which usually means that it would have some relevance to the user's life. If a potential transgressor wished to guess the password, his task would be comparatively simple if the user were allowed to choose freely.

Figure 10.1

ON LINE ACCESS CHECKOUT

1. Can the system be accessed by terminal?

2. Are there strict authorisation and identification procedures to prevent access by an unauthorised person via a terminal?

3. Is a log maintained of all terminal activity?

4. Are these logs reviewed regularly?

5. Is each terminal uniquely identifiable to the system?

6. Is terminal access restricted by:
    (a) physical locks?
    (b) password/identity checks?

7. Are terminals automatically polled for activity?

8. Are terminals automatically logged-off when not in use?

9. Is there a time limit after which open or inactive terminals are logged off?

10. Are physical terminals dedicated to specific user functions?

11. Are there any spare terminals? If so, are they secure from unauthorised use?

12. Is all on line access subject to supervision and monitoring by an appropriately-qualified System Controller?

If users *are* allowed to choose passwords a list of 'forbidden' passwords should be produced. These should include the common passwords used on many occasions (FRED—for no apparent reason—is an example) as well as passwords which apply to specific users, such as: their name; spouses or children's names; pets' names; telephone numbers etc.

A set of procedures must be produced, and its use monitored, which ensures an acceptable level of security over passwords. These procedures should include:

*   the naming convention described above, which will be enforced by software;
*   issuing procedures;
*   actions in the event of a breach of security;
*   if applicable, different procedures applying to data with different security levels;
*   frequency of, and procedures for, changing passwords.

These should be supported by software which will enforce compliance with the procedures, for example by:

- issuing warnings in the 'run up' period before changes are needed;
- locking users out as a last resort if passwords are not changed. Reinstatement will be allowed by entry of a supervisor's password, after which the user's password must be changed before any further activity is attempted.

A continuous training program is needed to ensure that users handle passwords correctly.

An individual should be appointed who is responsible for the monitoring of all activities related to the use and issue of passwords.

Appendix 6 provides examples of the procedures which must be laid down, monitored and enforced.

10.4   Other Identification Methods

In cases where data is highly sensitive, the use of a password (something known by the operators) can be enhanced further by the addition of extra techniques, based on:

- something unique to the person, such as handwriting, fingerprints, retina patterns, voice prints;
- something possessed by the person, such as cards, badges, tokens or keys.

11 Securing the Customers' Cash

11.1 ATM Security

The use of Automated Teller Machines (ATMs) has created a revolution in banking. They are now a familiar sight in most towns and cities, allowing round-the-clock access to a bank account for statements to be ordered or withdrawals made without the need to step inside a bank.

Although a boon to the person in the street, they can be a security headache to banks and other financial institutions.

Usually exposed and often inadequately lit, they are an inviting target for the urban criminal. Both the customer and the ATM itself are open to attack.

There are now very few occasions on which the press is unable to publish details of at least one attempted or actual crime at an ATM. The increasing trend towards violence against ATM users, in order to steal comparatively small amounts of money, is disturbing; while the more ludicrous use of brute force in attempts to pull ATMs physically from bank walls generates questions about the mental health of the potential beneficiaries.

Security measures have been devised to make ATM withdrawals safer for the customer and bank. These include 'Lobby' or 'Vestibule Banking'. ATMs are either sited within a bank doorway or a protective glass kiosk is built round the existing dispenser to protect the customer while withdrawals are being made. Security partitioning for these booths can provide several levels of protection—from anti-bandit to bullet-resistant grades.

Entry can be controlled by a card access control system which can be programmed to accept the customer's cash card and Personal Identification Number (PIN).

A well-lit vestibule/lobby can act not only as a strong deterrent against crime but can also significantly increase customer confidence.

The potential for fraudulent use of credit and cash cards by unauthorised people at ATMs is an increasing concern for banks, building societies and customers alike, highlighting the need for a method of confirming the identity of the withdrawer. Some American banks use pin-hole cameras, sited in the wall at shoulder height, which discreetly photograph every withdrawal and record the date and time of the transaction. However, pin-hole cameras cannot record whether a customer is being forced to make a withdrawal. In this case, Closed Circuit Television (CCTV) can be programmed to operate continually or, alternatively, to be triggered by card insertion, a panic button or PIN entry under duress. These CCTV systems can record at ten speeds offering two to 480 hours of filmed transactions, and can send a slow-scan image over the telephone lines to a remote security site.

Customer security is only one part of the problem. The storage area behind the ATM where safes can hold large quantities of cash also requires protection. Surprisingly, many safes housing ATMs offer minimal protection against direct attack, and certainly less than would normally be required given the value of currencies stored in them.

However, a number of international standards are now coming into force which require greatly enhanced security. This, coupled with a requirement for much thinner walls, has generated a totally new design concept. The safes can be designed with wall thicknesses as low as 25mm, although manufactured with a precision to match the tolerances required for the assembly of the electronics.

A range of vibration detectors are specifically designed to detect any attempt to attack ATM safes. These detectors are programmed to ignore normal environmental noises but will generate an alarm in response to sustained vibration. The detectors can be linked to an intelligent alarm control system, which offers flexible security for the safe and its surroundings by allowing authorised entry to the safe for servicing or cash replacement while protecting against unauthorised interference.

The alarm signal is linked to a centre which co-ordinates reactions to alarms from all major security installations by remote link.

11.2   Card and PIN Number Security

In order to avoid misuse of stolen ATM cards and PIN numbers, care must be taken to:

- ensure that issue only takes place after a series of authorisation checks. These must always be complied with—no short cuts must be taken;
- protect the postal 'chain' from bank to authorised customer.

The cards should be handled and processed under dual control from the time at which the account is created, through the embossing process to the point at which the cards are posted. Each card must be individually accounted for at all stages in this process.

Where the bank generates the PINs the staff dealing with PINs and cards must be segregated, as must those responsible for the destruction of returned cards and PINs. A controlled cycle of separate card and PIN mailing, with investigation of any customers who do not reply in a fixed period, will also help to detect mislaid items.

If the customer chooses the PIN, some of the potential employee fraud problems can be avoided. However it must be remembered that the magnetic strip can be used without the PIN in electronic point-of-sale environments, and cards must therefore be guarded and recorded at all stages up to and including the issue point.

The increase in fraud from stolen cards and PINs is continuing, aided by the proliferation of ATMs and point-of-sale outlets. Cards and PINs continue to be intercepted in the mail, while customers habitually attempt to make life a little simpler by carrying their PINs close to their cards. During a review of 'captured' cards in a US bank, one in four were found to have the PIN written on the card.

Some useful techniques to reduce the incidence of these frauds are:

- use of registered mail in areas which have a high incidence of theft;
- where possible, invite customers to collect cards and PINs at branches rather than using the postal service;
- prompt procedures to cancel cards which have been reported as stolen, backed by constant education of customers to ensure speedy reporting;
- the system should highlight exceptional activity on an account. The definition of this activity may vary from bank to bank, or even within customer categories. It must be carefully determined to ensure that subsequent investigation is not delayed or confused owing to the generation of a large volume of information on obviously valid transactions.

A description of a knowledge-based system designed to trap fraudulent transactions is given later in this chapter.

11.3 Intelligent Cards—the Smart and the Supersmart!

The magnetically-encoded and embossed plastic card is being replaced in many countries by more secure identification products such as the smart card. These cards are more sophisticated than the standard plastic card in that each contains a microchip which can store and process information related to the issuer and owner, in such a way that the information may not be illicitly modified. The cards are also more difficult to reproduce without access to stocks of the embedded microchip.

The smart card employs micro-electronics, computing and cryptography techniques to produce a personal token which demonstrates a high level of functionality and security.

Although the smart card is similar in some respects to a conventional plastic card, it contains an embedded microchip and exposed contacts by which it can be plugged into a terminal. The microchip on the early smart cards contained only memory cells, which could be used as secure data stores. Modern smart cards also incorporate a processor, providing facilities which enable them to:

- process data, in order to authenticate the card in a terminal;
- identify the card holder;
- encrypt and decrypt messages;
- generate electronic signatures for transactions originated by the card holder.

Standards completed or under development cover the physical size and shape of the card, assignment and location of the microchip contacts, electrical signal parameters, and the various communications protocols over the transfer of messages to and from the card. Recently, a contactless smart card has emerged; data transfer between the card and a terminal is achieved by inductive coupling, eliminating the requirement for exposed metal contacts.

Although smart cards are in common use in a variety of worldwide applications, they have been slow in gaining a foothold in the United Kingdom retail banking environment, mainly on the grounds of cost.

The supersmart card is a more complex version of the smart card. In addition to the features expected from a smart card, it contains:

- a one- or two-line alphanumeric, liquid crystal display (LCD);
- a small keypad.

These features give it the appearance and functionality of a pocket calculator. However, the inclusion of an eight-bit CPU and a 64 K-bit memory provides the facilities of a complete personal terminal.

The keyboard and display may be used to authorise transactions on a bank account and perform calculations on account data. Transaction details may be stored and processed on the card. The card may also provide added personal services such as a notebook, address and telephone directory, clock/calendar, calculator, and reminder service.

The user may also provide authorisations to a third party by connecting the card into the third party's terminal. The cardholder will be provided with a display of the authorised transaction, and will then confirm or deny the authorisation by inputting data at the terminal.

11.4 Knowledge-Based Systems to Combat Fraud

Knowledge-based systems (KBS) have had a chequered history. As the first commercial spin-off from artificial intelligence (AI), their development was stunted by the hiatus in UK research funding for AI caused by the Lighthill report (1972). It took ten years for UK KBS research to recover from this setback, and by that time the UK lead had been surrendered to USA researchers. A KBS development technique had been adopted called 'rapid prototyping', which involves coding computer systems directly from acquired knowledge, without initial analysis or design. The performance of the system is then improved by involving the expert in interaction with the prototype system.

Figure 11.1

AN OUTLINE OF THE KADS METHOD OF KBS DEVELOPMENT

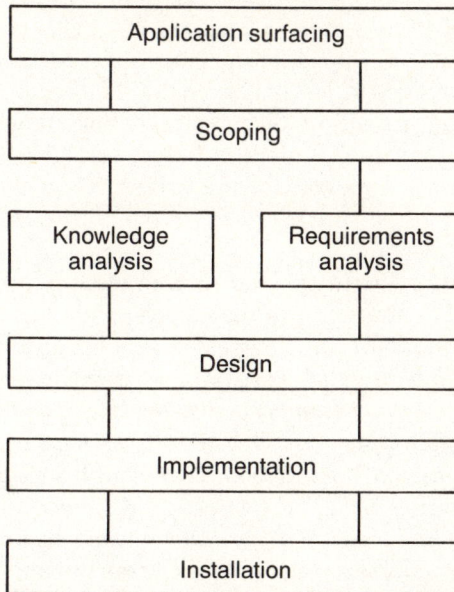

```
┌─────────────────────────────────────┐
│        Application surfacing         │
└─────────────────────────────────────┘

┌─────────────────────────────────────┐
│              Scoping                 │
└─────────────────────────────────────┘

┌──────────────────┐  ┌──────────────────┐
│    Knowledge     │  │   Requirements   │
│    analysis      │  │    analysis      │
└──────────────────┘  └──────────────────┘

┌─────────────────────────────────────┐
│              Design                  │
└─────────────────────────────────────┘

┌─────────────────────────────────────┐
│           Implementation             │
└─────────────────────────────────────┘

┌─────────────────────────────────────┐
│             Installation             │
└─────────────────────────────────────┘
```

At around this time, third generation computer systems were benefitting from analysis and design methodologies such as SSADM (Structured Systems Analysis and Design Methodology). In an attempt to ensure that KBS development did not make the same mistakes as conventional systems development, the EEC sponsored a research project (Esprit project 12) to investigate the possibility of a methodology for KBS analysis and design. This led, through Esprit projects 304, 1098 and currently 5248, to KADS [1]—the methodology for KBS development. Like SSADM, KADS stresses the need for careful, thorough analysis and design before any consideration is given to coding and maintenance. KADS is a model driven methodology, with a descriptive representation of inference types known as Interpretation models. Fraudwatch, the KBS developed by Touche Ross for Barclaycard, was developed using the KADS methodology.

A KBS can contribute to security in a number of ways. When volumes of data are immense, and any one item could be vulnerable, it can apply 'quick and dirty' checks to weed out those which show irregularities. These can then be further investigated at a later time. They can provide an effective means of detecting fraudulent behaviour by highlighting unauthorised access to computer systems, unauthorised opening of new accounts, sudden reactivation of dormant accounts and untypical usage of a live account. These systems can deduce or 'infer' irregular or untypical behaviour in computer systems, bank accounts and telephone networks. In fact the approach has benefits in any medium where normal and abnormal behaviour patterns can be identified, and where the update and manipulation of massive amounts of data is typical.

Fraudwatch [2, 3] is a system that concentrates on identifying potentially fraudulent transactions on classic Barclaycards. The core concept of the development is that it is impossible to have a credit card account without having a behavioural norm for that account. In theory, this norm can be placed anywhere on a scale of nil usage to completely random usage. In practice, all accounts exhibit a pattern based around volume and value of transactions in any given month, for the period over which historical data is available to the system. This means that the norms are constrained and readily definable.

This would not be sufficient for the KBS to identify potential fraud if the norms were applied as absolutes. Instead, each account has a norm, and every transaction on that account can be assessed in relation to this. For example: *one transaction of 50 per cent of credit limit would register as suspicious on an account which had a normal monthly activity of 20 per cent of its credit limit on between eight and 12 transactions, at a set of merchant types which excluded that of the transaction under assessment.* However, it would be less suspicious *if the credit limit were small, the transaction remained the only one over a period of time, or was transacted at a merchant type which attracted little or no fraud.* It would of course arouse no suspicion on an account where *the monthly norm was one transaction of 50 per cent of credit limit at that specific merchant.*

The protection offered by adopting such a system lies in highlighting a

Figure 11.2

THE INFERENCE MODEL FOR FRAUD ASSESSMENT

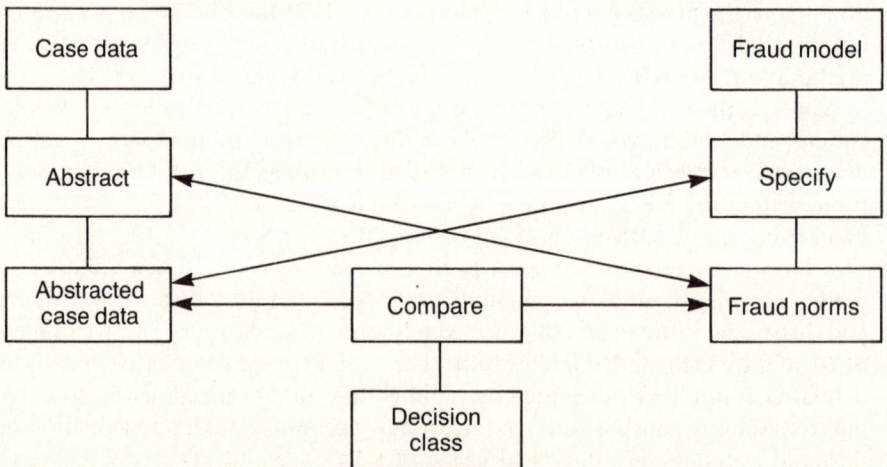

Figure 11.3

EMBEDDED LOG MONITORING KBS

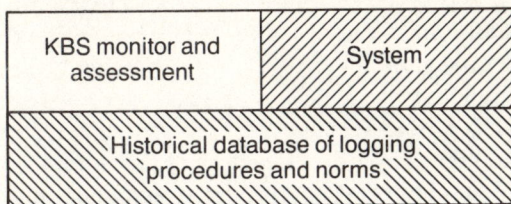

KBS monitor and assessment	System
Historical database of logging procedures and norms	

smaller number of possible frauds, from the hundreds of thousands of daily transactions for the further investigation of the fraud department. In so doing, it allows proactivity in detecting fraud for the first time. It is a complementary activity to that of credit scoring—in that it detects rather than prevents—and can thus cover those cases where prevention has failed.

A further application of these techniques to the secure operation of computer systems and installations is shown in the diagram above. It is possible to infer the validity of logging attempts by monitoring each logon, and assessing it for 'fit' with a norm of logons constructed over a period of time and stored in a historical database. In this case, a surprise logon attempt—for example, via telephone and modem at 0230 hours by an employee whose password had only ever been used during normal working hours, using an on-site terminal—could generate a security call to that employee's home number, while leading the 'phantom' attempt in ever decreasing circles around some fictitious piece of operating system code. If no contact could be made with the genuine password holder, a number of tactics could be devised to ensure security; for example, use of a second KBS to monitor all the activities of this user, and breaking communication if certain criteria were met.

The Fraudwatch pilot KBS developed for Barclaycard in 1989 consists of two programs:

SELECT applies rudimentary fraud criteria to the entire set of cardholder accounts. The program is deliberately pessimistic, identifying all accounts which display the slimmest evidence of fraudulent card use. Its purpose is to act as an initial 'filter', reducing the huge cardholder database to a more manageable set of accounts.

The ASSESS program then examines these accounts in greater detail using the distilled knowledge of Barclays' fraud experts, including models of normal and fraudulent card use, to identify accounts with purchasing patterns that are characteristic of fraud. The result is a set of suspicious accounts and transactions which can be examined, and if necessary investigated, by staff in the Fraud Department.

The system was tested for a week in early December 1989 using 10 per cent of the cardholder database (representing several hundred thousand accounts) chosen at random. Over the five-day period, 386 accounts were identified as potentially fraudulent. The Fraud Department managed to contact 309 of the 386 cardholders, and seven of these accounts were eventually confirmed as fraudulent. In addition, of the 77 accounts where the Fraud Department was unable to contact the cardholder, three were classified by the bank as highly likely to be fraudulent.

The calls were very well received by the customers who were contacted.

It was estimated that the cost of developing the system would be recovered within a year of implementation through reductions in fraud losses. It is believed that further savings could be made by integrating the system with the authorisation procedures of the bank.

12 If the Worst Happens: Disaster Recovery and Insurance

12.1 Disaster Recovery

'We have not bothered to produce a Disaster Plan—we have not had any disasters and I do not see why we should have any in future.'

The manager of a large UK computer installation who tempted fate by making this comment is not the only person who follows this philosophy. In his case fate retaliated by inflicting a reasonably large disaster on his computer centre. He reacted in the time-honoured fashion, by following the famous rules laid down by the anonymous poet: 'When in danger or in doubt, wave your arms and scream and shout.' In the absence of any other method of coping, he had very few alternatives. However, it should be added that this technique was not very effective!

Financial organisations which have still not been persuaded of the intrinsic value of contingency planning may be influenced by the fact that many regulatory bodies, including the Bank of England and the Building Societies Commission, are becoming increasingly enthusiastic in recommending this safeguard.

Disaster recovery does not merely relate to computers. Bearing in mind that a disaster is not usually selective, a disaster plan should be produced for the complete organisation. The key to disaster planning is to minimise the need for thought and decision-making when the disaster actually happens.

When a disruption occurs it is essential for an organisation to have recovery procedures which enable it to cope with everything from a major disaster to a minor 'hiccup'. In some cases loss of the information-processing facility can have more serious effects than loss of the more obvious assets and profit-making functions; there are organisations whose contingency plan in the event of a complete loss of computer facilities would be to go bankrupt.

The incidence of major catastrophe is low but the consequences can be extreme.

The potential impact of the loss of a data centre is usually not fully appreciated. Disaster plans are rarely in evidence and—even when they have been developed—are probably incomplete and of limited value. Even though a complete, accurate plan may have been detailed some time ago, very few organisations perform a regular review to confirm the plan's validity.

A disaster plan encompasses far more than a sound backup routine and a reasonable alternative site. It cannot be drawn up properly without commitment by senior management, DP staff and users. Of the three, the latter are the most usually forgotten.

The plan must ensure that all resources such as:

- people;
- hardware;
- software;
- data;
- paper;
- instructions;
- plans;
- inventories;
- transport.

can be made available to provide an alternative service in good time;

It must also be detailed enough—and plain enough—to follow easily in an emergency and under stress. Staff will not have time to ask questions when the disaster happens.

To recover from a disaster, the organisation will need a plan, people and money. In addition to replacement of software, equipment and data the plan will need to address such aspects as:

- interim staffing for operations and support;
- user department procedures and staffing;
- supplies of consumables and transportation arrangements.

In order to draw up the plan all business functions must be reviewed, and management must identify the level of service that is acceptable in the event of a disaster. The procedures needed to obtain that level are then agreed and form the basis of the plan.

A variety of 'hot', 'cold' and 'mobile' restart services, which may provide a cost-effective alternative, are available from hardware manufacturers and specialist organisations, providing the necessary assurance without a need for otherwise redundant hardware and premises. Examples of these are the ICL Disaster Survival and Thorn EMI Datashield services.

One requirement which is often omitted is the need to obtain the agreement of employees to perform the emergency activities. It is too late to commence negotiation when a disaster occurs, and the terms and conditions under which staff will work must be agreed and documented at an early stage.

Once the plan has been produced, a number of factors—such as passage of time, or changes in the business or technical environment—will quickly combine to make it impractical, invalid or outdated. It must be:

- regularly reviewed to ensure that changing circumstances have not made it ineffective;
- frequently tested in detail to ensure that it is workable and properly understood;
- consistent in terms of its cost against the benefits of preserving an acceptable level of service.

A 'skeleton' disaster plan is given in Appendix 7.

Try the Disaster Recovery Checkout in Figure 12.1 to assess the vulnerability of your organisation.

Figure 12.1

DISASTER RECOVERY CHECKOUT

1. Has a recovery plan been developed, tested and maintained which will allow processing to continue, assuming different levels of disruption?

2. Does the plan allow for the re-establishment of the IT function using duplicated facilities?

3. Is there a contingency plan for each critical application?

4. Have the user departments been involved in the development of contingency plans and in their testing?

5. How often and completely is the plan tested?

6. Has the plan been tested recently?

7. Are copies of the plan held at remote, secure locations?

8. If the plan involves the use of another organisation's computer facilities, is there a firm, contractual agreement?

9. Are all the people who were involved in the most recent test of the contingency plan still in post?

10. Does the contingency plan include:

    (a) an exact description of the circumstances which constitute a disaster?

    (b) the names of those authorised to declare a disaster situation?

    (c) the names and telephone numbers of the officers of the organisation who will:

    – control;
    – operate;

    the plan?

    (d) the names and telephone numbers of any other people who must be informed?

    (e) details of travel arrangements for media, instructions and personnel?

    (f) protection for security copies at all times, including while in transit?

Figure 12.1 cont'd

DISASTER RECOVERY CHECKOUT *(cont'd)*

(g) location of keys of remote secure locations and details of authorisation arrangements?

(h) provision of maps, instructions and any necessary equipment (e.g. trolleys)?

11. Does a priority list for jobs exist to ensure that the most important are performed?

12. Has a decision been made on which applications must be recovered and the timescale in which this must be achieved?

13. Is a security copy of each of the following stored in a strong room at a separate, secure location:

(a) data files?

(b) software programs?

(c) all relevant documentation?

14. Is the backup afforded by (13) above adequate to ensure that all necessary information is available to retrieve the situation in the event of loss of any information at the main computer centre?

15. Are security copies of data and programs adequately labelled?

16. Are source documents retained by the user until the appropriate security copies reach the remote stores?

17. Is copy documentation amended at the same time as the original? Is this checked?

18. To what extent can the organisation operate manually?

19. Is essential backup data regularly checked to ensure readability?

20. Are *all* personnel familiar with the plan in general and their part in particular? When they change jobs are they trained in the relevant aspects of the plan?

21. Is there a record of staff on duty?

22. Can a log be duplicated at a remote site?

23. Has agreement been made with the Finance Department regarding responsibility for authorising contingency activities?

24. Does the contingency plan include activities in the event of a remote disaster e.g. at a warehouse or branch?

25. Does the long term or total disaster plan provide for operation of key on line systems? If not, is there batch backup for any on line system?

26. Is the plan regularly reviewed and updated in the light of current requirements?

12.2   Insurance

It is worth pointing out at this stage that insurance is not an alternative to preventive and detective security measures—indeed if an adequate level of security did not exist in an installation it would be extremely difficult to obtain cover. If an insurance company were persuaded that security was sufficient to form the basis of a contract, proof that security procedures were not followed might be a valid reason for non-settlement of a claim.

Once these provisos are accepted, the assurance that losses will be repaid provides an extra level of confidence. Recovery of service after a disaster can be extremely expensive, and the comforting feeling provided by the knowledge that others will pay for this should not be underestimated.

Policies can cover:

- material damage of the computer and its ancillary equipment, which can be taken out against:
  - a standard list of perils;
  - all risks;
- breakdown insurance (usually on an all-risks basis);
- consequential loss (business interruption), covering loss of data, which includes loss of fees, cost of the extra work needed to recreate the data and loss of profit;
- legal liability:
  - employees for loss or injury;
  - third parties for damage caused by staff negligence or fraud.

Excess coverage is wasteful as the insurers will only pay out for the actual loss. If computer insurance is handled separately from the other business insurances carried by the organisation there may be a costly overlap. Even more important, there may be gaps. These difficulties can be avoided by considering computer insurance as part of the general business insurance carried, although specialist help will be required in identifying the risks.

Material Damage

This type of insurance covers losses arising directly from external events and internal breakdown. An all-risks policy gives cover against accidental damage for risks such as fire, explosion, theft, water, storm damage, malfunction of other equipment, vandalism and malicious damage. However, it does not cover every risk imaginable by the insured; it is still important to read the policy. Cheaper cover can be obtained by excluding some risks, using a 'selected perils' policy.

If the equipment is hired, the user organisation would not normally be expected to insure against material damage, except perhaps for negligence.

It is possible to obtain insurance for breakdown or malfunctioning of equipment which can supplement the benefits obtainable under maintenance contracts.

The fundamental principle of insurance is indemnity, which can best be described as exact financial compensation. An indemnity policy restores the insured to the same financial position after a loss as he enjoyed prior to the loss. It does not allow him to make a profit from his loss, so depreciation and loss of value by wear and tear will be taken into account. There is therefore no point in insuring an asset for more than its current value. If, on the other hand, the sum insured is less than the current value then full indemnity will not be given, the insured carrying the residue of the risk.

If the policy is for 90 per cent of the value of the item, then the insured will receive only 90 per cent of any loss sustained. In the event of total or partial loss the insured is automatically penalised by the inadequacy of the sum insured.

It is sometimes possible to obtain cover on a 'replacement as new' basis. This concession modifies the indemnity principle, but is much more expensive since the premium will cover the full replacement cost of the asset.

A major problem in the computer industry is posed by obsolete equipment. Situations occur in which a system running perfectly, with no business reason for an upgrade, can suddenly become redundant owing to the breakdown of a component which is no longer manufactured.

It is essential to ensure that the sum insured is regularly upgraded to remain in line with current value. Both under- and over-insurance should be avoided. The former leaves losses unprotected: the latter wastes money.

A common feature of insurance policies is an excess clause, which is designed to avoid small claims. The insurer pays only that part of a claim for damage which is in excess of some fixed amount. The damage up to this amount is the responsibility of the insured. Excess clauses by which the insured retains a significant portion of the risk are common in business.

As an alternative to an excess, the policy may operate on a franchise basis, in which case the insurer pays the whole claim only if it is over an agreed value. Damage which is less than the amount of the franchise is the responsibility of the insured.

Consequential Loss (Business Interruption)

This class of insurance is also called 'Loss of Profits Insurance'. If the computer installation suffers damage the system may not be able to function normally. The business will be interrupted and financial losses will be incurred.

These will include loss of revenue and loss of profit, caused by inability to produce goods or services. There will also be increased cost of working owing to costs of another machine, extra staff, overtime pay, transport and accommodation.

Business interruption may also be caused by denial of access or loss of power supplies. Business interruption insurance can provide cover for all these financial losses. There is no obligation to take out consequential loss insurance for all the risks which are covered in a material damage policy, but the two are usually linked. The period of cover and the total sum insured for business interruption losses must be based on realistic estimates of the losses and costs that may be encountered.

Another aspect of this is the 'time franchise' where liability is not undertaken until an agreed time period has elapsed. If business interruption exceeds the time limit, payment will be made covering the total period of the interruption.

Losses and costs continue for a long time after the event. To allow for this, cover is provided for a fixed period (the indemnity period), the length of which is defined in the policy. During the indemnity period the insurer is liable for the specified costs and losses, which then revert to the insured. The usual 12 months is often inadequate, and two years may be much more sensible. When considering the period, it should be rememberd that too little cover is often crippling and may cause business failure.

Employee Liability

The risks to a company from its personnel are many and varied. Injuries to staff must be covered by an Employer's Liability Policy, and to others by Public Liability Insurance. Absence of employees can be covered by a Health and Sickness Policy. Dishonest acts can be covered by a Fidelity Guarantee Policy. Risks from staff negligence can be covered by a professional indemnity policy, as can those arising from breach of duty.

The *UK Consumer Protection Act*, as well as similar legislation in all EC countries, imposes liability for personal injury or loss of personal property on a strict liability basis. There is no requirement for the victim to prove negligence or lack of care; liability resides with those responsible for the product. Offloading the responsibility is not always a practical proposition, and coverage for this liability must always be considered.

If an organisation carries on a business of building equipment which is then sold to others, professional indemnity for errors and omissions is needed. The insurer will require confirmation that reasonable care is taken, and that the insured's liability is limited—as far as possible—in his contract with his customers.

Special care ought to be given to personnel risks in abnormal circumstances, such as working at standby sites. Even where employees are covered when working elsewhere, it will be necessary to cover any damage they might cause to the equipment and facilities at the site. This may be covered in a contract between the two organisations, but in many cases the arrangement is concluded hurriedly between two data processing managers without a formal agreement.

An important aspect of insurance of all kinds is the principle of 'utmost good faith'. Each party to the contract of insurance is under a duty to disclose all material facts to the other. A material fact is one that could have a bearing on the assessment of the risks. For example, if the site contains a store of combustible material, this is likely to be pertinent to any assessment of the fire risk. Similarly, an undisclosed history of system breakdowns and faults may provide a reason for non-payment of claims on a Business Interruption policy.

If material facts are withheld the policy may be declared invalid when the facts come to light. The insured is not penalised for not revealing facts that he did not know, and could not reasonably be expected to know. Usually the policy contains conditions that require the insured to notify the insurer of any changes which could have a bearing on the risk. In case of doubt it is best to consult the insurer.

The Systems Perils Policy
This policy, which has been available from Lloyd's Underwriters for some years, insures computer users against risks such as:

- loss of system availability;
- loss of data;
- loss of revenue caused by, for instance, inability to collect payments on time or—in the case of a bureau—to earn money;
- liability to penalty clauses owing to failure to perform promised tasks;
- theft of money or property;
- loss of goodwill.

The policy covers damage to computer and communications equipment, data and software plus gross revenue interruption loss and additional costs following:

- deliberate sabotage or manipulation;
- accidental corruption or loss of data and software;
- failure of telecommunications and market information services;
- damage to equipment including fire, explosion, theft;
- flood and other natural disasters;
- breakdown;
- failure of electricity;
- prevention of access.

The policy also covers consequential loss arising from a breakdown of the insured's computer and communications equipment.

The policy was originally designed for financial institutions but has now been extended to a more general clientele.

Hogg Insurance Brokers' Computassure
This provides cover against all, or a combination of, the following:

Material Damage. 'All risks' of physical loss or damage to all computing equipment and storage media. Its features include:

- generic property schedules and sums insured;
- automatic cover for new additions;

- automatic transit cover;
- day one average;
- reinstatement without betterment penalty;
- repair investigation costs;
- full contingent breakdown cover.

Data and Software. The cost of re-researching and reprogramming software lost or corrupted by accidental or deliberate means, including the actions of computer viruses and logic bombs.

Business Interruption. Increased costs of working (including uneconomic costs), loss of profit, lost research and development expenditure, lost interest or fines and damages caused by cessation of processing following:

- physical loss or damage to computing equipment;
- failure of electricity;
- failure of telecommunications services;
- loss or corruption of data or software;
- hardware failure (including the failure of unmaintained equipment, subject to increased time excesses);
- the accidental or deliberate introduction of programming code designed by its author to cause an interruption to processing;
- failure of temperature and humidity equipment;
- denial of access as a result of damage in the vicinity, or the order of a statutory authority to safeguard life.

Book Debts. The value of outstanding debt balances that are unrecoverable because of the accidental or malicious loss or corruption of computer data.

Damage to Work in Progress. Damage to work in progress owing to deliberate or accidental corruption of software controlling a manufacturing process.

Fraud and Embezzlement. Fraud and embezzlement by employees, third-party computer fraud, fraud by contract employees, ex-employees and consultants. Two significant aspects of this policy are:

- The culprit does not have to be identified by name;
- Accounting systems declared on the proposal form are not warranted into the policy—a minefield in any company affected by the continuing changes introduced by the computerisation process.

The Lloyd's Electronic and Computer Crime Policy
In the early 1970s many bankers' fund-transfer operations were converted from teletypewriter to electronic systems. These operations were comparatively secure because of the general ignorance of a bank's systems which had the effect of protecting banks against computer fraud. However, the advent of personal computers and the ability to 'tap' into systems illegally has greatly reduced the use of ignorance as a security measure.

The original 'Bankers Blanket Bond' fidelity cover for frauds by bank employees was extended early in the 1980s to cover loss owing to fraudulent input of electronic data or computer instructions to the assured's computer by means of:

- unauthorised access to a terminal;
- fraudulent preparation of data tapes;
- fraudulent preparation of computer programs;
- obtaining access to a bank's communication lines.

The policy also covered the fraudulent use of electronic communication systems by alteration of messages or misuse of authorisation.

However this policy only covered banks against frauds by their employees. Further policies extended cover to frauds by ex-employees, consultants, contractors and suppliers' engineers, and new policies extending cover to non-banking organisations are under consideration.

A review of security must usually be performed by outside risk assessors before a policy can be agreed.

The current Lloyd's Electronic and Computer Crime Policy contains seven standard agreements, although 'specials' can be tailor-made for specific clients.

Agreement 1 covers losses caused by:

- fraudulent input of data into:
  - the victim's computer system or service bureau;
  - an Electronic Funds Transfer system;
  - a 'customer communication system' providing direct access by customers to the assured's system;
- fraudulent modification or destruction of data in any of the above systems.

Agreement 2 covers losses incurred owing to fraudulent preparation of program instructions. It should be noted that an exclusion clause specifically excludes loss resulting from fraudulent coding in programs developed for sale to, or sold to, multiple customers at the time of their acquisition from a vendor or consultant. Since this applies to many of the systems in use today the areas of exclusion could be significant. In addition, where a program has been developed for another customer and modified for the assured, there may be no cover.

Agreement 3 covers:

- attempted or actual malicious destruction of data stored in the assured's computer system or that of a bureau;
- deliberate or accidental loss of the assured's electronic media while in storage or in the custody of an authorised person.

There are a number of restrictions to this policy, notably in the following areas:

- loss of potential income will only be covered if the data represents negotiable instruments or similar 'Evidence of Debt';
- electronic funds may not be covered.

Agreement 4 covers transactions fraudulently input to—or modified before or during—transmission to the assured by:

- an electronic communication system;
- an automated Clearing House;
- by tested telex or similar methods.

Agreement 5 covers losses incurred by a customer owing to fraudulent input, modification or destruction of electronic data being stored, processed or transmitted by the assured's bureau services.

Agreement 6 covers the reverse situation to Agreement 4, covering

Figure 12.2

INSURANCE CHECKOUT

1. Is insurance considered as complementary to other controls?
2. Is insurance calculated at replacement cost?
3. Is the computer cover adequate?
4. Has consideration been given to all insurance risks including:
   (a) material damage to machine and equipment?
   (b) consequential loss due to system breakdown?
   (c) third party liability?
   (d) employee loss or injury?
   (e) employee fidelity insurance?
   (f) breach of Data Protection Act?
   (g) interruptions of transmission or amendments to data by third parties (hackers)?
   (h) amendments to, or destruction or loss of files or databases?
6. Have insurance policies been reviewed by auditors or risk assessment specialists?
7. Is insurance cover reviewed regularly in the light of changing circumstances:
   - new hardware, software etc?
   - changing business or social circumstances?
8. Are premiums/cover regularly compared with
   (a) other insurers?
   (b) similar installations?

customers of the assured who incur losses after receipt of fraudulent transactions.

Agreement 7 covers loss incurred owing to fraudulent telephone instructions by an unauthorised person.

Monitoring Changing Insurance Requirements

Insurance risks will change progressively, both within the organisation as a whole and in its IT activities. The insurance position must be reviewed frequently to identify any new exposures and arrange adequate cover.

Insurance must never be looked at as the only necessary solution to an organisation's security problems. In the event of a disaster, merely waiting for the cheque to arrive is not an acceptable alternative to a series of well-rehearsed recovery measures. Indeed, many organisations could lose their customers and their businesses before payment was made. However, the knowledge that the cheque *will* arrive can be a powerful motivating force, enabling management to carry on with the recovery procedures in the confidence that, at some stage, life will be worth living again!

13 Microcomputer Security

13.1 Threats and Vulnerabilities

The development of solid-state microcircuitry and the miniaturisation of storage media led in the 1980s to the increased use of cheap, compact computers which could operate in individual user departments. As the decade progressed they became increasingly powerful and flexible, and their use and application has increased dramatically.

The cheapness of stand-alone microcomputers often led to their being purchased without the control and monitoring procedures established in most organisations for capital spending projects. Indeed, many powerful personal computers (PCs) were purchased using the office petty cash, which required a comparatively low level of authorisation. However, many of these machines are capable of full-scale processing and can operate with real-time systems and databases. They have the potential to cause as many problems as mainframes while, in many cases, being operated by personnel who have little knowledge of the controls and disciplines required in a large IT department.

As stand-alone PC usage has increased, other needs have been identified. These include:

- a requirement for many users to access the same data or use the same peripherals;
- the need to transfer data from a mainframe to PCs for further local processing, possibly followed by the return of the results to the mainframe.

Parallel developments in network processing have created the technology to satisfy these requirements. PCs are now increasingly being linked to each other and to mainframes, performing complex business activities and downloading and manipulating sensitive corporate information.

A Local Area Network (LAN) allows facilities such as processing, storage, printing, information retrieval and electronic mail to be shared by multiple PCs in a comparatively small geographic area. The network can, in turn, be linked using 'bridges' to create a Wide Area Network (WAN) in which a user can access data on any of the component LANs.

The improved cost-effectiveness of using a microcomputer to perform some processing while allowing quick access to vast quantities of information on the host mainframe has been demonstrated in many organisations, and can be seen as an attractive business option. Many PC software packages can directly access data and facilities running on the mainframe. A database 'front-end' can be held on a PC, linked to more comprehensive storage and processing facilities on the mainframe, allowing selection and manipulation of central data via the user's machine. Some details of the security aspects of these features can be found in Chapter Seven.

Further developments are taking place. Optical disks can now provide storage in gigabytes, providing massive databases which can be shared using networks. Fax gateways allow users to fax files to individuals or groups.

The development of microtechnology has created a wide variety of tangible benefits. Business users are finding that flexible, cost-effective computing is available, and in many cases control of processing has reverted to the user after many years of remote, apparently bureaucratic and sometimes arbitrary decision-making by a central data processing department.

However, the benefits of micros—from stand-alone PCs to complex networked environments—are accompanied by a wide range of security problems. Increased risk and vulnerability are inherent in:

- the technology;
- the methods used to develop the techniques and applications;
- the way in which the systems are operated.

In many cases one person—particularly in a stand-alone environment—will have responsibility for operating the machine, retaining the files and distributing the output. The same person was probably responsible for choosing the machine and its software, and writes any necessary programs on an ad hoc basis. The segregation of duties expected in a mainframe installation will probably not exist and there may be little or no control over processing or media storage.

If the security objectives cannot be met by separation of duties, the major control over the computing functions will be provided by supervision. Even though the 'supervisor' may not be a specialist he should receive control reports which must be produced by all systems. The reports will cover such areas as:

- exception conditions identified by the system;
- machine usage statistics;
- reconciliation reports.

The dangers of the 'one man band' should be identified and guarded against:

- backup staff should be trained and regularly tested in practice;
- all systems and operating procedures should be documented and copies held at a remote site;

Figure 13.1

CORPORATE MICROCOMPUTER USAGE – MANAGEMENT'S RESPONSIBILITY

1. Agree and enforce policies on the acquisition and use of microcomputers.

2. Set microcomputer acquisition criteria which should include:
    - the highest practical level of standardisation
    - purchase of hardware, software, supplies and services only from reputable organisations
    - cost/benefit considerations

3. Ensure adequate documentation of all systems and operating procedures

4. Agree and enforce access rules over data held on, or processed by, microcomputers, particularly bearing in mind:
    - the Data Protection Act (1984)
    - the Computer Misuse Act (1990)

5. Ensure that all use of microcomputers is documented, monitored and properly controlled

6. Never say: IT'S ONLY A PC!

- fallback systems (manual if necessary) should be available;
- fallback equipment should be purchased.

Despite the low cost of these machines it is essential that the organisation should have a co-ordinated policy for their purchase and use, and that this should be adhered to.

It must be stressed that the necessary level of security depends on what the computer is expected to do, not how much it costs or who is running it. From a practical point of view, effective control need not be costly when set against the cost of recovery from a disaster (or even from a mere problem).

An earlier chapter in this book described the major security issues as:

- privacy of confidential data and software;
- protection against unauthorised use of computer systems and equipment;
- assurance that authorised work is correctly processed, and transmitted to the intended recipient;
- protection of stored data and software from corruption, loss or amendment;
- continuation of processing in the event of a hardware or software breakdown.

These concerns apply to the PC environment to the same extent as to larger machines and networks. The adoption of adequate security measures must be preceded by an assessment of the risk involved, since only when this is complete can a realistic understanding of the security requirements be achieved. Requirements will vary from system to system, depending on such aspects as:

- the sensitivity of the data being processed, stored and transferred;
- the technical complexity of the system;
- the vulnerability of the system components.

Historically, PC hardware manufacturers have placed little emphasis on security; processor speed, video graphics and disk size have been the key selling points. The initial response to PC security was to introduce a physical keyboard lock to the PC as a primitive form of system protection. However, although people usually switch the machine off, few ever remember to lock it and remove the key. Where a number of users make use of the same PC this can be even more impractical. Such shared use also rules out simple solutions such as locking away or disabling the equipment.

Application software suppliers have been lax in building security controls even where the data is extremely sensitive. A number of years elapsed before Lotus introduced password protection to their top selling spreadsheet package, while few accounting package suppliers currently provide effective protection.

The growth of PC security product add-ons can be seen as a reaction to the weakness of currently-available hardware and software systems, and a recognition of the size of the problem. Unfortunately, the use of technology to solve a largely procedural problem such as system security means that many companies fail to cover all threats and operate under an illusion of safety.

When looking at specific security products the level of security offered must be appropriate to the requirements. Low-risk environments may only require password access control, whereas high-risk data may require encryption.

Since the PC is reasonably resilient, needs no special environment in which to operate and is relatively easy to replace, threats to PC systems usually concern unauthorised access and loss or damage to data. Nevertheless, this cannot be taken for granted and a security review should check the vulnerability of the organisation to all threats. Where PCs are linked to other systems, these must also be reviewed.

In addition to the organisational controls referred to earlier, a combination of physical and software security measures will be required, the level of security depending primarily on the value and sensitivity of the data processed. However, it must be remembered that PC hardware, software and ancillary equipment are valuable corporate assets and must be protected against simple theft.

Examples of physical controls are:

- fastening the PC to a desk;
- placing machines which process sensitive data in lockable rooms;

- provision of safes for the secure storage of backups;
- use of keyboard locks;
- formal procedures for registering the acquisition, movement and disposal of PCs;
- maintenance of a register of PC hardware and software, with frequent verification;
- removing data from the PC hard disk after each use.

13.2   Security Techniques

Since PCs are user-orientated tools, it is not surprising that in-house development of software often takes place in a much less controlled and disciplined manner than that found in larger environments. End-users rarely have their code checked, archived or properly documented and they rarely follow an agreed software development methodology. They can act as analyst, programmer, documentor and ultimate end-user, often making it very difficult for other users to understand an application which may be inaccurate, incomplete or simply missing.

Building-in system controls is a good way to encourage data security. At the design stage this may mean viewing the development tool, package or operating system in terms of the security controls it offers. For instance, if managed properly, systems which run on OS/2 or UNIX can operate in a more secure and stable environment than MS-DOS.

PC security products are broadly divided between the hardware and software varieties, the former being generally the more secure. A popular strategy for software products is a 'loader' or 'shell' which wraps itself around the operating system and applies predetermined authorisation criteria to all operations requested by users.

In general, software security measures are slower than hardware devices. Complex encryption algorithms take a long time to process, and even the fastest software cannot match the speed of a custom-built chip whose sole purpose is data encryption.

Hardware security devices can take the form of add-in boards that occupy standard expansion slots, ROM chips plugged straight into the motherboard or 'dongles' which plug into the serial or parallel port. Such systems generally intervene as soon as the machine is switched on, before any activity can take place.

On the basis that patents make public technical specifications, many hardware security device manufacturers have decided not to register their product designs. This is a sensible precaution against attempts to 'reverse-engineer' particular hardware chips or boards. However, some hardware devices can be bypassed by simply removing the device, altering a DIP switch setting or removing the hard-disk drive to another machine. Only hardware boards or other devices which actually scramble the hard-disk system area are proof against this sort of interference.

Before looking at the particular features of a security product it is very important to establish that the supplier is reputable and that the security tool has some history of use. Once investment has been made in a particular hardware or software tool the costs of alternatives, taking into account retraining and configuration time, can be high.

Details of the key features of PC security products are given in Appendix 8.

13.3   Viruses

A virus is a program which infects other programs by modifying them to include a copy of itself. Many organisations have been struck by viruses before they have understood what they are, let alone learnt the necessary methods for dealing with them. The nature of the damage a virus can do is limited only by the imagination of the inventor. Viruses can re-infect programs after they have apparently been destroyed, and are capable of travelling nationally and internationally, infecting every system they contact.

The current perception of a virus-producer as an intellectual 'prankster' was given a sharp reassessment late in 1989 when an apparent demonstration disk loaded software which threatened to destroy the users' data unless a fee was paid. This may have been the first serious attempt at crime as distinct from mischief. It will not be the last.

One objective in the Red Brigade manifesto is the destruction of computer systems. CLODO, referred to earlier, exists for this single purpose; its previous attempts have been violent, but introduction of a virus may be more effective.

Signs of a virus are:

- an increase in the size of .EXE or .COM files;
- an inability to run program software;
- the computer unexpectedly attempting to write to a floppy disk drive when software is being installed or used;
- anything unusual, such as strange characters on the screen or application programs 'hanging up' when in use.

Once infected, software is available to identify, and recover from, the damage caused and clear the disks holding it. There are also software packages which, with a greater or lesser level of success, will check and report on the presence of viruses. However, nothing will take the place of the preventive 'housekeeping' measures which should, if followed consistently, prevent a virus from reaching the system. These include the following.

Preventive Measures
- Strictly control the acquisition, loading and use of software, particularly games;
- Write protect all data diskettes once data has been copied onto them.

- Use the 'copy' rather than 'diskcopy' command to avoid copying the boot sector from an infected diskette onto another diskette.
- Do not download executable files from other systems without careful testing.
- If you should accidentally try to 'boot' from a floppy (perhaps because a data diskette has been left in the floppy drive), turn the machine off immediately you see the 'Non-system disk or system disk error' message. Do not replace the disk to try again.
- Do not let other people use your machine.
- When you are sure that your machine is clean, install virus-checking software.

The above procedures should be accompanied by the following activities:

Detective Measures
- Test your programs periodically to see if they have changed.
- Always look very carefully for signs of viruses, such as an increase in file size or the appearance of 'bad' sectors on the hard disk.

The effect of a virus will be lessened by using the following procedures:

Recovery Measures
- If you believe that your machine has a virus, reboot from a clean floppy (one that has never been write-enabled) otherwise the virus will still have control of your machine.
- Isolate an infected computer until its data storage can be electronically wiped clean and reloaded with untainted software.
- Do not take measures to eradicate the virus without making sure that you have a copy of it, since destroying the evidence will make it even more difficult to trace its source and destination.
- System managers should develop plans for quick removal from service of all copies of a suspect program, and immediate backup of all related data. These plans should be made known to all users, and tested and reviewed periodically.
- Create backup copies of all important data before installing new software.

14 Risk Analysis Packages

14.1 Introduction

A number of risk analysis packages can be used to simplify and standardise security reviews. The software will usually call on a database of experience, prioritise risks and vulnerabilities and suggest remedies for security weaknesses. Such packages do not replace experienced security staff, but provide a structure for reviews and a justification for recommendations as well as performing the calculations involved in achieving an objective assessment of risks and countermeasures. Examples of these are Riskpac, Security By Analysis, MARION and CRAMM.

14.2 CRAMM Overview

The CRAMM Risk Analysis and Management Method was devised originally for the CCTA for use in Government departments. It has proved to have wider applications and is now being used to assess risks and countermeasures in IT installations and networks in the public and private sectors. It uses as a basis the following concepts.

Assets. An asset of an IT system, or potential system, can be:

- physical, for example:
  - hardware units;
  - air conditioning plant;
- software, for example:
  - operating systems;
  - utilities;
  - application systems;
- data.

Each asset must be identified and valued.

'Data assets' are 'valued' on a qualitative scale of one to ten against the four main security impacts of: disclosure; modification; unavailability; and destruction.

Physical assets are valued at their replacement costs, which are subsequently converted into the same range of values (one to ten) as the data assets.

Software assets are valued at their replacement costs and on a qualitative scale against:

- disclosure;
- modification;
- unavailability;

Threats. These can be accidental (for example, 'acts of God' such as fire and flood, or staff error), or deliberate (from permanent staff, or outsiders). The likely threats to the assets must be identified and their levels assessed;
Vulnerabilities. The likely vulnerabilities, or weaknesses of a system (or potential system) which could be exploited by the threats must be identified and their levels assessed. Examples of vulnerabilities are:

- building access too 'open';
- poor locks on doors or cabinets;
- documents not marked or registered;
- dial-in lines;
- links to unprotected networks;
- 'loopholes' in software;

Risks. The levels of risks to a system or projected system from the four security impacts are assessed by combining the asset values with the levels of threats and vulnerabilities.

The risk management aspect is performed by applying security counter-measures to a level and in a number justified by the assessment of each risk.

Countermeasures selected to protect assets from identified threats would normally be in a combination selected from more than one aspect of security. There are seven of these:

- *Non-technical:* physical; personnel; documentation; procedural;
- *Technical:* hardware; software; communications.

The product is software-based, running on an IBM or compatible PC, and was launched in the Government 'unclassified but sensitive' domain in Janu-

Figure 14.1

RISK ANALYSIS AND MANAGEMENT

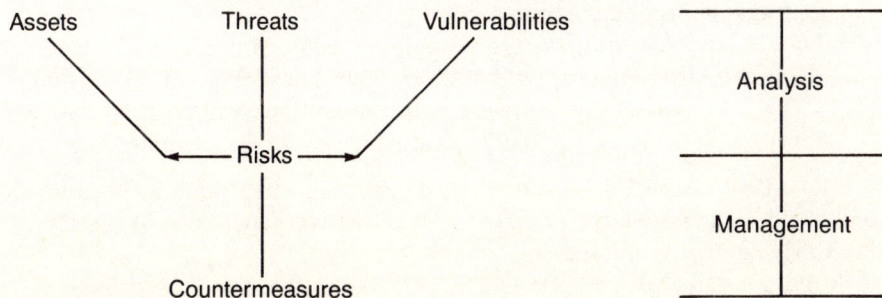

ary 1988. Early in 1989 the first non-Government courses took place, and a number of businesses are now using it in a wide variety of security reviews.

The methodology comprises a staged, or modular, approach. The first two stages address analysis of the risk, while the third addresses management of risk through the implementation of countermeasures.

CRAMM also offers the manager the ability to 'backtrack' to see exactly what contributed to the recommendation of a particular countermeasure or countermeasures. This would identify the impacts of concern and the scenarios which led to those impacts, the threats and vulnerabilities addressed, the justification for identification of particular levels identified, and the related asset(s) which the countermeasures are designed to protect.

The advantages of CRAMM can be summarised as follows:

- there is 'common metric' guidance to assist reviewers to obtain objective qualitative valuation of data assets for the four major impacts. (This has been particularly popular with government users).
- There is objective *qualitative* assessment of the threats to, and vulnerabilities of, specific groups of assets.
- There is a combination of qualitative values for assets, and threat and vulnerability ratings, to form numeric indications of risks.
- Numeric indications of risks are matched to specific detailed countermeasures.
- No presumptions are made as to the need for previously-implemented countermeasures; the justification for existing countermeasures is examined leading to possible cost savings.
- A baseline (or code of good practice) level of countermeasures is always required, based on the premise that all systems must have some value even if it is minimal.
- Extensive and readily-understandable management help facilities are provided.

The CRAMM methodology provides a disciplined framework in which security staff and auditors can perform reviews in an efficient and effective manner. In the public service, CRAMM is used comprehensively by security staff and internal audit teams, since:

- its principles are similar to those applied in Government audits of application systems and computer installations;
- because the data on risks, vulnerabilities and countermeasures held on the CRAMM database is based on the knowledge of Government security experts, the software will guide inexperienced employees through their reviews, providing valuable 'on-the-job' training.

CRAMM Version 2.0, developed by Touche Ross in 1990, now includes an enhanced database which reflects a comprehensive experience of security in both private and public sectors.

A more detailed description of CRAMM is provided in Appendix 9.

15   Managing Security

15.1   Who is Responsible?

The Board of Directors

The Board of Directors in a commercial enterprise—or their equivalents in the public service—have overall responsibility for all aspects of the organisation's operations, which must include security. Legal action (in the event of, for example, breaches of the *Data Protection Act*; *Financial Services Act* irregularities; civil actions for damages) would be aimed initially at the directors, whoever was directly responsible for the breach.

Their responsibilities include setting the required level of security awareness, communicating it to employees—by example in addition to more formal methods—and monitoring its achievement.

User and IT Management

Computer security is ultimately the responsibility of senior management. They must ensure that:

- an IT security policy is established;
- all employees are made aware of, and understand, the organisation's security objectives;
- an environment is created in which all employees and visitors are security conscious;
- appropriate security procedures are set up, strictly enforced and adhered to.

Specific responsibilities must be delegated for the security of:

- hardware;
- software;
- data;
- documentation;
- communications;
- personnel;
- environment;

- physical access to premises;
- logical access to systems;
- standby and recovery.

System Designers
These are responsible for ensuring that an adequate combination of application controls is built into each system.

Programmers
These must write the program steps necessary to create application controls and confirm, by testing, that they perform their function adequately.

Operators
These are the 'front line' in computer security. Although their security procedures should be documented in detail, they have the ultimate choice in their hands—to obey or not to obey!

Internal Auditors
The internal auditor's primary responsibility is to assist management by monitoring and appraising internal control (see chapter 16). Internal control is defined as the methods and measures established by management within a business to:

- safeguard its assets;
- ensure the reliability of its records;
- promote operational efficiency;
- encourage adherence to documented policies.

Their security-related responsibilities will typically include:

- active involvement in systems development, ensuring that:
  - adequate controls are incorporated;
  - the development project is properly controlled;
- reviews of application systems to confirm existence of, and compliance with, adequate controls;
- reviews of the security policy in order to confirm adequacy of, and compliance with, security procedures.

External Auditors
In order to provide an opinion on the accuracy of the company's financial statements, external auditors must be able to rely on the computer security procedures, and many of their audit tests will be aimed at establishing the level of confidence they can place in them.

A more detailed description of auditors' duties is provided in Chapter 16.

All employees have a duty to observe and enforce the security policy and

Figure 15.1

SECURITY TASKS

The Board	1. Appoint and monitor the performance of the Security Officer
	2. Approve and authorise the Security Policy
	3. Review security reports from the Security Officer and auditors
	4. Approve security arrangements
Security Officer	1. Produce draft Security Policy for Board agreement
	2. Ensure that each department has adequate security procedures and that these are consistent with the Security Policy
	3. Review compliance with these procedures
	4. Maintain the Security Manual, including risk/control assessments for all functions
	5. Record, and take action on, reported security breaches
	6. Make regular reports to the Board
Departmental Heads	1. Set up agreed security procedures
	2. Ensure compliance by departmental staff
	3. Ensure awareness of security requirements
	4. Inform the Security Officer of breaches of security
Internal Auditors	Review the work of the Security Officer.

---

procedures, and awareness sessions and training programmes must be tailor-made to the specific responsibilities of each group.

A brief description of the security responsibilities in an organisation is given in Figure 15.1.

15.2 The Information Security Officer

Although everyone has a responsibility for security at one level or another, it is important to identify a specific officer with responsibility for all aspects of

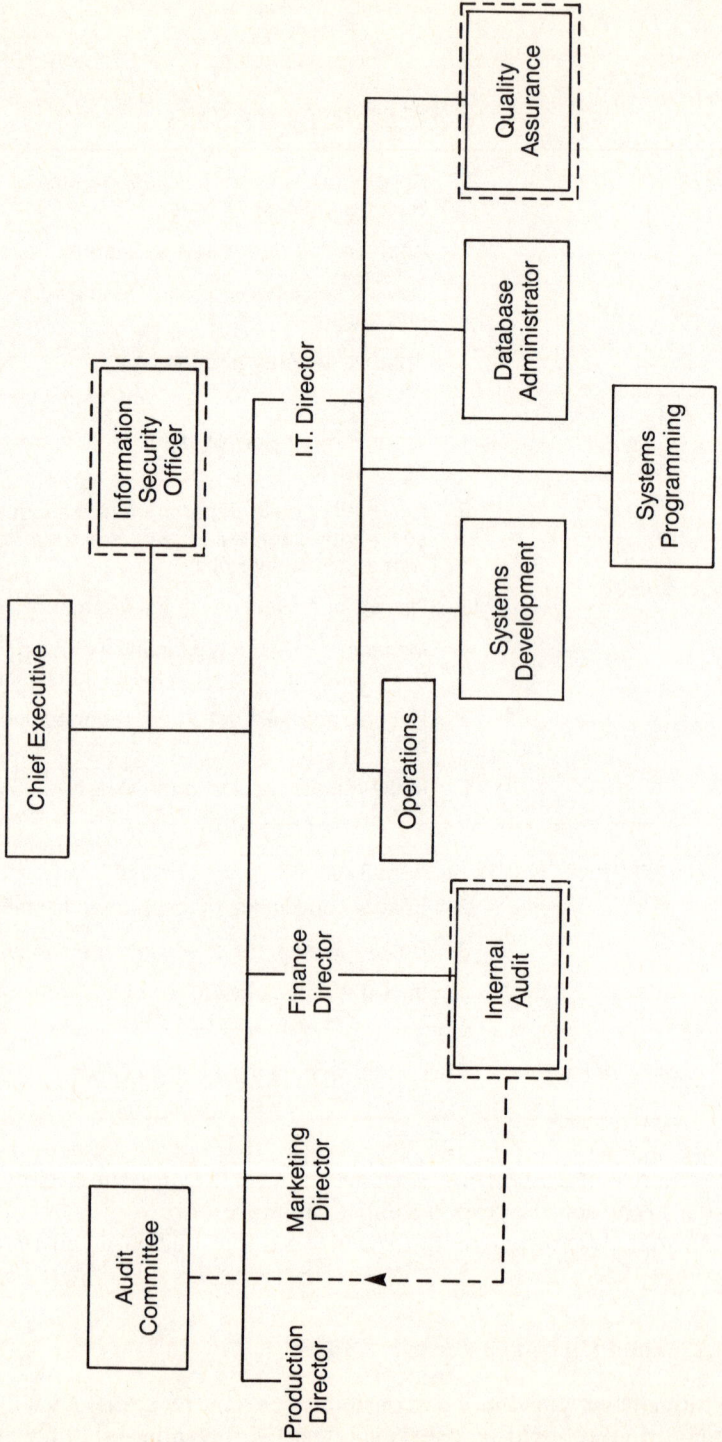

Figure 15.2

SECURITY IN THE ORGANISATION – 1

information security. Although the term 'security officer' suggests a man in a peaked cap, the reality is very different; in many organisations the title used—such as Security Manager or Security Administrator—reflects a need to avoid this assumption. The level of authority required means that a senior official is needed. He may be organisationally separate, or form part of a larger function such as risk management, but he must be able to demonstrate complete independence from any organisational structure, possibly by means of a reporting link to the chief executive or to board level. Figures 15.2 and 15.3 show two alternative organisational arrangements which demonstrate this requirement. The varied range of areas covered requires wide technical and business knowledge. In addition, the personal qualities required suggest that only saints need apply!

In many organisations this is a full-time job, in others it is an important part-time function. This will depend on the size and complexity of the organisation.

The titles 'Information Systems Security Officer', 'DP Security Officer' and 'Information Security Officer', have been used among others to describe the

Figure 15.3

SECURITY IN THE ORGANISATION – 2

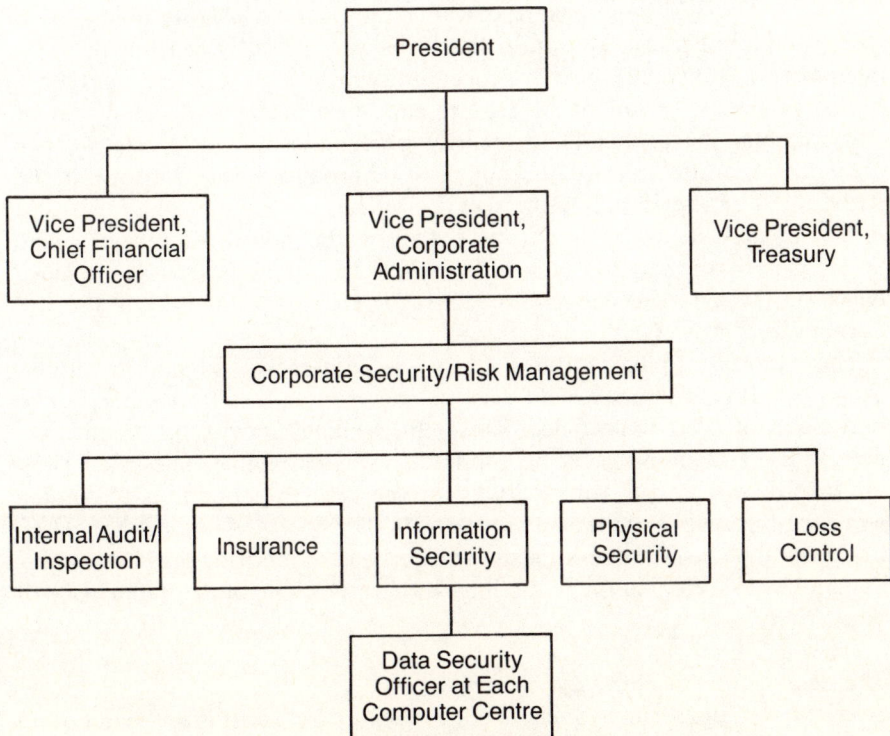

President

Vice President, Chief Financial Officer

Vice President, Corporate Administration

Vice President, Treasury

Corporate Security/Risk Management

Internal Audit/ Inspection

Insurance

Information Security

Physical Security

Loss Control

Data Security Officer at Each Computer Centre

function. The last-mentioned is possibly the most relevant since it suggests responsibility for all information in an organisation, regardless of the source or the medium used, making no differentiation between computer and manually-produced data. The responsibility of the post can extend further to take in responsibility for the overall security of the business organisation, and will typically include the security aspects of the following areas:

- organisation;
- personnel;
- physical security;
- system availability;
- data security;
- systems development and maintenance;
- communications systems (voice, data, electronic mail);
- IT operations (computer and network);
- risk management;
- job control and scheduling.

The security officer's background will typically be diverse, with varied experience in IT and, where relevant, in network operations and development. A wide understanding and experience of security matters is also essential, together with detailed knowledge of the organisation and the business world in which it exists.

His first task will be to ensure that a comprehensive security policy exists (see Chapter Three). He must then ensure that all departments have adequate, documented, security procedures which follow the rules laid down by the policy. A review of all departments must take place, conducted by departmental management. If security procedures do not exist, are not documented or are inadequate, they must be produced or revised within the department and reviewed by the security officer.

The documents will only be accepted by the board after review and acceptance by the security officer. He will then compile a security checklist based on the agreed security procedures for each department, and use this during future reviews.

The task of producing the security procedures should not be underestimated. If procedures do not exist management and staff may need to be persuaded of their importance. Once this 'selling' activity has been completed, the procedures must be produced in a reasonable timescale. Their production will be the responsibility of the relevant department, but the security officer will be intimately involved in the process. Among other activities, he will be responsible for setting targets and monitoring progress, and—in many cases—continually reminding those responsible of the importance of this activity.

The Duties of the Security Officer
A brief list of the security officer's duties is given below. It is not exhaustive,

merely providing a 'skeleton' around which each organisation will build its own specific requirements.

- Preparation of a plan covering reviews of all security subjects over a period acceptable to the board;
- Agreement of the security review plan with the board;
- Discussion and agreement of security procedures for each department;
- Using the appropriate checklist, performance of security reviews in accordance with the plan;
- Reporting to the board on results of the review;
- Prompt investigation of reported breaches of security;
- Liaison on a regular basis with all departments on security matters;
- Updating the security manual in accordance with any relevant change in circumstances;
- Liaison with internal and external auditors;
- Maintenance of the following documents: departmental security procedures; security checklists; register of computer users and applications; log of security breaches and responses.

In order to perform effectively, the security officer will require a regular inflow of information, including details of the following:

- new hardware, application systems, operating software and communications equipment;
- new areas of technical involvement;
- changes in business environment;
- external events and climate of opinion;
- security breaches.

15.3   The Security Review

A single security review is of limited value since it represents only a snapshot of the position at a specific time. To be effective, security must be reviewed on a recurring basis.

The first review of any function, department or system is a traumatic activity requiring the expenditure of a great deal of time, commitment and patience by many people. However, once the review—and the implementation of any necessary recommendations—is complete, succeeding reviews will be restricted to:

- updating security requirements in the light of changed circumstances (for example, new business areas, new hardware and software, different methods);
- confirming that the procedures are followed.

These ongoing reviews will be the responsibility of the security officer, who will require complete, understandable documentation of the original review.

The security officer's activities in turn must be documented, providing a full audit trail by which management, auditors and others can monitor his progress.

A security assignment will typically fall into a number of stages, as follows:

- familiarisation;
- identification of threats;
- risk evaluation;
- evaluation of existing protection;
- assessment of weaknesses;
- recommendations for improvement.

However, a security review is not a solitary activity. Many reviews have failed because management expected the security officer to perform the review without assistance from other experts in the organisation. Although he will provide the organisation and methodology, and be finally responsible for the review's effectiveness, he is not necessarily an expert in the business of the firm or its IT functions. A true understanding, and realistic prioritisation, of the risks to the business (as well as the effects of any security measures) can only be achieved by 'pooling' the experience of line management, IT specialists and the security officer. Despite the difficulty of organising the simultaneous attendance of these experts, the expertise of this 'security triumvirate' must be tapped to ensure that the review is firmly based on practical knowlege. The history of the organisation, problems in similar firms and installations, and sound commercial judgment will be applied during 'brainstorming' sessions, which must be carefully controlled and documented by the security officer. Although these will take place primarily during the early stages of threat/risk identification and assessment, limited involvement in specific areas of countermeasure identification will ensure that recommendations emerge as a consensus, rather than an imposed solution.

Familiarisation

The first step is to understand the overall business objectives of the systems under review, followed by identification of the underlying security objectives relating to those systems. As an example, a payroll system may have a number of business objectives including:

- to calculate monthly salary payments for all staff;
- to notify each member of staff of his gross pay and net pay for the month, and how the two are related.

Security objectives for the same system might include ensuring that:

- all payroll calculations and payments are confidential;
- no payment is made without the chief accountant's authority.

These objectives should be reviewed to ensure that, if they were met in full, an acceptable level of security would be achieved. If not, other more comprehensive objectives must be defined. The review then becomes an examination of how far the objectives are met in practice.

As well as understanding a system's objectives, the reviewer must also appreciate what it actually does, how it works and the environment in which it operates. This will help to confirm that the objectives are realistic and will form the basis of a detailed risk analysis.

Identification of Threats

In conducting a security review it is necessary to establish first what needs to be protected (assets, reputation etc) and the consequences of failure to provide adequate protection. Specific threats to the organisation should be identified. For each threat it is necessary to specify:

- how it could happen;
- the likelihood of it happening;
- the possible consequences of it happening.

The list of threats should be kept under review throughout the project.

An additional but quite separate method of identifying threats in a specific system is the use of a 'tiger team' of experts who will attempt to break the security in order to access, read, amend, purge or otherwise sabotage the data and programs. By thinking themselves into the roles of saboteurs they will act in unorthodox ways, identifying weaknesses which may not be detected by a more orthodox approach.

Risk Evaluation

A scale of priorities should be agreed, by experienced management and staff of relevant departments, based on the 'mix' of the following factors which apply to the organisation:

- loss of business;
- loss of assets;
- loss of reputation;
- loss of public confidence or goodwill;
- loss from legal actions.

A position on the scale is then applied to each identified risk.

Those threats where the potential loss is trivial or non-existent can be ignored. Equally, where the chance of the occurrence of a particular threat is negligible then it too should be ignored. For example it would be unwise to ignore earthquake damage as a threat to a computer installation in San Francisco but reasonable to ignore it as a threat in London.

Evaluation of Existing Protection

The next phase is to identify any existing protection against each of the specific threats which have been identified.

In general, protection falls into five main classes. These are measures which:

- prevent the occurrence of a threat;
- make its occurrence less likely;
- help detect its occurrence;
- help recover from it;
- mitigate its effect on the organisation.

While prevention is self-evidently preferable to recovery, there is still a requirement for detection and recovery procedures to support preventive measures.

A common mistake is to assume that protection is totally effective and so to ignore backup controls and recovery procedures. Very few preventive controls can be relied on absolutely. The ideal approach to security is the 'onion skin' approach, in which the failure of any security measure will not leave an asset completely unprotected since another aspect of security will take the strain (see Figure 1.5).

The use of a matrix which cross-relates threats and controls is a valuable technique for documenting the protection available for each class of threat, and an example is shown as Figure 15.4. However, lists of specific threats and controls can become very long and the task of manually compiling the cross-relationships becomes tedious and prone to error. Fortunately, software is available which can perform these activities efficiently with the aid of database techniques. This has the following benefits:

- Automatic cross-referencing of the converse relationships. For example, if a list of all security features for each threat has been compiled then a corresponding list of all threats contained by each feature can be produced automatically.
- Easier updating and recomputation of the threats or controls affected by a changed control or threat.
- Automatic listing of selected threats or controls with their corresponding controls or threats decoded.

It is important that the protection that exists is as effective as possible. This requires the following conditions to be fulfilled.

The procedure shuld be intended to deal with the threat. There may be procedures which contribute to security but unless they are recognised as such they are not truly security measures, since their significance is not fully understood. If this occurs, the procedure might be amended or discontinued without consideration of the security implications.

The procedure shuld be properly enforced. The reviewer will need to investigate the way in which the security measure is being carried out, and judge the adequacy of its enforcement.

Where the security protection comprises a passive contingency, it should be reliable. Many security measures are in the form of contingency plans or provisions. For effective security these must be relied upon to work when needed. This requires them to be regularly tested, as realistically as possible, to ensure they can be relied upon. An untested security plan is not an effective security measure.

Security measures should be formalised. In order to be effective, security measures should be known to all people who are involved, should be documented and should be subject to regular review.

Skill and imagination are required to determine the extent to which weaknesses in security measures should be strengthened. Experience and judgment are required in most cases to determine whether the degree of threat containment is adequate and whether the cost of improvements to controls is justifiable.

Assessment of Weaknesses
For each possible threat, the reviewer will decide the adequacy of the available protection. A healthy degree of scepticism is needed in this exercise. The reviewer should adopt an attitude of needing to be convinced that adequate security exists.

In most cases it is not possible to remove the threat entirely. The aim is to reduce the threat to an acceptable level. This involves reducing the probability of its occurrence, or reducing the loss involved if it does occur.

Having done this, a prioritised list of 'residual' weaknesses can be drawn up.

Recommendations for Improvement
Recommendations must be:

- *Effective.* The measures must pass the criteria used for existing measures, and be:
  - intended to deal with the weakness;
  - adequate to control the weakness entirely if properly enforced;
  - enforceable;
  - reliable;
  - formally adopted;
- *Efficient.* Any recommendations for improvements to security must be capable of justification in cost terms. Enquiries will be necessary to estimate the total cost of the solution, including any additional maintenance costs, labour costs, etc.

Figure 15.4

RISK ANALYSIS MATRIX	THREATS										
SECURITY PROCEDURES	1	2	3	4	5	6	7	8	9	10	11
1. Key pad access control to computer room	●	●	●								
2. Card reader control to computer room	●	●	●								
3. Staff photo-identification cards	●	●	●								
4. Security staff (day and night)	●	●	●								
5. Surveillance equipment	●	●	●								
6. Night checks on computer room by security	●	●	●								
7. Authorisation required for week-end working	●	●	●								
8. Register of micro-computer equipment		●									
9. Minimum of two operators during night shift	●	●	●								
10. Checking of staff identification cards at reception points		●	●								
11. Spot checks on vehicles leaving site		●									
12. Secure disposal of paper waste							●				
13. Back-up equipment (e.g. generator & air-conditioning)										●	
14. Halon detection-extinguishing equipment										●	
15. Fire proof safe for holding tapes										●	
16. Full fire training for all staff who use computer room										●	
17. Regular testing of fire procedures (e.g. evacuations)										●	
18. Posting of fire notices in computer room and support areas										●	
19. Dismissal procedures	●	●	●								
20. Taking up of references for prospective employees	●		●								
21. Formal leaving interviews for all computer staff			●								
22. Similar recruitment controls for contract & permanent staff	●										
23. Review of grievance procedures										●	
24. Back-up copies & off-site archiving of computer data			●			●					
25. Two copies of all back-ups taken at different times			●			●					●
26. Password system				●	●	●					
27. File protection facilities				●		●					

Figure 15.4 contd

RISK ANALYSIS MATRIX
(contd.)

	1	2	3	4	5	6	7	8	9	10	11
THREATS											
28. Restriction of sensitive applications to specific terminals				●		●					
29. Education of users regarding access control procedures				●							
30. Reporting of unauthorised access attempts				●							
31. Guidelines on types of passwords to be used				●							
32. Restriction of access by type of login				●							
33. Controlled usage of 'WHOIS' 'SETDEF' 'SHOWUSER' commands				●	●	●					
34. Batch controls and data validation checks					●						●
35. Reporting of computer usage by department					●						
36. Control of standing data amendments					●						
37. Reporting of access attempts to user areas					●						
38. Random checking of important accounts data					●						
39. Random review of computer usage by department					●						
40. Closed user group under P.S.S.						●					
41. Procedures for transfer of programs to production						●		●			●
42. Procedures for the control of personnel reports							●				
43. Standards for program development, maintenance and documentation								●			
44. Deletion of sensitive print files once reports printed							●				
45. System change control procedures									●		
46. Disaster plan										●	
47. Application of testing procedures										●	

Key to Threats
1 – Malicious damage
2 – Theft of equipment
3 – Theft of data
4 – Disclosure of sensitive data
5 – Fraud
6 – Sabotage of data and programs
7 – Unauthorised access to confidential computer output
8 – Application system faults caused by incorrect maintenance
9 – System faults caused by lack of configuration control
10 – Temporary or permanent loss of computer or communications
11 – Accidental data corruption

Figure 15.5

EXAMPLE: RISK ANALYSIS SHEET

CATEGORY: INTERRUPTION OF SERVICE

Threat: Incorrect Program or Version

Method of Occurrence Accidental or deliberate loading and running of incorrect program or version in the live system. This could be a new version which is not yet authorised, an old version loaded by mistake or an unauthorised program deliberately placed in the live system in the place of the correct program.

Risk of Occurrence Low/Medium.

Effect of Risk Low for accidental risk.
Potentially high for deliberate action.

Existing Controls Software Library procedures.

Coverage Inadequate control over transfer from testing to live environment.
Inadequate access control to system.

Compliance Software library procedures not always followed.

Possible Additional Controls
1. Restriction of access to live files within Operations department.
2. Certification and handover to Operations.
3. Procedures for authorising access to building, computer room, documents etc.
4. Security awareness and training.
5. Prevent development staff from accessing live system.
6. Software library procedures audit.
7. Program version control.

Recommendations The above additional controls should be implemented.

16 The Auditor

16.1 Introduction

Throughout the lengthy history of the auditing profession, which can be traced back to 4000 BC, the primary objective has remained the same: the need to confirm that records are complete, accurate and verifiable. The increasing complexity of processing and communications systems has naturally increased the difficulty of achieving this objective. Transaction processing and transfer take place at breathtaking speeds. Changes to data and programs take place very quickly, often destroying historical data, in some cases without providing paper backup. In this environment the auditor will find it difficult to verify the integrity of corporate databases and software using manual techniques.

The basic requirements for audit reviews in an IT environment are the same as those needed for any other branch of auditing: observation, interviewing and a liberal helping of scepticism! Although the objectives remain the same, the techniques and procedures involved in achieving them have changed considerably in 6000 years. The responsibilities of internal and external audit have expanded dramatically in the last 30 years and both now apply audit techniques which use the power and speed of the computer to enable security and control to be tested more thoroughly than otherwise possible.

16.2 Internal Audit

The Internal Audit Department has historically reported to the chief accountant or finance director, although the increasing development of non-financial audits such as value for money (VFM) and environmental audit, together with the growth of computer audit has made this approach seem less reasonable. The need for an adequate level of authority requires that the head of internal audit reports to a senior director on a day-to-day basis, while the need for independence has, in many cases, provided a separate reporting role to an audit committee. Examples are given in the Organisation Charts shown in Figures 15.2 and 15.3.

In any discussion of an internal auditor's responsibilities, the term 'internal control' will occur with monotonous regularity. The scope of internal auditing will usually include the evaluation and monitoring of 'systems and mechanisms of internal control'—a short phrase which is capable of extremely wide application.

In most organisations the term would be seen to include the organisational structure and all methods and procedures adopted to:

- safeguard assets and ensure the propriety of liabilities;
- maintain adherence to management policies and external regulations;
- ensure that records, financial statements and management information are accurate and reliable;
- confirm that the results of corporate activities are consistent with their objectives;
- ensure that resources are used effectively and efficiently in the service of the organisation's objectives.

The word 'control' can describe a number of widely-differing features. Control can be provided by:

- a physical device;
- a procedure;
- a software package;
- specific coding in applications or system software;
- the organisation of the business functions and people.

The security measures in a business or other organisation can therefore be seen as components of its internal control structure, and an effective internal audit function as a potent monitor and analyser of the effectiveness of security.

The *Statement of Responsibilities* of the Institute of Internal Auditors describes internal auditing as 'an independent appraisal acivity ...' and as 'a control which functions by examining and evaluating the adequacy and effectiveness of other controls.' The requirement to demonstrate independence from both auditees and routine control functions can create several dilemmas for the internal auditor who has no statutory powers and whose job specification is determined by management. In some cases internal auditors have been given—or have drifted into taking—responsibility for functions which conflict with their status as impartial observers. Examples of these activities are:

- design and, in some cases, programming of applications control procedures;
- regular monitoring of system logs for evidence of illegal access or processing;
- destruction of spoilt cheques.

Each of the above activities has been performed by auditors who were eager to prove their value to their employers, despite the fact that by doing so

Figure 16.1

THE PECKING ORDER

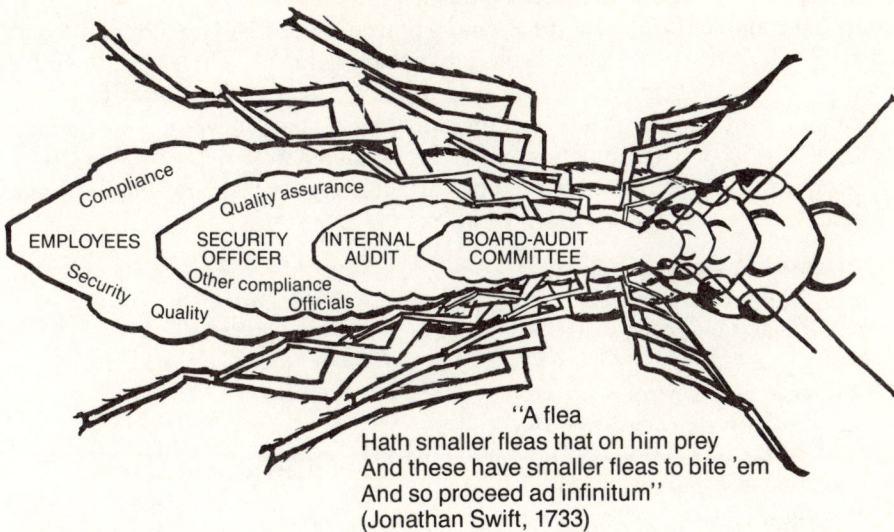

Compliance
Quality assurance

EMPLOYEES | SECURITY OFFICER | INTERNAL AUDIT | BOARD-AUDIT COMMITTEE

Security
Other compliance Officials
Quality

"A flea
Hath smaller fleas that on him prey
And these have smaller fleas to bite 'em
And so proceed ad infinitum"
(Jonathan Swift, 1733)

they became a component of the internal control they were employed to monitor. However, guidance on handling these problems is provided by the national and international auditing organisations, and most internal audit departments strike a productive, effective balance between the need for impartiality and their status as employees of the audited organisation.

The object of an auditor's investigations is twofold:

- to reach an opinion on the adequacy of existing controls to prevent, detect or mitigate the effects of significant risks;
- to investigate the extent to which the controls are used or complied with.

The question of which risks are significant will finally be answered by management using the only yardstick possible: significance to the continued and future prosperity of the business. However, in order to reach these conclusions a large quantity of information is required, and this will often be provided by a detailed risk analysis.

16.3   IT Controls

The controls over computer systems are usually classified in three categories.

Application System Controls
IT Installation Controls
Systems Development and Maintenance Controls

Application System Controls
This term refers to the programmed and manual procedures which ensure that valid transactions are processed and recorded completely, accurately, only once and in the correct timescale. Application controls are not applied in a similar fashion to all systems—suitable combinations are selected based on the security requirements of each system. In this aspect they differ from the 'general' controls over EDP installations and systems development, which should apply consistently in a computer environment.

Application system controls can be further categorised under the headings Input, Processing, and Output. Some examples are:

- input controls:
  - validation or 'reasonability' checks for transactions;
  - batch controls;
  - check digits;
- processing controls:
  - run to run reconciliation:
  - crossfooting checks to confirm data consistency;
  - verification of permanent data;
- output controls:
  - input–output reconciliation;
  - confirmation of completeness of output, for example by 'Nil Return' reports, page numbering and 'Start' or 'End' pages.

A more detailed description of these, and other, controls is provided in Chapter Eight.

Installation Controls
These act as a consistent framework to all applications. In the absence of a secure environment, application controls could be bypassed and would therefore be unable to provide the required levels of assurance. The necessary environment could be provided by such security measures as:

- segregation of duties;
- supervision and monitoring of activities;
- controls over access to buildings, hardware, programs and data;
- controls over hardware and system software;
- use of authorised standard operating instructions;
- controls over data and program libraries.

Systems Development Controls
These are essential to ensure that an implemented system has been developed in a properly-controlled manner. They include:

- a standard methodology for project performance and management;
- checkpoint stages at which deliverables can be reviewed against agreed objectives;

- formal quality assurance (QA) procedures;
- effective testing at all stages;
- detailed implementation planning throughout the project;
- application change control procedures.

Typically the auditor will perform audits of:

- an individual application system, considering:
  - programmed controls;
  - user procedures;
  - system operation and data control;
  - control over program changes and enhancements;
- a computer installation, including investigation of:
  - organisation and personnel controls;
  - physical security;
  - system availability;
  - data integrity;
  - communications;
  - software development and maintenance;
  - system operation and control;
  - insurance arrangements;
- a systems development project, confirming that:
  - adequate programmed controls are included in the system;
  - control procedures are designed to support the systems;
  - the project is properly managed and controlled (this will include an evaluation of QA and an assessment of the degree to which the auditor can rely on QA findings);
- specific audits of, for example:
  - a communications network;
  - an ATM network;
  - the interface with a bureau or VADS service.

Internal audit's activities in an IT environment will cover much of the ground performed during a security review. However, the emphasis is different. If security reviews are performed by others, the auditor will see them as components of internal control. His concern will then be to ensure that they take place sufficiently frequently, that they are comprehensive and that they are properly performed and documented. For a description of the auditor's activities in this environment, readers should refer to Section 16.6.

16.4 The Application System Audit

The application audit comprises the following activities. The stages apply to any system, whether computerised or manual, but the techniques will differ.

Define Objectives and Scope of the Audit
The general objective of an application audit is to verify those processes and controls necessary to make the applications free from significant risks. However, detailed terms of reference must be produced at this stage to enable the audit to be planned and monitored effectively. This document will define the scope of the work to be performed and identify any constraints.

Develop Understanding of, and Document, the System
At this 'information gathering' stage a number of activities will take place in order to provide sufficient understanding of the system to enable the auditor to identify the required controls. These activities will include:

- studying existing documentation, such as systems descriptions and operating and user manuals;
- interviewing relevant management and personnel;
- creating the necessary audit files by copying or, if not available in an accepted format, producing the relevant documents.

Although at this stage the auditor is primarily concerned with the collection of information about the system, he will also be forming a judgment on the adequacy of the organisation's documentation standards.

Once the system has been documented the auditor may scrutinise a limited number of examples of completed transactions, tracing them from input documents via control registers to the related output, in order to confirm his understanding.

Identify and Evaluate Controls
The information collected at the previous stage is now used to identify and reach a conclusion on the existence and quality of controls. The auditor must ask the following questions:

- Does the system appear to provide the required results?
- Which controls must the auditor verify in order to determine the confidence he can place in the system?
- What investigations of apparent weaknesses should be made?

Design and Perform Audit Tests
After identifying and evaluating the controls, the auditor will choose the appropriate methods of testing their effectiveness. The tests will:

- verify the accuracy of the results of processing;
- perform specific tests of critical processes and controls;
- confirm that control procedures are complied with.

It is essential that these tests:

- use a representative sample of data;

- also include examples of unusual transactions; for example, invalid transactions and those which exceed the boundaries of normal items.

Reporting and Follow-up
On completion of the tests the auditor must document and evaluate the results. This process will result in an identification of any weaknesses in internal control and a measure of their impact on the business.

The draft report produced from the review will contain a description of the identified weaknesses and specific recommendations for correcting the defects. After reviewing the report with audit and EDP management the final report will be produced.

The final stage will be a review of the audit—and the auditee's responses—in order to identify a plan and schedule for follow-up action, which should be documented for future use.

In order to record computer-based controls the auditor will include the following in his documentation:

- flowcharts of the EDP and clerical processes;
- examples of input documents and output reports;
- layouts of all master and transaction files;
- tables or lists defining the codes used by the system;
- copies of error and exception reports;
- descriptions of the circumstances in which each error message will be output, and the actions to be taken.

Testing of controls is typically performed using the following techniques:

- confirming output with outside parties, such as customers, suppliers or banks;
- comparison with files maintained by independent departments, or with the physical items represented by the files (stock, fixed assets etc);
- reasonableness and edit tests of items within files (credit balances, excessive payments etc);
- an integrated test facility, which integrates test data with a 'live' processing environment;
- snapshot techniques, which provide a selective transaction trail;
- parallel simulation, where 'live' transactions and records are independently reprocessed and compared with the original results.

16.5   Internal Audit in Systems Development

The benefits of early involvement in development projects have ensured a lively debate among audit practitioners, since it is primarily in this area that the audit requirements to provide both independence and value for money can appear to be in conflict.

Since the auditor's advice on control matters will be incorporated in the finished system, he may not be seen to provide the assurance of impartiality required by management, no matter how strenuously he attempts to be unbiased in practice. A further danger exists in the possibility that system designers may believe their responsibility for designing adequate controls has been delegated to the auditor.

Neither of the above difficulties should be considered as insoluble when balanced against the undoubted advantages of audit involvement. The internal auditor can never be said to be completely independent, since his scope and responsibilities are determined by management. His historical auditing of current systems usually results in recommendations for improving controls. Once incorporated, his recommendations become part of the system upon which, in turn, he may be required to comment later. The parallel with development auditing is obvious, and provides a clear example that this audit approach is not new. However, any fears which remain can be allayed by ensuring that different auditors are responsible for the systems development and 'live' system audits.

The auditor must ensure that the systems designers understand that his involvement does not in any way reduce their responsibility to design adequate application system controls, and the document laying down the details of his involvement must make this plain.

The time-consuming nature of an auditor's involvement in the development phases must be considered, and sufficient time budgeted for active involvement in at least the critical phases of development.

The benefits of audit involvement at this stage are impressive. Adequate controls can be built into the system from the start, when they are comparatively cheap to install, rather than after implementation when they would be much more expensive. A survey in the early 1980s found that costs increase dramatically if the auditor is not involved at the earliest stage. It was found that a control, in general, costs:

- four times as much to include if added after the system specification is complete;
- eight times as much after the programs have been written;
- twelve times after testing is complete;
- sixteen times after implementation.

The increased costs of systems development since that time ensure that the figures will be no smaller in the 1990s! Audit involvement during the development stage also brings benefits to the auditor, by providing training and understanding of the system. This understanding should provide a basis on which the nature of subsequent audit involvement can be determined.

Although each organisation must consider the above factors, the generally accepted opinion is that—since the internal auditor is never completely independent—it is usually in the interests of his employer to compromise a little more to ensure that adequate controls will exist in the system, and that those controls will be installed as inexpensively as possible.

16.6   Auditing the Security Function

Security is a line management function, responsible for recommending, evaluating, and overseeing the implementation of security measures; while internal audit is an independent monitoring function.

The two should work closely together, sharing information in the following ways:

- An auditor should be included in the security committee;
- Auditors should review security procedures before implementation;
- Reports on security reviews should be sent to the Audit Department;
- A member of the security officer's staff should assist the auditors during their security audits and respond to audit comments on security matters.

The auditors will routinely review the effectiveness and independence of the information security function. Based on the results of these reviews, they will determine the extent to which they can rely on the security function as a control. A checklist (such as that shown in Figure 16.2) may be used for this purpose. The more effective the security officer is at developing security programs, reviewing security measures and increasing security awareness, and the greater his independence from the information providers, the more reliance can be placed on security as a component of internal control.

During this review the auditors will investigate the major controls over corporate data, such as:

- password controls;
- physical security over critical resources;
- security parameter file settings.

Their assessments of the Security Department's controls will be affected by the level of:

- completeness of documented security procedures;
- departmental and corporate compliance with security procedures;
- follow-up on potential security exposures
- validity of system users;
- access restriction to sensitive commands and files.

16.7   External Audit

The external auditor's overall objectives for company audits are laid down by law—in the United Kingdom by the *Companies Act* and other statutes (eg *Banking* and *Building Society Acts*) related to the conduct of business. More detailed requirements and guidance are provided by the various accounting and auditing institutes and bodies. External auditors are required to provide an independent opinion on the fairness and truthfulness of the

Figure 16.2

SECURITY CHECKOUT

1. Does your organisation have a Security Policy?

2. Is it documented and regularly reviewed? (*NB:* If not, Answer NO to Question 1)

3. Does a senior member of staff have a specific responsibility for risk management?

4. Have the detailed responsibilities been described in his/her job specification?

5. Are all potential risks regularly identified, documented and evaluated?

6. Are existing security measures similarly evaluated?

7. Does your organisation have an Information Security Officer?

8. Is information classified according to its security status?

9. Is there an employee security awareness scheme in operation?

10. Is the Information Security Officer:
    - independent of line management?
    - at an appropriate level of seniority?

11. Are his/her responsibilities:
    - documented?
    - regularly reviewed at Board level?

12. Does the installation use the following on-line security software features:
    - on-line monitoring?
    - program library management?

13. Do controls exist to prevent unauthorised access to production data files and program libraries?

14. Do systems software facilities allow for the enforcement of data access rules?

15. Are audit trails of system access provided?

16. Are password files, authorisation tables, and key software stored secure from read-and-write access?

17. Are confidential passwords used?

18. Are adequate password administration procedures followed, including:
    - proper authorisation of each user?
    - frequent changes of passwords?
    - prompt suppression of passwords on resignation or dismissal?
    - periodic review for redundant passwords?
    - unauthorised access attempts documented and followed up?

auditee's financial statements. Their interest in evaluating internal controls, primarily of a financial nature, usually relates to the level of confidence they wish to take from those controls. However, Sections 39 of the *Banking Act* and 71 of the *Building Societies Act*, as well as requirements of the SROs set up by the *Financial Services Act* specifically require external auditors to report on internal control.

The external audit of UK public organisations is also covered by relevant statutes, although in general the auditors have wider responsibilities in value for money (VFM) audits, which cover efficiency, economy and effectiveness. The relevant Acts are:

Local Government and Finance Act (1983)
Audit requirements for local authority audits under this Act are specified in a code of practice; this sets out the nature of the audits and requires the auditors to report on matters of public interest (for example, lack of value for money, misconduct, fraud). External audit of Local Authorities is the responsibility of the Audit Commission, although some of the audits may be undertaken by commercial accountancy firms.

NHS and Community Care Act (1990)/Local Government Housing Act (1989)
Under this legislation the external audit of Health Authorities was defined, regulated and placed under the control of the Audit Commission.

National Audit Office Act (1983)
This legislation replaced aspects of earlier Acts in the regulation of central government audits. The Act also gave a statutory basis for value for money audits in the central government sector for the first time.

Although the internal auditor is, unlike the external auditor, responsible to management, the common requirement to study internal control leads to a similar approach to the investigation of security procedures and techniques. In many cases the methods and procedures of each are the same, although internal audit may focus on a wider range of issues or have a lower 'materiality' threshold. The external auditor will normally evaluate the competence of internal audit and, in the event of a satisfactory evaluation, may reduce the amount of detailed work required by relying on the results of internal audit activities.

16.8   The US Experience

The responsibilities of the external auditor in the USA cover similar ground to those in the UK, although the statutory environment in which they operate differs.

Internal audit in the USA also has the same objectives and responsibilities as in the UK. However, a number of developments in criminal law and national regulations have ensured managements' undivided attention to their auditors' recommendations for improvements in security.

The *Foreign Corrupt Practices Act (1977)* contains provisions which require all companies to maintain an adequate system of internal accounting controls and records of financial transactions. In the event of bribery being proved on the part of any member of the organisation, evidence of proper control and recording of transactions would assist in proving that the organisation had no corporate responsibility, thereby avoiding or mitigating the draconian punishments which can be imposed.

The Proposed Rules on managements' responsibilities issued by the Securities and Exchange Commission (SEC) in 1988 will—if they become mandatory—further strengthen the role and authority of the internal audit function in investigating adequacy and compliance with systems of internal control. The rules require a statement in every company's annual report which would include a description of management's assessment of the effectiveness of internal control and its response to any significant recommendations on the subject by internal and external auditors.

US banks are also subject to audit by the National Bank Examiners and the Federal Reserve Bank, both of whose requirements refer to the need for an acceptable level of security.

It should be emphasised that the above requirements do not merely apply to companies which reside physically in the USA. Other organisations which are required to comply in the same way include:

- foreign branches of US companies;
- foreign companies registered with the SEC;
- the many UK and other organisations in the financial services sector owned by US companies.

In many cases this causes conflicts with the requirements of the host country, which are currently unresolved.

17 Security Aspects of Compliance Reviews

17.1 Compliance Officers

Financial organisations have needed to demonstrate compliance with a wide variety of regulations for many years. However, the *UK Financial Services Act (1986)* and its many descendants created a need for professional officers, who may be full time or part time, depending on the size of the firm and other factors. They will have a variety of responsibilities, including:

- identification and implementation of methods satisfying reporting requirements;
- assessment of the firm's compliance with relevant laws and regulations;
- identifying and informing others of the impact of new regulations, or of existing regulations on new business;
- investigation of complaints;
- identification of breaches;
- liaison with regulators;
- organisation of compliance training.

Principle 9 of SIB's *Statements of Principle* (April 1990) reads:

'A firm should organise and control its internal affairs in a responsible manner, keeping proper records, and where the firm employs staff or is responsible for the conduct of investment business by others, should have adequate arrangements to ensure that they are suitable, adequately trained and properly supervised and that it has well-defined compliance procedures.'

The document *Professional Standards and Guidelines for Compliance Officers*, which was published by the Chartered Association of Certified Accountants in collaboration with the SIB in December 1990, provides guidance on responsibility for compliance and the necessary activities and organisation.

Visiting investigators from regulatory authorities will often review compliance arrangements, focussing on such areas as capital adequacy assessments, client money control, the levels of remuneration from trading and adherence to responsibilities contained in client agreements. However, they will also wish to review compliance with the requirements related to internal controls, systems development and maintenance, audit trails, documentation and security of records. The compliance officer will need to include all the above matters in his review programme.

17.2 Compliance Reviews

The IT-related requirements which should be considered by a compliance review fall into three major categories:

- a) application system features which will produce accurate information for clients and regulatory authorities;
- b) the provision of an acceptable security environment in which the systems can be expected to operate correctly, ensuring that the information provided is correct;
- c) adequate documentation of the standards, procedures and controls implied by (b).

The detailed requirements covered by categories (b) and (c), as well as some of those included in (a), are also required in the interests of security, efficiency and the provision of an effective service to clients. These objectives can be achieved by, for example:

- providing improved management information;
- installing flexible methods of creating ad hoc reports;
- repairing the deficiencies identified by internal and external audit.

17.3 TSA Regulations: Security Aspects

Some of the security implications of the original regulations of The Securities Association (TSA) Regulations which now forms part of The Securities and Futures Association, are given below.

- 1) In order to comply with the rules, systems must be capable of recording a variety of details of orders, instructions, execution, clients etc—with all that this implies in terms of:
  - file or database structures;
  - storage capacity;
  - response times.

- 2) Software is needed to provide access to, and reports from, the records. Installations must be sufficiently flexible to provide any required processing, while IT operations must be effective enough to despatch the results to clients or SROs in the prescribed timescale.

3) It will be necessary to review existing retention procedures on a regular basis to provide continuing assurance that data will be retained for the required period and—even more important—that it can be identified, reclaimed and used when required. Sophisticated software may be needed to manage archival and retrieval of data on a rolling three-year basis.

4) Strict control of access to records is essential to maintain 'Chinese Walls'. This requires:

- a good access control system;
- procedures which ensure that passwords are issued, used and controlled in a secure manner.

The best software in the world is useless if the staff do not treat their passwords with respect, and the procedures must be reinforced by sound security training.

5) Security over access to off-line data, whether in the Media Library, backup stores, printed form or microfilm is equally important, although more often forgotten. Access to computer equipment and terminals must be restricted on a 'need-to-use' basis.

6) The penalties for inability to trade, provide information or comply in the many other ways required are stringent. The need for a plan for resumption of business in the event of the many problems which may occur (from a major catastrophe to a minor 'glitch') is now self-evident. If a disaster plan has not been produced this must be done without delay. If a plan already exists, a few questions should be asked such as:

- Is it adequate?
- Is it up to date?
- Has it been tested?
- Is it regularly reviewed?

Unless the organisation can answer 'Yes' to all the above questions the resources used in the production of the plan have been wasted.

7) The TSA regulations refer to a need to:

- establish and maintain systems of internal controls;
- establish an adequate audit trail;
- maintain procedures for the maintenance, security, privacy and preservation of records.

The implications of these statements are enormous, although none of the many requirements covered by them are unique to the SROs. If these subjects have not already been addressed, frenzied activity may be necessary. Certainly, a comprehensive security review is essential on a regular basis.

Compliance officers may perform other security functions by confirming that systems and installations are following the rules laid down by the VAT and Inland Revenue authorities, in addition to the more down-to-earth requirements of the fire authorities and Health and Safety Executive. Another function could be that of ensuring compliance with the *Data Protection Act*.

Appendix 1: SWIFT

Society for Worldwide Interbank Financial Telecommunication (S.W.I.F.T.)

S.W.I.F.T. is a co-operative society, owned by the international banking community, which operates a communications network providing its members with fast, responsive and secure worldwide transmission of financial messages. These include:

- customer transfers;
- bank transfers;
- credit/debit advices;
- credit/debit confirmations;
- securities transactions;
- statements;
- foreign exchange and securities dealings;
- documentary credits;

as well as system messages which enable users and the system to communicate.

The network currently connects over 3000 users in 84 countries and transmits an average of 1.35 million messages per day, peaking to 1.5 million at times. The traffic growth increased in 1989 by 16 per cent to over 296 million messages, and this trend is expected to continue or increase, particularly owing to the increased range of message types supported by SWIFT and the greater use of automated processing at banks.

In addition to its main service of message processing and transmission, S.W.I.F.T. is active in other areas through two subsidiaries: S.W.I.F.T. Terminal Services (STS), which supplies network-compatible terminals and software to almost 70 per cent of network users, and S.W.I.F.T. Service Partners (SSP) which offers specialised financial services such as ECU netting. SSP also caters for the specialised needs of specific segments of the Society's membership, including non-bank financial institutions.

The first banks converted to the new SWIFT II System in 1990, and cutover is taking place on a country by country basis.

Perhaps the most important benefit of SWIFT II is its ability to handle the growing volume of messages quickly and efficiently, allowing any amount of extra capacity to be added to meet future user demand.

The Network

The network functions are performed by two operating centres serving regional processors in different countries. Each regional processor acts as the local concentrating point, operating on a 'store and forward' basis. The operating centres validate the messages, acknowledge their receipt, store copies of them and control delivery.

Users are connected to their regional processors via public switched or private leased lines, with their choice of equipment which must comply with S.W.I.F.T. standards.

Messages may be input manually to the sender's SWIFT terminal or be generated by the sender's internal computer system and transferred to its SWIFT terminal. The SWIFT terminal then transmits each message to the regional processor in the sender's country. From there the message goes to the operating centre controlling that regional processor, and from there to the regional processor of the receiver's country (possibly via another operating centre). The output regional processor delivers the message to the receiver's terminal from where it is transferred into the receiver's internal computer system or printed in the receiver's operational area or locally in the processing department.

In SWIFT I the network functions are performed by two operating centres serving regional processors in the different member countries. It is a centralised system with the majority of the functions and most of the control exercised by the central system which resides in the operating centres.

The new SWIFT II decentralised modular network, based on Unisys CP2000 front-end processors with Unisys A Series equipment in regional and operating centres, uses transaction processing, providing greater flexibility and ensuring that, as traffic increases, processing capacity can easily be enhanced.

SWIFT Security

All users are provided with overall SWIFT network security by the application of principles which are, and always have been, considered primary requirements. These cover:

- *integrity*, which relates to the authorised use of the system and the accuracy, completeness and accountability of all messages and transactions;
- *confidentiality*, the restriction of access to sensitive data during transmission, processing and storage; the term 'sensitive data' covers messages and transactions, as well as information relating to the operation of the system and organisation;
- *availability*, through:

- – the prevention and early detection of denial of service (or reduced service levels) to the users for whatever reason;
- – building resilience into the system;
- *reliability*, meaning:
  - – the degree to which systems conform to their requirements;
  - – the physical security of the assets necessary to make and keep systems operational;
- *accountability*: the ability to inform users accurately and in an acceptable timescale if a compromise in any of the above objectives occurs, and who has the responsibility for processing the message at any one stage.

These objectives are achieved by applying proven developments in the areas of computer security and control, as well as intensive application of effective computer audit.

Data confidentiality in SWIFT is achieved primarily by encryption of all data. This entails the use of encryption devices on all links and circuits controlled by SWIFT, and the encryption of data in storage by means of proprietary encryption algorithms. Additionally, all functions which access data still being processed are protected by means of one-time passwords under the control of the security department. These controls also contribute to data integrity since they prevent access to data, which could result in inadvertent or fraudulent modification, regardless of the shortness of the time period in which data could be intercepted and/or manipulated.

Typical data integrity controls are unique sequencing of all messages, dual storage and real-time acknowledgement to the user, indicating the time of arrival. However, by far the most important data integrity control is the message authentication procedure between sender and receiver. Authentication consists of a digital signature which is based on the contents of the message and the identity of the sender. Both the sender and receiver have exchanged a set of bilateral keys before transmission. The digital signature, known as the authenticator, will change if even a single bit is changed in the contents of the message. When it is recalculated by the receiver and compared with the authenticator provided by the sender, the authenticity of the contents—as well as the authenticity of the sender—is guaranteed. Other important controls for data and functional integrity are the use of one-time passwords for gaining access to the system; and non-repudiation, which is assured by obtaining proof of identification of sender and of receipt.

SWIFT availability is achieved by several measures, many of which are built into the organisation in the form of contingency planning. Other typical availability controls are the duplication and, in some cases, triplication of equipment, extensive recovery schemes and automatic rerouting in the event of failure of some network nodes. Physical controls such as access control, environment detectors, an uninterruptible power supply (UPS) and back-up generators also contribute to the system's availability.

Many of the controls used by SWIFT to ensure availability are not common, and their purpose is not immediately obvious. For example, the time-out control indirectly contributes to availability because it highlights any system or network failure quickly, allowing speedy remedial activities to take place. This function illustrates a general design principle for controls, applied wherever possible in the system, by which all elements of the network are continuously monitored for proper functioning. Each element of the system is required to transmit traffic continuously, or generate dummy traffic where necessary, so that absence of traffic immediately indicates a failure.

Error pattern recognition has been implemented in SWIFT to protect the system against the careless or untrained operator. It also contributes to integrity if the apparently careless operator is really trying to penetrate the system. If a pattern of errors is recognised on any terminal and threshold values are exceeded, the terminal will be disconnected automatically.

Assurance that the correct level of security has been achieved is provided by intensive internal and external audit. Internal audit performs a continual review of all critical SWIFT features, covering the organisation, hardware, software, regional and central operations, physical security and all system changes and enhancements. They were also deeply involved in ensuring that the security objectives for SWIFT II were identified and achieved, and that the development project was properly controlled. External auditors perform wide-ranging reviews, and their view of the level of security and control is included in each annual report.

SWIFT II Security Features

SWIFT I was designed with centralisation of control in mind. SWIFT II is a distributed system, and security and control aspects have changed accordingly. The new development has also provided an opportunity to install additional security features, some of which are described below.

Improved Access Controls
Although the one-time password principle is still considered well above par for security in commercial systems, the passwords travel through the system and could be exposed as a result of the failure of other controls, or if errors or omissions occurred. The design of SWIFT II enables system access functions to be separated from those functions which control the use of a particular application. There are two levels of access:

- the basic LOGIN, which enables a user to access the SWIFT II system;
- SELECT, which controls access to specific applications.

To improve the security of access to the system, the random and response keys in SWIFT II LOGIN and SELECT tables are not transmitted over the network. Instead, they are used by the user terminal and SWIFT in every access procedure, to generate unique security codes which are exchanged and verified by both parties.

User-to-user message authentication is fully supported in SWIFT II exactly as in SWIFT I. Authentication keys already exchanged between correspondents remain effective, regardless of whether either or both users have cut over to the SWIFT II system.

In addition, a filter principle will be applied to all password-based accesses from users, operators and administrators. This will allow greater control over the capabilities of the many varieties of users of the system.

Improved Service Reliability

All messages passing around the SWIFT II system do so using proven store-and-forward techniques. That is, before a message is sent from one part of the system to the next, a copy is retained by the sending computer until the receiving computer acknowledges safe receipt of the complete message. This principle is applied to every part of the system and provides for a reliable service.

All computers within the SWIFT II system have at least one standby processor. This provides extensive hardware backup resources throughout the system.

Certain data transmission paths within the system are duplicated to ensure continued service in the event of single path failures.

In SWIFT II, the system control processor (SCP) constantly monitors the integrity of the system, dynamically allocating resources as required. The SWIFT II system provides facilities such that—should a failure occur somewhere in the network—traffic may be automatically diverted via standby resources with little effect upon the rest of the network.

All SWIFT II messages are stored on two separate storage media. Should a system failure occur, users should not need to retransmit messages—input messages already acknowledged by SWIFT will be retrieved from either the primary storage media or its backup. Extreme cases of loss of messages from all storage media, requiring re-input by users, are far less likely to occur than in SWIFT I.

Reliability of service is further improved by the requirement that all CBTs connected to SWIFT II must formally acknowledge safe receipt and storage of all output messages. Until such an acknowledgement is received by SWIFT, a message is not considered to have been delivered successfully and will remain in the delivery queue for that terminal.

End-to-end Integrity

To satisfy the continuing guarantee that every piece of information—at any point in the exchange process—will remain complete and correct, checksum systems have been expanded to take into account any possible transfer of information from initiation to reception.

End-to-end Confirmation
The final proof of delivery in SWIFT I is based on the correct completion of a telecommunications protocol which is continuously monitored and recoverable. In SWIFT II an additional acknowledgement is required at the application level of the receiver's system by means of an explicit and retrievable message.

End-to-end Encryption
In addition to line and file encryption as applied in SWIFT I, the new system will use software to encrypt any piece of sensitive information before it is stored anywhere. As a result, any user message on the telecommunication lines will have been 'double encrypted', once by software and once by hardware.

A mandatory checksum is added to all SWIFT II banking and system messages to enable the receiver (whether SWIFT or a user) to verify that a message text has not been corrupted owing to system malfunction or undetected transmission error. This is a system enhancement and does not replace the user-to-user message authentication process.

On-line Audit and Control
The system will provide more automated and on-line access routes for auditors and supervisory staff to enable verification of all security and control aspects of the system to be performed immediately.

Improved Status Information
A major improvement for the users will be the provision of more detailed information on messages, connections and system status. The user will also have more opportunity to tailor the information to his control needs.

Bank Security Requirements
1) Segregation of Duties. Functions which should be the responsibility of separate individuals or teams are:

- Security officer/Administration—the person(s) designated to receive LOGIN Tables from SWIFT. The tables are distributed in two parts, and optimum security is achieved if each is received by different individuals. They are then held in safe storage and passed to operational staff as necessary. In many banks this is the responsibility of the chief accountant and/or chief inspector, who would also control the Master Password but should not be involved in SWIFT Operations or any aspect of payment processing.
- SWIFT Operations are responsible for the control and handling of the interface, their activities consisting primarily of performing the necessary "logins" and "logouts". SWIFT recommends that two officers hold the separate parts of the login table, and this must be seen as the ideal

situation. If this rule is not followed, a high level of physical and logical access control is essential.

- Custody of authentication keys. In many banks this is a function of the employee responsible for Telex test key authentication.
- Transaction processing. This is a two or three-stage activity, each stage of which should ideally be performed by separate individuals:
  - data entry;
  - verification;
  - authorisation and release to SWIFT.

Release to the SWIFT network is sometimes completed in the verification step. However, it is recommended that the three-stage process, undertaken by separate individuals, is invoked when large-value transactions (say greater than £100,000) are being processed.

In smaller banks some of the above functions are performed by the same person. However, it is generally understood that the greater the degree of separation, the lower the risk.

2) Logical Access Control. Transaction-processing must be subject to very specific User-id/password control, limiting privileges on a 'need-to-use' basis. It is important to ensure that this restriction applies not only to operatives but also to management. Officers who perform authentication should not be allowed to create and process transaction data.

Use of workstations must be controlled. As a minimum, application users must logout at the end of a session or whenever the terminal is not in use. Preferably, the system should enforce this.

Access to live data should be strictly controlled. Under most circumstances development staff should not be allowed to do this. If under extraordinary circumstances this is essential, authorisation must be given for this occasion only at high (possibly vice president) level. The resulting activities should be witnessed and a print or audit log of the 'before' and 'after' conditions of the data produced and independently reviewed.

SWIFT will, in future, offer new products such as EDI and Interbank File Transfer, which may be dealt with by bank employees who have not in the past been subject to the strict controls expected in payment processing. It will be necessary, in these cases, to be aware of the need to apply relevant security measures and perform the necessary training in good time. The value of limiting logical access controls for specific applications to specific work-stations in specific departments should also be considered.

3) Control of Paper Output. In many bank systems, although messages for despatch are generated automatically, the receipt and processing of incoming messages is performed manually. In these circumstances the paper must be controlled as carefully as the electronic data, ensuring that printouts are not altered or lost in transit and that a transaction is effected without delay.

All reports—in whatever form (paper, microfiche etc)—must be stored securely and in a manner which will allow easy retrieval even after an extended period. Queries are possible many months after a transaction is believed by one party to have been correctly accomplished, and the ability to trace contentious items quickly is essential. These requirements also, of course, apply to the electronic 'message database' holding transaction information; which must be downloaded, backed up and archived.

4) Error Reports. Reports of possible errors from SWIFT—such as PDMs/ PDEs (Possible Duplicate Messages/Entries) and Missing Input or Output Sequence Numbers (ISNs/OSNs)—will be received and a series of procedures are needed to ensure that they are treated correctly. An item flagged as a PDM may in fact reach the destination before the original, arriving out of sequence owing to internal SWIFT procedures. The bank system will need manual or system controls which will ensure that even in these circumstances, the message is processed only once. Missing ISN/OSN reports must also be followed up to investigate all flagged or missing numbers.

5) Encryption. At present, data is encrypted by SWIFT at the sender's Regional Processor (RP) and decrypted at the RP of the receiving bank. The banks may use STENs to encrypt data on their leased lines to the RPs, although this is not at present available to PSTN users. However, the fact that the PSTNs transmit other data with Funds Transfer messages provides a measure of protection, since the messages will be difficult to select from this extraneous information. In addition, only PSTN employees will know of the routing used, thus limiting the number of potential interceptors.

User Security Enhancement (USE) Project
The 'two-way' handshake between SWIFT and the bank's Terminal Interface Device (TID) requires MAC'd codes to be exchanged. Although secure and technically sound, this control relies on the cumbersome and risky use of paper tables in banks. This, together with the problems inherent in the exchange of Bilateral Keys, is addressed by SWIFT's User Security Enhancement (USE) which is currently under development and expected to be available in 1993. Using high-technology, tamper-resistant devices (the Integrated Circuit Card [ICC] and Secure Card Reader [SCR]), to be installed in the bank's premises, authentication key administration and SWIFT logins will become automated. It is expected that, by removing the need for paper communications and tables, greater security and a reduction of the administrative burden will be achieved.

The first phase of the USE project is the new user-to-user authentication algorithm. The algorithm, which is longer and inherently more secure, will be mandatory from September 1991.

Two other features—Login Table Replacement (LTR) and Bilateral Key Exchange (BKE)—are also under development.

Login Table Replacement removes the need for SWIFT-generated paper login tables to be sent to each bank, then stored safely for possible multiple references throughout the SWIFT 'working day'. Information on paper is, by its nature, insecure in that it is easily copied, mislaid, damaged or memorised.

LTR provides an optional automatic login facility which:

- helps to clear incoming queues prior to the beginning of the business day;
- avoids traffic queues where an operator has not notified a system line failure.

There are attendant security concerns, for example:

- an unattended ICC needs a high degree of physical security;
- since some interface devices do not always identify line failures, dependence on the device could result in long outages with large queue build-ups. It is essential that the cause of all failures should be identified and resolved.

Bilateral key exchange. BKE resembles the method used for Telex test keys. Currently, any bank wishing to send SWIFT messages must exchange authentication keys with the receiving bank. This is achieved by sending paper documents through the post; a method which is subject to loss or delay and is extremely time-consuming. BKE will automate this, creating new message types to transmit the keys via the SWIFT network.

BKE increases the security of bilateral key exchange by totally removing the need for paper exchange between banks. In addition to the problems inherent in using paper there are other significant concerns in the key exchange process. These relate to the method by which the communication/ letter is authorised and physically demonstrated to have been authorised to the receiving bank. Authorising written signatures are:

- almost impossible to verify, particularly by another bank;
- inevitably authorised outside the secured 'test-key' area.

A number of message authentication failures are a direct result of either incorrect entry of a key in one of the banks, or failure to activate the key at the correct time. Some banks address this problem by generating low-value SWIFT message types (MT199s). Discrepancies are therefore picked up immediately. This practice is not, however, widespread and so a significant number of actual payment messages fail authentication.

The negative aspects of this are twofold:

- the costs of:
  - investigating and correcting the erroneous key;
  - delayed payments;
- the risks involved in acting on payment instructions which have failed authentication without waiting for a successful retransmission, on the assumption that the key exchange/update process has failed.

The supplier of the terminal (CBT)—for example STS, Wang, DEC or IBM—may provide value-added services such as audit trails, improved error-handling or the facility to trigger key exchanges selectively when certain criteria (such as the date or a specific number of uses of the key) are met.

The Structure of the SWIFT II Message Flow

1) Having gained access to the SWIFT II Network, User A sends a message to the IRP, destined for User B.

2) IRP performs validation checks on the header, text and trailer of the message; checks that the ISN is correct and sends the message, along with a Message Input Reference (MIR) and validation result to the ISP.

3) The ISP safestores the incoming message to disk.

4) The ISP sends a confirmation to the IRP, signifying that the message, as received, is safely stored.

5) On receipt of this confirmation from the ISP, the IRP sends a Positive Acknowledgement (ACK) or Negative Acknowledgement (NAK) to User A, giving notification of message acceptance or rejection.
   On receipt of an ACK, the user is assured that SWIFT II has accepted responsibility for the delivery of that message. If a NAK is sent, this indicates that the message, although safestored (and hence retrievable), has not been accepted by SWIFT for delivery.

6) Having accepted a message, the ISP determines (from its user database) which RP is the prime RP for User B and sends a copy of the message across the network to this RP (the ORP).

7) The ORP temporarily stores the message on disk, and places it in one of the user-defined output queues for User B, where it is held awaiting delivery. The message will remain on hold until a logical terminal (LT) at User B's destination has logged-in for output and has asked to receive output messages from that particular output queue.

8) Before attempting to deliver the message, the ORP assigns an OSN and creates a unique Message Output Reference (MOR) for that delivery attempt. ORP sends the MOR to User B's owning SP (OSP) and awaits authorisation from the OSP before attempting delivery.

9) The OSP checks that the MOR assigned (and hence the OSN) is valid for that particular LT, and records it in safestore.

10) The OSP sends a confirmation to the ORP, authorising it to attempt to deliver the message using that MOR.

11) ORP outputs the message to the appropriate LT using the MOR authorised by OSP.

SWIFT II MESSAGE FLOW

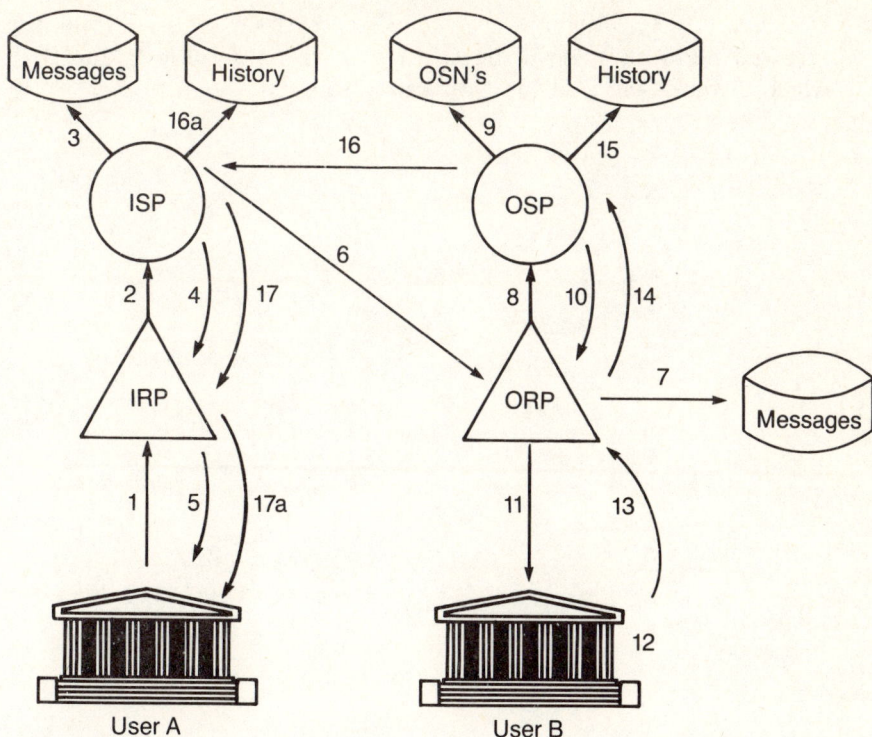

NOTES:

    IRP =   Input Regional Processor
    ISP =   Input Slice Processor
    ORP =   Output Regional Processor
    OSP =   Output Slice Processor

12) User B receives the output message via the appropriate LT and safestores it.

13) If the destination LT considers the message to have been properly received (ie, checksums agree) a positive User Acknowledgement (UAK) is sent to the ORP, confirming safe receipt. If the destination LT rejects the delivered message, a User Negative Acknowledgement (UNK) is returned to the ORP and the message is considered to be undelivered.

14) The ORP creates a delivery history from the UAK/UNK and sends this to the OSP.

15) The OSP updates the message history with the result of this delivery attempt and records this in safestore.

16) The OSP sends a copy of the message history to the ISP for reconciliation, and the ISP also safestores the message history (16a).

17) If Delivery Notification has been requested by User A, the ISP (having received notification from the OSP) sends a notification to the IRP, which forwards the Delivery Notification to User A (17a).

Appendix 2: The UK Data Protection Act (1984)

Background

The Act allowed the United Kingdom to ratify the Council of Europe Convention on Data Protection which was signed by the UK in 1982. It also established an independent public registrar to meet fears concerning the existence and purposes of computerised personal information systems.

It is worth noting that the Act's provisions are not as all-embracing as those of similar acts passed by the West German and Swedish governments. The common principles in the laws of all Organisation of Economic Co-operation and Development (OECD) countries are:

- There should be limits to the collection of 'personal data' and the data should be obtained lawfully and fairly, with the knowledge or consent of the subject where appropriate. The subject, in this case, is the person about whom the data is being collected;
- Data should be relevant to the purposes for which it is collected, as well as accurate, complete and up-to-date;
- The purposes of collecting the data should be specified when the data is collected and again whenever the purposes change. The new purposes must be compatible with the old ones;
- The data must not, in general, be used for purposes other than those for which it was collected;
- Data should be protected by reasonable safeguards against loss or unauthorised access, destruction, use, modification, or disclosure. In other words, data security should be provided;
- It should be possible to find out what personal record systems exist, their main purposes and the names of the persons who are responsible for controlling the records;
- Individuals should be able to find out whether a databank has information about them; and, if so, be able to gain access to it. The subject should also be able to challenge the data, and, if it is incorrect, have it altered.

Provisions of the Act

In summary the Act regulates the computer processing and storage of data relating to individuals. Its aim is to ensure that personal data is accurate, appropriate to its declared purpose and kept securely. Individuals are given rights of access to computerised data about them and can enforce correction of inaccurate data.

Both end users and computer bureaux are covered by the Act—the former are fully responsible for the relevance, accuracy and security of the personal data they hold, while the latter are only responsible for the provision of adequate security.

The Data Protection Registrar is responsible for the enforcement of the Act. All systems that hold personal data must be registered, and it is an offence to process unregistered data. Users who contravene the Act's principles can be removed from the register and so disqualified from holding personal data, as can any organisation whose security is judged by the Registrar to be 'inappropriate'.

A number of exemptions were agreed, of which the most significant are:

- payroll and accounting systems;
- mailing lists;
- word processing.

However, only the 'pure' payroll and accounting systems are exempt. If the system provides other information it may lose the protection of the relevant section.

The intensive publicity which accompanied the appearance of the Act encouraged a reasonable level of awareness, if not complete compliance. However, a survey carried out on behalf of the Registrar in 1990 showed a decline in awareness among small businesses of their need to register from 70 per cent in 1986 to 51 per cent. Awareness among the wider computer-using community had declined from 75 per cent to 70 per cent in the same period. The Registrar found it necessary to issue a warning that he prosecutes data users who do not seek registration, and that the courts had found against the defendants in all cases brought so far.

General awareness among the public is evidenced by the increasing numbers of complaints, and prosecutions of some financial organisations are imminent. The Registrar has also drawn attention to possible breaches of the Act by credit agencies who recommend denial of credit to a resident of premises shared with, or previously lived in, by a person whose details they hold. Although this is common practice among many agencies it may constitute misuse of personal data, and a legal battle is currently pending.

A further concern is the potential for abuse in the 'matching' of data, possibly held by a number of computer users, bringing it together for purposes unrelated to that of its original capture.

Some details of the measures proposed by the European Commission to harmonise and extend National laws on the subject are provided in Appendix 14.

Appendix 3: Designated Investment Exchanges

Amsterdam Port and Potato Terminal Market (NLKKAS-Amsterdam Futures Clearing House)
Association of International Bond Dealers
Australian Stock Exchange
Bourse de Commerce (Lille-Roubaix-Tourcoing)
Bourse de Commerce (Paris)
Chicago Board Options Exchange
Chicago Board of Trade
Chicago Mercantile Exchange
Coffee, Sugar and Cocoa Exchange Inc.
Commodity Exchange Inc.
European Options Exchange
Financiele Termijnmarket Amsterdam
Hong Kong Stock Exchange
Irish Futures and Options Exchange (IFOX)
Johannesburg Stock Exchange
Kansas City Board of Trade
Marché à Terme des Instruments Financiers, Paris
Midwest Stock Exchange
Minneapolis Grain Exchange
Montreal Stock Exchange
New York Cotton Exchange (including the Citrus Associates of the New York Cotton Exchange)
New York Futures Exchange
New York Mercantile Exchange
New York Stock Exchange
New Zealand Futures Exchange
Pacific Stock Exchange
Paris Stock Exchange
Philadelphia Board of Trade
Philadelphia Stock Exchange
Singapore International Monetary Exchange
Singapore Stock Exchange

Stockholm Options Market
Sydney Futures Exchange
Tokyo Stock Exchange
Toronto Stock Exchange
Toronto Futures Exchange
United States Stock Exchange
Vancouver Stock Exchange

Appendix 4: Gas Fire-extinguishing Systems

Halon 1211

Bromochlorodifluoremethane (BCF) is odourless and gives no warning of its presence. The maximum concentration in air to which humans can be exposed for one minute without ill effects is 4–5 per cent. This is insufficient for fire-fighting and below the usual design concentration for BCF systems, which is 5–8 per cent. The toxic effects include:

- dizziness;
- impaired co-ordination;
- reduced mental activity;
- irregular heartbeat.

Humans should never be exposed to BCF at the levels needed for fire-fighting.

Halon 1301

Bromotrifluoromethane (BTM), also known as Pyroforane 1301. Slightly safer and less toxic than BCF. This is the most commonly-used substance, being generally preferred to BCF and CO_2. Halon 1301 has no smell and gives no warning.

At concentrations above 5–7 per cent it may cause irritation of the eyes. Short-term exposure to a concentration of 6 per cent is unlikely to produce undue effects in a human, although concentration above 10 per cent can produce marked disturbance to the central nervous system. Unnecessary exposure should be avoided.

The Health and Safety Executive Guidance Note GS16 covers automatic operation for total flooding using Halon 1301. It is permitted in normal circumstances (except during maintenance) provided:

- the achieved concentration in air after discharge must be no more than 6 per cent by volume;

- the system should not activate unless signals are received from two separate detection points;
- time delay is provided for escape after the alarm is given (30 seconds is suggested as adequate);
- a 'panic button' is provided to prevent release where necessary.

Since Halon 1301 is produced as a by-product of the manufacture of CFCs, it is not expected to be available after 1993.

It should also be noted that the corrosive hydrogen bromide caused by the effect of fire on Halon will damage hardware.

Carbon dioxide (CO_2)

Thirty per cent concentration is needed to extinguish a fire. CO_2 is an asphyxiant which is lethal in far lower quantities than that necessary to extinguish a fire.

Seven per cent concentration will lead to stimulation of respiration. Ten per cent depresses the respiratory system and causes:

- headache;
- visual disturbance;
- ringing in the ears;
- tremor

followed by unconsciousness.

A concentration of 30 per cent produces immediate asphyxiation.

CO_2 gas-flooding systems must be locked off when people are present.

Rapid cooling of the air occurs on introduction of CO_2, leading to condensation of moisture on equipment and media. The cooling effect is certain and severe, and is known as 'thermal shock'.

Appendix 5: The OSI Security Architecture

Services

The OSI Security Architecture defines the following services:

- *Peer Entity Authentication.* This service, which is provided at the establishment of a connection, aims to provide assurance that no unauthorised user is attempting to masquerade as an authorised user or to replay a previous connection;
- *Access Control.* This provides protection against unauthorised use of a resource. It can be based on identity (through the use of a password) or on credentials (through the use of a terminal access point). Access control can be applied in common, as in the case of a Closed User Group, or on an entity-by-entity basis;
- *Data Confidentiality.* This service aims to protect data from unauthorised disclosure;
- *Data Integrity.* This counters active threats and ensures that the data received is the same as that which was sent;
- *Data Origin Authentication.* This service provides layer-by-layer corroboration that the source of the data is who it is claimed to be;
- *Non-Repudiation of Origin.* This provides the recipient with proof of the origin of the data. In this way the recipient is protected from any attempt by the sender to deny sending the data or its contents;
- *Non-Repudiation of Delivery.* This is a similar service but provided to the sender. It prevents the receiver from falsely denying that he has received the data or its contents.

Mechanisms

The mechanisms by which these services are provided include the following:

- *Encryption* can be used to provide confidentiality either of data or of traffic flow information. In addition, by means of a cryptographic check function, elements of the data integrity service can be provided. Encryption can also be used to complement other security mechanisms. It is no accident that encryption appears at the head of this list, since it is the key to most effective security systems;

- *Digital Signatures*. Non-repudiation services can be achieved in two ways:
  - by signing a data unit. This can be done either by encrypting the data unit or by producing a cryptographic check function of the data unit, using the signatory's private information as a private key;
  - by verifying a signed data unit—possibly to the satisfaction of a third party. In this case, the user is seeking to verify that only the unique holder of the private information could have produced the signature. To do this he will use procedures and information which are publicly available but from which the signatory's private information cannot be deduced;
- *Access Control Mechanisms*. By using the authenticated identity or other credentials of a user, the access rights of the user may be determined and hence controlled. Any unauthorised attempt to gain access will result in a rejection. Ideally, such an unauthorised attempt should be automatically reported for alarm and audit purposes. Such mechanisms typically involve passwords or other security labels or devices;
- *Modification Detection Techniques*. It is usually not practicable to prevent data being changed while in transit. Security mechanisms are therefore restricted to detecting that such changes have occurred. This generally involves the transmission of a block check sequence or some other check function. Protection of the integrity of a sequence of data units will additionally require some form of sequence numbering and may also use timestamping;
- Authentication Exchange. Mechanisms in this area may comprise any or all of transmitted passwords, cryptographic techniques or handshaking protocols;
- Traffic Padding. This involves the addition of spurious data to a message. To protect against the analysis of traffic flow, this data is inserted by the sending application and removed by the receiving application;
- Routing Control. This mechanism provides for routes to be chosen so as only to use physically secure networks or links. Another feature of the mechanism is that it allows communicating systems to request alternative routing in specific cases in circumstances which include:
  - detection of a successful attempt to manipulate data;
  - optionally for certain types of data; or
  - when a particular 'quality of service' is required for a specific application;
- *Notarisation*, where assurance as to data integrity and, in certain cases, elements of authentication and non-repudiation can be provided by means of a trusted third party holding the necessary information. As an example, the sender could transmit a message tagged with his own digital

signature. The recipient, on receipt of the transmission, would send a message to the third party containing both his own signature and that received from the sender. The trusted third party would therefore be able to provide a non-repudiation service.

Appendix 6: Password procedures

An Example

It is the responsibility of departmental managers to ensure that all staff are aware of, and act in accordance with, the following procedures.

1) A departmental register should be maintained listing those staff authorised to have access to any software or data held on a computer. This register should also indicate the computer to which access is authorised, the nature of the authorisation and the dates on which that user has changed his password.

2) A departmental register should be kept indicating the nature of all computer applications and the procedures to which these applications are subject.

   Copies of both registers will be held by the information security officer, who must be notified of all changes.

3) Departmental managers must report to the information security officer any actions relating to unauthorised access to a computer, the files on the computer, or any misuse of the equipment.

4) Each user should have a password known only to that user, and that password must be changed at intervals not exceeding two months. The password must not be communicated to other persons.

5) This password should be of at least five characters and should not incorporate the user's identifier.

6) For a user with access to several machines, a password common to all machines may be used but that password must be changed at intervals not exceeding two months.

7) All data of commercial value or a sensitive nature should have a protection level which ensures other users cannot read, copy or alter the data. Additionally the directory holding the data should be protected to ensure other users cannot establish the file names.

8) For technical data with no commercial value and not of a sensitive nature, protection should be such that its recovery can be readily achieved should it be deleted. It must also be protected from loss or change by other users.

9) Any user suspecting his files have been accessed by unauthorised persons must report such matters to his department manager with details of the associated evidence.

10) All users must be aware that unauthorised attempts to access computer files are forbidden. Failure to comply with this instruction will result in company disciplinary procedures being invoked and may also render the offender liable to prosecution under the *Computer Misuse Act (1990)*.

Appendix 7: Contents of a Disaster Recovery Plan

Introduction

This sets out the initial definitions to be applied, and outlines management objectives. Contents will include:

- *Assumptions.* This should classify the category of disaster, defining job functions and responsibilities for individuals in each different case. The assumptions should define key priorities and responsibilities
- *How to use the plan*;
- *Updating the plan*;
- *Authorised distribution list.*

Staff

A section bringing together available resources and identifying alternatives is needed. It will give emergency telephone numbers, skills etc:

- *Names* of the personnel involved in the recovery process, with a description of the responsibilities of each.
- *Organisation:* normal, and during contingency operation. This may involve two entirely separate DP departments—one at an alternative site maintaining the service, another planning and implementing replacement equipment etc.
- *Communications*: initial notification of disaster; reporting structures and communication links.

Equipment

A list of existing equipment, augmented by contingency needs, should be established. The list should consider all items, including such mundane equipment as desks, chairs and typewriters. The following would be covered:

- Mainframe(s) and peripherals;

- Off-line processing hardware;
- Specialist output equipment such as COM (computer output on microfiche) units;
- reproduction;
- telephone fax and electronic mail services;
- teleprocessing networks, covering:
  - transmission lines;
  - teleprocessing software;
  - teleprocessing hardware;
- office furniture;
- typewriters and calculators.

Physical Environment

Considerations include:

- floor space;
- power;
- air-conditioning;
- lighting;
- location.

Operational Procedures

The following documentation should be stored off-site:

- priority run list;
- operations manual;
- computer run schedules;
- restart procedures.

Software

Off-site duplicate copies of:

- application program libraries;
- systems software including:
  - operating system files;
  - utilities;
  - database and communications software;
- all related documentation.

Transport

During disaster recovery, transport of personnel, deliveries and mail may become a key issue. The following should be included in this section:

- list of vehicles (required and available);
- alternative sources of vehicles;
- vehicles and personnel needed to replace transmission facilities;
- mail/delivery service needs.

Supplies

These should include:

- computer operations requirements;
- clerical operations requirements.

User Department Plans

All user departments likely to be affected by loss of IT facilities should draw up fall-back and contingency plans for their own operations, which must be co-ordinated with those of the DP centre to ensure consistency and workability.

Appendix 8: Key Features of PC Security Products

Introduction

Lists of suppliers and their products quickly become out-of-date. Rather than provide yet another, the following gives a brief introduction to some of the features of PC security tools.

IBM, and a few other manufacturers, use MCA as the internal bus architecture of the PC. (The bus is the internal transport mechanism by which the PC communicates with itself and connected peripherals.) Others, such as Compaq, use the standard PC bus and the new EISA architecture. With all modern PC hardware products, be wary of possible MCA/PC bus slot compatibility problems.

Locks

Generally, locks are not a very secure method of securing the PC against unauthorised use. They invariably cause problems when more than one person requires access to the machine, and are often left off. Keys are easily lost.

Log and Filter

Security packages can be configured to collect information about the usage of the PC they are attached to. An audit facility can provide statistics on individual users or on PC usage in general. Programs which can filter the log to extract a restricted view of the data—based on a specified time period, user name or event type—are much easier to use.

Audit logs can often grow very large and easily fill up valuable disk space. Procedures for periodic clear-down of logs should be set up and agreed with system managers.

Encryption

The official encryption standard—Data Encryption Standard (DES)—is generally more secure than data scrambled or encrypted under a proprietary algorithm. Where only proprietary encryption is available it is very important to select a well-established, reputable supplier. If something goes wrong with the encryption your data can be lost for ever. Ensure that any encryption system has the option of 'clear text' storage to diskette as well as in the encrypted format.

It is important to recognise that while most products offer effective encryption security against casual snoopers, few are strong enough to withstand an attack by a highly competent cryptographer.

Remember that it can be difficult to automate the encryption process. Encryption is usually carried out by running a command or program outside the application you actually use. You may then wait some time while your files are encrypted.

Time-Slotting

Some systems in which shift-work patterns are in operation can benefit from time-slotting (allowing use of a system to specific users only during a predetermined period). However, such configurations should only be set up with care in case vital access to the machine is denied.

Maximum Access Attempts and Lockout

Some packages allow the administrator to limit the number of invalid log-on attempts, three being the most common default. Further attempts may actually suspend activity on the workstation or PC concerned. Audit logs should record this.

Timeout

If users neglect to logout or switch off the machine when leaving it unattended, any passer-by could gain access to their data. For this reason, many programs automatically lock the keyboard or log the user out after a specified period of inactivity.

Maximum Users

It is important to choose a product which allows for growth in the number of users.

Groups

Associating users with groups or project identifiers can be a quick way of setting up appropriate permissions where several users require a similar level of access; each user still has his/her own password but within the group all share common privileges. This can also help in tracking related work for billing or statistical purposes.

Temporary Lock

A temporary lock gives users the chance to leave their workstation without having to go through the lengthy initialisation routine when they return. Typically, the screen is blanked until the user re-enters his or her password.

Secure Deletion

When DOS processes a delete command it merely marks the file as unavailable; data remains on the disk until it is overwritten by a new file and is therefore retrievable until this occurs. Several security deletion packages provide irretrievable deletion, which usually works by overwriting the file space occupied.

Network Capability

Network protection is generally only possible where the device can recognise logical drives. Protection and security of electronic mail may well come from the actual application.

Executive Protection

DOS version 3.0 and succeeding versions allow programs to be executed without first being read. This allows users to run programs, but not to copy them.

Dongle Protection

Hardware dongles are becoming increasingly popular as a quick and cheap method of protecting software or data. In terms of convenience they have many advantages over hardware boards which need to be installed inside the machine. Generally they work by running a program on the directory or file that needs to be protected. With software protection some dongles require lines of code to be added to the actual application programs.

Power Failure Protection

Automatic shutdown following power failure is available to critical systems where data corruption could result. Such products work with uninterruptable power supplies (UPS) to save files, exit programs and log out of the PC or network session.

Appendix 9: CRAMM

Introduction

The CRAMM Risk Analysis and Management Method was commissioned by HM Government's Central Computer and Telecommunications Agency (CCTA). It is a method for identifying all the justified protective measures to protect IT systems used for processing valuable or sensitive data. Experience with CRAMM has proved that it can be used with equal success in the public and private sectors.

CRAMM meets the stringent criteria set by CCTA for a security methodology. These included requirements that CRAMM should:

- be capable of handling systems and networks of all sizes, types and complexities;
- cover all aspects of security;
- be quick and easy to understand and use;
- include an automated support tool;
- provide a database of countermeasures.

CRAMM and the Risk Management Model

CRAMM was designed to match the traditional model of risk management. This commences with risk analysis, which involves identifying assets, assessing the threats to which they are subject and how vulnerable they are to those threats. After the risks have been assessed, the next task is risk management, which involves identifying appropriate countermeasures to address the risks.

CRAMM is divided into three stages. Stage 1 (Asset Identification and Valuation) and Stage 2 (Threats, Vulnerabilities and Risks) correspond to the Risk Analysis phase of the model, while Risk Management is addressed at Stage 3 (Countermeasures)—see Figure 14.1. The following sections explain the processes involved in each stage in more detail.

Stage 1

During Stage 1 the reviewer asks the question: 'What assets need to be protected?'

The first step is to establish a boundary for the review. This may be stated, for instance, in terms of particular systems; or it may restrict the review to looking at certain locations within a networked system. Management should agree the review boundary and the reviewer should ensure that it is adhered to, so that the review can be effectively planned and controlled.

The assets within the review boundary are then identified. Assets include physical assets, data assets and software. There is some flexibility in the level of detail to which assets are identified and grouped for the purpose of later steps within CRAMM; this will depend to an extent on the size and complexity of the system.

All the identified assets are now valued. Physical and software assets are valued in terms of replacement cost; data (and sometimes also software) is valued in relation to the impacts of destruction, unavailability, disclosure and modification. For each impact, the possible effects of the worst realistic scenario are measured using a series of guidelines (for example, breach of commercial confidentiality or financial loss). In some cases the worst effect could be qualitative rather than quantitative (for example, 'Managing Director resigns', which is normally seen as a bad effect). To ensure comparability, scores are converted to a scale of one to ten.

Dependencies between data, software and physical assets are then established. For instance, if a firm stands to lose £2m if data held on its mainframe is disclosed to outsiders, the mainframe has a 'dependent asset value' of £2m for this impact.

CRAMM places emphasis on a continual management review process. When asset values have been established for all assets against all impacts, Stage 1 is complete and the findings are agreed with management. Ensuring the accuracy of the model of the system is essential as mistakes are much easier to rectify now than at later stages of CRAMM. A review meeting should also be used to ensure continuing management commitment to the review.

Stage 2

During Stage 2 the reviewer asks the question: 'What level of protection is required?'

CRAMM has a standard table of threats relating to particular types of assets. This is compared with the actual assets identified at Stage 1 so that a set of relationships are established for the review. The reviewer may amend the relationships which have been set up automatically if this will better reflect the actual threats to the assets being considered.

For every threat/asset combination now established, system-generated questionnaires will then be completed to assess both the threat of an unwanted incident impacting the asset, and the vulnerability should the threat materialise. Threats and vulnerabilities are assessed as high, medium or low.

CRAMM uses a matrix to combine every asset value with the threat and vulnerability assessments relating to that asset. The result is a security requirement which measures the extent to which each asset needs to be protected against the various threats.

Stage 3

During Stage 3 the reviewer asks the question: 'Which countermeasures will provide the required level of protection?'

CRAMM has a database of more than 1000 countermeasures, covering all aspects of security, which relate directly to the threats. As part of their work involving the maintenance and continuing development of CRAMM, the Touche Ross consultancy firm has completed a review of this database and incorporated enhancements which mean that CRAMM's countermeasures reflect the latest developments in IT security practice.

CRAMM will select countermeasures which should be installed on the basis of the security requirements calculated at Stage 2. The higher the security requirement, the more stringent the level of security that will be recommended.

The reviewer will compare the countermeasures recommended with those actually installed. After entering the findings from this exercise into the package, it is possible to produce reports listing outstanding countermeasure recommendations. An action plan for implementing recommendations will then be agreed.

The CRAMM software can produce a number of other reports, including management reports which summarise the main issues arising from the review and list the main areas of security concern and the recommended counter-measures. The reviewer may, however, prefer to use these as the basis for a tailor-made report which can take into account the needs and house style of the organisation under review.

Tools to Help Analyse the Results of a CRAMM Review

CRAMM provides a full audit trail. If the need for a particular counter-measure is questioned, a report can be produced detailing the security requirement which gave rise to that countermeasure. The 'backtrack' process then identifies the particular threat and vulnerability ratings, and asset values, which contributed to the requirement; and will further analyse the asset values by individual assets.

Another powerful tool is the 'What-If?' facility. This enables the reviewer to investigate the impact of changes to the system in terms of additional countermeasure requirements, or countermeasures that need no longer be installed. As an example, removing from the system an asset which carries a high cost of disclosure is likely to reduce the need for some of the countermeasures against system infiltration.

CRAMM can prioritise the recommended countermeasures. This facility uses a number of factors to rank countermeasures into 'best buys'—each countermeasure providing an indication of whether its implementation cost is likely to be low, medium or high, and a measure of its effectiveness at addressing risk. These are combined with a measure of the number of assets the countermeasure will help to protect, and an indication of the type of countermeasure. (For instance, a countermeasure that helps to reduce a threat will be given greater priority than one which merely assists recovery after a threat has materialised.) The resulting ranked list of countermeasures is useful in helping management to improve security in the most cost-effective way.

CRAMM and Developing Systems

One of the objectives behind the development of CRAMM was that it should be applicable to both existing and developing systems. To assist users of CRAMM in a systems development environment, Touche Ross has developed an interface between CRAMM and SSADM (Structured Systems Analysis and Design Methodology).

This interface enables the reviewer to set up a number of parallel reviews for the same project. At key stages in the development, a choice is made between different project options and the chosen option is then carried forward to the next stage of the development.

The CRAMM reviewer will not always be able to obtain firm data when conducting a review at an early stage of systems development. Nonetheless, if CRAMM is to be used effectively all aspects of security should be considered together. It may be difficult to reach a firm assessment of risk in certain areas, but those risks may well be significant and need consideration at an early stage. The threat and vulnerability questionnaires therefore incorporate guidance on their completion while a system is still proposed or under development; in certain cases alternative approaches to obtaining or estimating answers are suggested or alternative questions used to assess the threat.

By avoiding the use of jargon specific to SSADM, the CRAMM/developing systems interface is also useful for reviews of systems being developed using other methodologies.

The main source of guidance on using CRAMM in an SSADM environment is incorporated into the CRAMM User Guide and the CRAMM/

SSADM Subject Guide. The latter gives guidance on the way in which the reviewer should use CRAMM at each of the stages of SSADM.

The facility to generate additional reviews from a review already set up within CRAMM, and to copy data between reviews, is also available when conducting a CRAMM review of existing systems. This is useful when, for instance, reviews of two or more similar hardware environments are being conducted simultaneously.

The Advantages of CRAMM

CRAMM provides a qualitative and objective assessment of the security measures needed to protect an organisation's IT systems from a range of threats. The CRAMM software support tool uses a scoring system which combines both quantitative and qualitative factors to assess risk. The resulting analysis is tailored to the needs of the organisation, thus combining a reliable and objective assessment with an approach that reflects the actual business environment.

CRAMM forces a rigorous review. Every aspect of security is covered, both in assessing threats and in selecting the relevant countermeasures. Technical aspects (for example hardware, software, communications) and non-technical aspects (for example physical, personnel, documentary, procedural) are all addressed. The extensive library of countermeasures, defined and updated by the UK's leading experts, supplements the skills of the reviewer and helps to ensure comprehensive but cost-justified levels of security.

CRAMM allows a risk assessment and management review to be carried out quickly and efficiently, since the software reduces the need for clerical activity. All the information relating to the review is maintained within the system and is easy to update. The user interface has been developed in accordance with the latest standards; the menu designs are Windows-based and user-friendly, allowing easy navigation around the package.

CRAMM produces a wide range of reports, showing both the data entered at different points in the review and the information which should be included in management reports. One of these is a standard management report targeted directly at management rather than the reviewer, although the reviewer may wish to adapt it to suit the house style of the organisation.

Appendix 10: The First Security Review

Introduction

The first security review in any organisation can be traumatic. There may be no security policy, standards or procedures. In their absence, compliance checking is obviously impossible and the major recommendations of the report must focus on the need to create the infrastructure for performing effective monitoring in future.

Even in this environment some examples of good practice may be found. A part of the 'selling technique' required to ensure good security lies in persuading management that some of the necessary standards already exist and complimentary references should therefore be made to those which can be extended and incorporated. Management must be persuaded, and a dash of flattery is an appropriate weapon.

The recommendations in the following sample report section concentrate on the need to provide the security policy and standards which are essential before effective security work can commence.

The organisation has been referred to as 'the company' and the decision-making body as 'the board'. Although some details of wording will vary from organisation to organisation, the following will cover the major areas to be addressed and the recommendations should be universally valid.

Principal Recommendations

Summary

1) Responsibility for security should be allocated to a security officer, who will report to the board. The security officer must have the authority to implement and enforce security measures throughout the company, and the skills to fulfil the requirements in a credible manner.
2) A firm-wide security policy must be developed.
3) Realistic security standards and procedures, consistent with the policy, must be designed.
4) Set up the infrastructure to disseminate, implement and support the security standards and procedures.

5) Implement them.
6) Monitor and enforce them.
7) Review the security policy, standards and procedures at intervals appropriate to the degree of change in the company's operations and use of IT.

Some of these activities can be carried out concurrently. Each is described in more detail below.

Assign Responsibility to a Security Officer
The security officer should take overall responsibility for implementing, monitoring and enforcing security throughout the company. He should report directly to the board. In view of the extent of the authority required to enable him to meet his responsibility, he should be a senior manager.

In practice the security officer will require a forum at director level at which security issues can be discussed and policies agreed. He will delegate the actual implementation, monitoring and enforcement of standards and procedures to line and IT management as appropriate, and monitor their achievement.

Develop a Security Policy
The security policy should consist of a high-level document describing the company's statement of intent, which should be supported by explanatory notes as necessary.

The policy should include all aspects of the firm's business, in addition to internal management and administration.

It should also refer to the different levels of risk associated with different categories of data, and give guidance on how the category into which a particular system or piece of data falls can be assessed. This is essential in order to assess the level of security techniques and procedures appropriate to each.

All employees should read and have access to the security policy document.

Design Realistic Standards and Procedures
The standards and procedures required are those which are necessary to implement and enforce the security policy.

Many of the required standards and procedures may already be in existence in some parts of the organisation, either as good practice followed by some individuals, or in manuals which at present are not widely followed. The security officer should be responsible for the completeness of the standards and procedures.

It will not be possible to ensure that recommended standards and procedures cover all relevant security requirements until the security policy has been developed and agreed.

Set up an Infrastructure
The following will be required:

- a job description for the security officer, and amendments to the job descriptions of those who should report to him on security issues. Their new responsibilities will include ensuring compliance at a local level with security standards;
- processes by which the security officer can receive the reports of those to whom he has delegated responsibilities, report to the board, and discuss and agree policy issues with relevant directors;
- production of documentation which is easy to use and readily available;
- a mechanism for reviewing and amending policy and procedures;
- amendments to existing standards and procedure manuals;
- amendments to induction and training courses for all staff;
- disciplinary measures which can be used, if necessary, to enforce standards and procedures.

Implement Standards and Procedures
Despite the diversity of many organisations, and the related communication problems, it is possible to achieve a high degree of awareness and consistency in procedures.

The implementation of security policy, standards and procedures could be dealt with through:

- a one-off programme of education and awareness. This might involve verbal presentations and less formal meetings, supported by written communications from the security officer;
- the permanent infrastructure descrbed previously.

Monitor and Enforce Standards and Procedures
The line and IT managers to whom the security officer delegates responsibility for monitoring and enforcing standards and procedures may in practice delegate aspects of this process to others. If so it is essential that the procedures for reporting and monitoring these activities are agreed, documented and enforced.

Examples of the application of these processes are:

- technical staff enforcing microcomputer procedures as the first contact point for a potential user;
- managers insisting on evidence of adequate Quality Assurance checking before signing off a user-produced spreadsheet;
- regular reviews of compliance with security procedures.

Review at Intervals
The security officer's job description should include reference to the requirement to review and update the security policy, standards and procedures at

intervals and on the introduction of significant changes in working practices. The frequency of reviews should be decided in advance in consultation with the board, as should their scope. The interval between reviews should be no longer than two years and the first should take place a maximum of one year after the implementation of standards.

In practice the security officer may commission suitable experts to conduct each review and report to him.

Appendix 11: Fraud Examples

Introduction

This Appendix describes a number of frauds which have taken place in financial organisations by direct use of, or with the assistance of, a computer system. The first section provides some details of the methods of perpetration and an indication of security measures which might have prevented, or aided discovery of, the crime. The second section ('Stop Press') provides only the limited information which can be made public and is included in its incomplete state to provide as complete a picture as possible of the lengths to which fraudsters have gone.

Readers may wish to use the contents of this Appendix to promote security-awareness in their organisations. The humility necessary for any improvement to take place may be generated by applying questions such as:

- Could this happen here?
- How?
- Are our security measures adequate to prevent/detect it?
- How can we improve them?

1.   Fraudulent Funds Transfer

Location: US Bank   *Value: $70 million*
In common with most EFT frauds, this crime was committed by employees of the victim bank acting at the point of entry to the system.

In this particular case the bank's staff were originally coerced, and later aided and abetted, by accomplished fraudsters. It is possible that this fraud may never have come to light (or taken longer to come to light, in which case the conspirators may have made good their escape) if the amounts involved had not been so spectacular.

The fraud exploited the rather simplistic manner in which money transfers were effected by the bank over the FedWire system. This was a simple process whereby a corporate treasurer would phone one of the two employees in the Wire Room of the bank to make a transfer request. A second employee in the Wire Room would then place a return call to the corporation involved and use a code to confirm the authenticity of the transaction. All the calls were recorded to provide the bank with a record of the authorisation of the transaction. The conspirator within the bank, a Wire Room operative, was aware of this system. However, he and his accomplices prepared their plan in such a manner that it would allow the employee to appear innocent. Despite this, these tapes provided the final evidence which led to the indictment of the individual concerned.

In laying their plans the group opened three bogus accounts with two Austrian banks in Vienna. They then set about identifying which of the US bank's customers routinely executed transactions of a size similar to the fraudulent payments they wished to enact. They eventually decided upon a securities house, an airline and an industrial company. The bank employees provided the names of individuals within these corporations who were authorised to request transfers. To gain the maximum lead time undetected, the group decided to commit the crime on a Friday, giving them over three clear days to avoid detection.

For their plan to work it was essential that the bank employee and co-conspirator was the person who 'confirmed' the transaction. Despite having to hang up on his accomplices on several occasions, this is exactly what happened. One of the conspirators telephoned the Wire Room from a hotel room and, speaking to an innocent employee, identified himself as an official from one of the 'targeted' corporations. The accomplice within the Wire Room then 'confirmed' the transaction, providing the code which he already knew from previous experience. In this manner the sums of $24,375,000, $19,750,000 and $25,000,000 were transferred via New York-based banks to the accounts in Vienna.

The fraudulent transfers were noticed early on Monday morning by two of the customers, who immediately notified the bank. (The bank in question has since stated that its own operations staff were already investigating the discrepancies at the time.) The bank's operations manager called in the FBI who played the Wire Room tapes. They noticed a similarity in the voice of the person confirming the codes for the three amounts.

Although it would not be unusual for a bank employee to confirm the three transactions, the same voice at the other end immediately alerted the investigators. Further investigations of the touch-tone dial tones associated with the confirming calls identified that the same number had been called on all three occasions.

The bank employee was questioned and subsequently confessed to his part in the crime. He later turned State's evidence and assisted in bringing the rest of his accomplices to justice.

2. Fraudulent Funds Transfer

Location: London-based International Bank   *Value: £5 million*
This fraud was perpetrated from the bank's backup system. It highlights the
need to be aware of the risks inherent in mirroring the live system too
accurately on a testing facility, and the need to 'desensitise' databases used in
this environment.

The bank in question used its backup system as a development and testing
facility. This is a perfectly valid approach and goes some way to mitigating the
cost of a duplicate computer configuration. An operator noticed that the
database on the backup system was a copy of the live system and contained a
file of Telex test keys which was used by the bank's funds transfer system.

Since the controls on the test system were far less stringent than those on
the production system, the operator had access to the application software
required to format and send a tested Telex. Since the test system remained
connected to the necessary communications circuits at all times (a conscious
decision by management in order to provide a speedy recovery should the
backup system be required) the foundations for an effective fraud had been
conveniently laid.

The operator ran the required software and issued a Telex requesting one
of the bank's correspondents to transfer £5 million to the account of an
accomplice.

This fraud could have been prevented if the test system database had been
desensitised by removing or changing the contents of the Telex test key file. A
more pragmatic approach to network connection would have prevented the
network being available. A better approach would have been to have
required a physical 'enabling' of network connection in a recovery situation.

3. Fraudulent Program Manipulation

Location: Bank   Value: $5 million
This case also demonstrates the importance of removing sensitive data from
'live' databases before allowing them to be used for program-testing
purposes. Using copies of 'live' databases for testing is a common and valid
approach adopted by many installations. However, before releasing such
copies, there should be controls in place to remove potentially sensitive
information beforehand.

This case occurred in an installation which did not have the above controls—and it cost them dearly. When testing a program on the development
system a programmer noticed that a table of codes used for making automated funds transfers was present on the database. Some simple checks soon
confirmed that he was working on a very recent copy of the database and,
hence, the codes were very likely to be valid.

The programmer inserted this information in his own program and submitted the software through the change control process, which was weak. Lack of a source code comparison mechanism within the change control process meant that the spurious code remained unidentified.

Once installed on the live system the program, when run, transferred $5 million to the programmer's account.

This case also underlines the need for strong change control procedures, which provide a last line of defence against this kind of fraud. However, had the database been desensitised in the first place, then the means by which the fraud took place would not have been available.

4. Fraudulent Accounting

Location: Bank   Value: £800,000

This fraud took place in a safe deposit company. The primary weakness exploited by the fraud was an inadequate segregation of duties. The nature of the safety deposit box business—where the contents of the box may not necessarily be identified—is extremely vulnerable to any kind of fraud involving misappropriation of goods. Even the depositors themselves, who often have personal reasons for keeping the nature of their deposits secret, are unwilling to report losses or become involved with investigations. Consequently, if a bank is to maintain its credibility and integrity in this type of business, strict segregation of duties is necessary.

In this case the operations manager had sole control over items in the safe deposit vaults and also of the accounting system used to record the various types of deposit. Over a period of three months the manager, on receipt of deposits, kept them himself or credited cash amounts to his own account. His access to the computer system also allowed him to move amounts to and from various accounts and thus disguise their source and identity. Because the manager also had responsibility for physically placing the deposits in the boxes his fraud was not noticed.

5. Unauthorised Access to Passwords

Location: Bank   *Value: £800,000*

This case concerned the use of emergency or privileged passwords, which were used to gain access to the necessary passwords to perform a funds transfer.

Many systems have a 'super user'. This is generally a user code and associated password which carry the very highest of system privileges. Such facilities are necessary in most systems to configure the system in the first place and to perform certain activities during systems failure. Normally the password is not known by one person but shared between two individuals, each knowing only half of the password.

During a system recovery an operator discovered the complete emergency password; we have not been able to determine the manner in which the password became known, although it is believed that it was noticed during its input. Having established the value of the emergency password the operator was then able to access the user password table. This table contained details of all user passwords and the system functions to which they gave access.

Armed with this information the operator ran the necessary application software to effect a funds transfer of £800,000.

The initial step towards this fraud (opportunistic sight of a high-privilege level password) is extremely difficult to prevent. With the current level of sophistication of password systems, the best that can be done is to place the onus on the person holding the password (or part of it) to ensure that no one is within reasonable viewing distance. Once access to a highly-privileged password such as this has been obtained the system is at the mercy of the holder.

6.   Fraudulent Input of Accounting Entries

Location: International Bank   *Value: £750,000*

An employee who had previously worked in IT was transferred to a line management position. He used his detailed knowledge of the system to process a series of journal entries which effected a transfer from reserves to a personal account in a foreign bank. Transfers of reserves were normally rejected and held in a suspense file awaiting clearance, but the fraudster made use of a batch resubmission procedure, normally used only in emergencies. This batch procedure was old and had not been updated in line with software enhancements made to the on-line input programs, which included instructions to reject entries which contained transfers from reserves.

The employee knew of this weakness and had also been given access to the systems input programs. When an opportunity presented itself he submitted a batch, containing spurious entries transferring amounts from the reserve account. The batch was deliberately constructed to fail with a reconciliation error between the batch header and the underlying entries. The first control in the batch input program was to reconcile the batch header to the underlying transactions, and if this failed to reject the batch without further validation of the transactions. He was then able to 'correct' the batch and reprocess it using the old resubmission procedure, thereby bypassing the control mentioned above.

This fraud could have been avoided had the generally-accepted control which prevents the same user from correcting and authorising his own input been in place.

It was not until the following day that the normal control procedures picked up the transactions. By this time the funds had already been transferred.

7. Fraudulent Accounting Entries

Location: Bank   *Value: £700,000*

Although this fraud involved the use of a computer, it should be described only as 'computer-related'. Manual procedures were weak and the computer system's power was merely used to hide the fact that frauds were taking place.

A departmental manager was given wide ranging systems facilities whilst at the same time retaining the sole authority for signing accounting entries. The opportunity for quick and substantial financial gain soon became apparent. He accessed the system which passed entries over corporate accounts, transferring the sums to his own account. Since the individual was able to authorise accounting entries, he did so; thus creating supporting documentation for the fraudulent entries. When the journal entries were checked the following day no suspicion was aroused because he was an authorised signatory.

This activity went on for several months. If a customer queried any of the transactions the manager pleaded a mistake and restored the amount. The manager eventually disappeared after embezzling £700,000.

The organisation involved was operating with several breaches of control within its internal systems. A two-stage input process with dual authorisation of accounting entries and verification of accounting entry input would have prevented this fraud.

8. Fraudulent Data Manipulation

Location: Insurance Company   *Value: £550,000*

This fraud used the company's pension and endowment plan system. It was perpetrated over a period of 14 years by a long-serving member of staff who abused his position in the liquidation department and took advantage of several weaknesses in the systems of internal control. As with a number of computer-related fraud cases, the fraud was conducted on the manual periphery of the system—no unauthorised access to the system was involved.

The fraud involved partial liquidation of 'dormant' pension and investment plans, that is plans which were still 'live' but on which there had been no activity for some considerable time.

The clerk used his position to insert fictitious input forms into batches of other valid transactions. These transactions created payment records under the dormant pension and investment schemes. Since:

- the on-line data capture program did not reconcile batch totals to input transactions; and
- there was no requirement for management authorisation of these transactions

the fradulent transactions were not noticed.

The clerk had previously opened building society accounts in the names used on the input document. After successful input to the system, payments in the form of cheques were automatically sent to the building society accounts previously opened. The clerk had also coded the input forms to indicate that there was no income tax liability, thereby avoiding any complications with the tax authorities. By limiting the amount of the transactions to less than £5,000 he knew that any internal checks were unlikely.

The clerk also had access to the processed input forms and copies of the cheque listings, and thus was able to destroy the audit trail of his activities. The cheque records were destroyed after reconciliation.

The individual's activities were finally discovered during an audit.

9.   Fraudulent Data Manipulation

Location: Securities Trader   *Value: £300,000*

This fraud has several interesting aspects; the first being that the controls in the institution involved were not in question. The weaknesses appeared to be within a service company. Another aspect of this case, which shows the reliance of financial organisations on information distribution services, should strike a cautionary note to both users and providers of these services.

The organisation involved subscribed to a database service which provided information on certain securities, including the current market price. An employee of the organisation, working in the computer department, discovered how to override the access controls in the service provider's system. He also learned how to update the database and used this knowledge to reduce the prices of certain securities. An update to this information triggered off a broadcast to the receiving systems of all subscribers to the service. The sudden reduction of price triggered off a spate of selling by dealers, consequently driving the price even lower.

The employee mentioned above was acting in collusion with an accomplice who was a trader with another organisation. They had previously rehearsed the mechanics of the fraud and his accomplice placed 'buy' orders for the securities in question, purchasing them at the artificially low price and selling them when the price stabilised.

The cost of the fraud given above is the actual cost to the organisation directly concerned. The total cost to other organisations—misled by the price quotes and consequently liquidating potentially profitable positions—remains unknown.

10.   Unauthorised Program Change and Data Manipulation

Location: Insurance Company   *Value: £300,000*

This fraud involved collusion by a number of individuals within the insurance company. Although it is more difficult to provide effective security measures over collusion it is certainly not impossible; tighter security over this company's change control and testing procedures could have prevented this fraud.

The employees worked in the claims department and the IT department. The fraud was initially enabled by a programmer/analyst amending a program which paid out claims under multistage policies, to credit the claims to the policies of the accomplices. The employee in the claims department then created fictitious claims on genuine insurance contracts, triggering off fraudulent disbursements.

If comprehensive acceptance and stress testing of program changes had taken place it is likely that the fraudulent activities of the programmer would have come to light. A source code comparison conducted against the previous version of the program would have highlighted the fraudulent code.

11.   Misquote of Foreign Exchange Rates

Location: Australian Bank   *Value: £200,000*

Although this case was not a fraud in the true sense, the lack of a simple control within the bank's computer system used for F/X rates dissemination caused a considerable loss, and provided a salutary lesson for all banks.

The bank in question had incorrectly posted the Australian dollar/Sri Lankan rupee exchange rate at 78.5 to the dollar. This rate was apparently four times higher than the current market rate. The bank's computer system did not provide tolerance checking on the input of new rates and consequently no warning was given to the inputter that these rates were at considerable variance to those previously quoted.

A customer of the bank noticed the inconsistency of the rates and purchased a large amount of rupees which he then sold at market rates to another bank. When the bank noticed the mistake it contacted the customer to recover the loss. The customer refused to co-operate and the bank instituted legal proceedings in an attempt to recover the money.

However, the Supreme Court ruled that it was the bank's responsibility to ensure the accuracy of its currency exchange rate quotes. Adding the observation that the bank's customer was not a professional in the Foreign Exchange market and therefore could not be expected to realise that the rate quoted was incorrect, the court denied the bank's attempts to recover their losses from the customer.

12.   Fraudulent Input and Data Manipulation

Location: UK Bank   *Value: £193,000*

This fraud was committed in a retail banking environment. The major security weaknesses were inadequate segregation of duties and a lack of 'after-the-event' authorisation procedures for transactions.

A clerk in the bank was able to process accounting entries over customers' accounts (which were not checked for authorised signatures or supporting documents). She also had sole control over computer equipment linked to the bank's central computer which was used to produce customer statements.

Over a period of six years she debited business accounts, transferring the money to her own account. She then intercepted the statements for these accounts and retyped them on the necessary special stationery (to which she had unrestricted access), omitting the fraudulent entries.

The fraud eventually came to light when she failed to intercept one statement and the customer queried the balance.

13. Fraudulent Program Manipulation

Location: Bank   *Value: £150,000*
This fraud was a true computer fraud in that it was effected by unauthorised software changes and perpetrated completely under program control.

The programmer modified a program which calculated employee profit-sharing. The modification reduced deductible amounts, transferring the difference between this amount and that which should have been calculated into the accounts of three accomplices (also employees of the bank). The fraud was only discovered several months after it took place.

Some details of this case are rather vague, in particular whether the programmer concerned actually gained access to the live system or made unauthorised changes to the program before its implementation. In either event, important security measures either failed to operate effectively or were not in place at all.

If the fraud was committed on the test system, then the installation change control procedures must clearly be suspect. A source code comparison (a method by which code changes to previous and current versions of programs may be identified) should have been performed and the results independently reviewed. Testing procedures also appear to have been weak. Changes to software should always be tested and the results reviewed independently. This control is especially important where the subject program is capable of transferring value from one account to another.

If the fraud was committed on the production system the answer is obvious—programmers should never be given access to the live system. If this is essential in specific circumstances there should be sufficient logging of activity to identify who was on the system and what they did. This must obviously be followed—speedily—by review of the logs.

14.   Plastic Card Fraud

Location: Finance Company   *Value: £60,000*

This fraud was ingenious in its simplicity. It is also worthy of note since, although the company involved followed generally accepted security procedures, collusion between dishonest employees managed to overcome the system of internal controls.

This company followed the generally-accepted 'good practice' of sending new cards to customers in a separate envelope to that of the PIN number. However, all mail passed through the same internal post room of the organisation. An employee of the company noticed that certain kinds of envelopes were used for the cards and the PIN numbers. A simple plot was then hatched between the employee and his accomplice, a Post Office employee.

The employee of the issuing company marked the relevant envelopes within the finance company's premises. His accomplice would remove these envelopes before delivering the company mail to the sorting office. The fraudsters used each card only once and then destroyed it to avoid detection.

15.   Internal Account Manipulation

Location: UK Building Society   *Value: £40,000*

This case highlights the potential vulnerability of a retail services organisation where cash is dispensed over the counter. Whereas funds involving international financial networks ultimately require the amounts to be converted to cash, in a retail environment the cash is readily available.

This case involved a building society cashier who transferred relatively small amounts from a number of investors' accounts to her own. The society's systems did not monitor activity over employee accounts, which would allow the source of credits to be verified. The branch procedures only required that the day's entries were balanced, and there was no requirement to compare individual account movements with source documents.

The fraud, which was perpetrated over a number of months, was discovered when a number of clients raised queries over their account balances and several of the transactions recorded against them. An absence of supporting source documentation prompted a review of previous accounting journals, and the cashier's account was identified as the recipient of the fraudulent transactions.

16.   Fraudulent Data Manipulation

Location: UK Insurance Company   *Value: £27,000*

The perpetrator of this fraud (which was committed over a number of years) was a senior clerk in a large branch office of the company. His principal duty was the reconciliation of incoming premium payments against policies sold through brokers or agents.

Reports showing mismatched postings and suspense items—as well as access to the central computer—were obtained via a terminal located in the clerk's office. Over a period of time a number of unmatched receipts built up. There was no regular review of the items in these suspense accounts, no independent checks on the timely clearance of the items and no scrutiny of accounting entries passed across the accounts.

In addition to his reconciliation responsibilities the clerk was allowed to pass accounting entries across the systems ledgers. He exploited this lack of segregation by transferring amounts out of the suspense accounts to other accounts to generate spurious overpayments.

The clerk also had the authority to request the drawing of cheques, and this was done under the guise of 'refunding' the false overpayment entries. The cheques drawn were raised manually by colleagues within the department and signed by senior persons outside the department. There was no independent check on the reason for raising a cheque or review of supporting documents.

The cheques were drawn in favour of a number of accomplices, who then 'laundered' the cheques through their own accounts.

17.   Fraudulent Data Manipulation

Location: Bank   *Value: £25,000*
This fraud was perpetrated on the central control system of an ATM network by an input clerk, who made unauthorised changes to the withdrawal limit of an accomplice. This, together with changes to other control-related data, allowed his accomplice to make over 100 withdrawals in a period of two months. In all, the total withdrawn was in the region of £25,000.

The controls in the bank's computer system were suspect. The system allowed updates to sensitive data (withdrawal limits) to be effected without subsequent independent verification. In addition, changes to customer information (cardholder details) were not reported and independently verified against supporting source documents. If this had been done, the unauthorised amendments might have been identified.

18.   Fraudulent Account Manipulation

Location: UK Building Society   *Value: £21,500*
This fraud was committed by a cashier who was experiencing financial difficulties.

In addition to dispensing and receiving cash, and recording the associated accounting entries on the society's computer, she was also able to set up accounts. Over the course of some months she created several fictitious accounts. The Passbooks (on which the investors' transactions and balances are recorded) were sent from the society's head office to the branch where the account was opened. The cashier intercepted these books before they were sent out from the branch.

She then began to transfer money from other investors' accounts into the bogus accounts. Using an innocent friend to make withdrawals, the cashier finally got her hands on the money.

The fraud came to light as a result of customer queries regarding their account balances and transactions being passed across them. The investigative procedures instigated by the society's internal auditors eventually pointed to the cashier as the perpetrator of the fraud.

Stop Press

1. *Fraudulent Program Manipulation*
Location: Bank   *Value: £2,150,000*
With the assistance of a project manager, a hacker gained access to a bank's videotex system. He was then able to open credit facilities which allowed three separate transfers of large amounts of cash (£450,000, £800,000 and £900,000).

2. *Fraudulent Data Manipulation and Funds Transfer*
Location: Bank   *Value: £1,400,000*
False guarantees were created which subsequently generated guarantee documents. These documents allowed rapid borrowings to be made because the bank in question thought that adequate collateral was on hand.

3. *Fraudulent Funds Transfer and Data Manipulation*
Location: Securities Dealer   *Value: £1,100,000*
By suppressing controls in a securities application the interest due was manipulated. The fraud went unnoticed for several weeks.

4. *Fraudulent Software Changes*
Location: Bank   *Value: £1,000,000*
By modifying the installation's access control program, access to the EFT system was obtained and £1 million was fraudulently transmitted.

5. *Unauthorised Access to Passwords*
Location: Bank   *Value: £800,000*
By using certain commands within a software package, the inspection and modification of certain sensitive data is possible. While these commands are password protected, the password is readable from the load module. By

exploiting this via a 'LIST' command, a system engineer was able to undertake a fraud to the value of £800,000.

6.   Fraudulent Program Amendments
Location: Bank   *Value: £750,000*
By modifying a program which maintained exchange rate tables, a fraud for £750,000 was perpetrated.

7.   ATM Fraud
Location: Bank   *Value: £600,000*
Following the breakdown of the central system controlling an ATM network, the cash dispensers were emptied using copied cards.

8.   Hacking
Location: Bank   *Value: £600,000*
The international network of a minicomputer manufacturer was hacked in order to use the manufacturer's remote support facilities. The hacker then gained access to the systems of a German bank and effected the transfer to a Paris-based bank of £600,000 which he then collected.

9.   Manipulation of System Parameters
Location: Bank   *Value: £600,000*
By making unauthorised changes to the expiry date in a program, a £600,000 fraud was committed.

10.   Fraudulent Program Amendment
Location: Insurance Company   *Value: £200,000*
A programmer modified a program to provide a higher rate of commission for a friend who was a broker. An estimated loss of £200,000 was incurred over a period of three years.

11.   Fraudulent Use of Systems Software Utilities
Location: Bank   *Value: £100,000*
Using the IBM utility TTRSPZAP, physical records were directly modified. Entries for £100,000 were then fraudulently processed.

12.   Manipulation of System Parameters
Location: Finance Company   *Value: £100,000*
A systems programmer bypassed the software which logs and monitors system usage, then processed several fraudulent transactions totalling £100,000.

13.   Plastic Card Fraud
Location: Bank   *Value: £800,000*
Forging of plastic cards and stealing PIN codes of several customers resulted

in an £800,000 fraud involving company accounts and Automated Teller Machines.

14.   Manipulation of Accounting Entries
Location: Bank   *Value: £40,000*

A bank manager disguised the financial problems of an ailing company (a director of which was a personal friend) by predating receipts and postdating payments on the company's account. Over a period of 18 months an interest loss of £40,000 was incurred by the bank.

15.   Credit Card Fraud
Location: Bank   *Value: £30,000*

The credit card and password of a customer were stolen by a clerk. The clerk raised the credit limit of the customer and withdrew cash from an automatic cash dispenser. Over a period of five months he stole £30,000.

Appendix 12: CHAPS

The Clearing Houses Automated Payment Scheme (CHAPS) is a system jointly operated on a co-operative basis by 13 of the major UK financial institutions using the national PSS (packet switched system). These institutions consist of clearing banks and the larger building societies. It is similar in concept to SWIFT but the overall principles differ in respect of its 'restricted' membership and the fact that its messages will actually transfer value between its members (whereas SWIFT messages take the form of an advice to transfer value). The actual transfer of funds takes place via designated accounts maintained at the Bank of England. The system, operated in the UK only, deals solely with sterling transfers—no foreign currency transactions are handled.

While there are only 13 members of CHAPS, each member bank is entitled to offer other banks (that is, the UK branches of foreign banks) facilities for making fast, efficient same-day value payments of sterling. The same-day value transfers via the Bank of England accounts are a major attraction of this service. Since the majority of member banks provide the facility to accept magnetic tape, settling via CHAPS is also attractive in terms of reducing manual payment processing overheads. The settlement banks also employ CHAPS to settle the nett Dr/Cr positions which arise via the clearing operations, thereby eliminating the manual aspects of Town Clearing.

The CHAPS software is processed on Tandem Non-Stop computers, an aspect made necessary by the high-reliability requirement. The obvious requirement is that of meeting the settlement deadlines set by the Bank of England; any interruption of this service could cause both banks and their customers serious cash shortage problems. Another, less obvious, effect is that the efficient working of the money markets could be distorted if a 'major player' were taken out by a system failure. Since the sums involved—particularly those related to clearings—are huge, the inability of a large financial institution to manage its position effectively could cause technical distortions in the marketplace in terms of interbank interest rates. The fault-tolerant architecture of the Tandem computers made them an attractive choice for this application.

Each CHAPS application system consists of two distinct suites of software; the banks' own application software and the standard CHAPS 'Gateway' software. The Gateway software was specified jointly between the banks and APACS (Association for Payment Clearing Services) and developed on their behalf by a major software consultancy. The functioning of, and controls within, the banks' 'approach' software is a matter for each individual bank and is determined by its approach to risk management. However, it would generally be concerned with the functions of payment input, verification, authorisation and, via an appropriate access control system, maintaining the necessary segregation of duties.

The Gateway software is primarily concerned with payment message integrity and control. The Gateway performs message time stamping, allocation of sequential numbers to each individual message and maintenance of running totals for each of the counterparties or settlement banks. For each payment sent or received by each individual settlement bank, the Gateway software maintains a nett Dr/Cr position in respect of all other settlement banks. Hence at the cut-off time each bank knows how much it owes to, or is owed by, each of the other settlement banks. In this manner an almost immediate reconciliation and consequent settlement can take place at the end of the business day.

All CHAPS messages are authenticated. The authentication and verification processes are effected by Tamper Resistant Modules (TRMs) attached to the Tandem mainframes. Each TRM performs the functions of key storage and management, authenticator production and authenticator validation. Since, as in SWIFT, the authenticator keys are unique between each settlement bank pair, the TRMs maintain and use several sets of keys. To preserve message confidentiality, all CHAPS messages are encrypted at their point of entry to the network.

A further control technique is implemented at the network level where, in order to provide a level of access control, all settlement banks belong to the same Closed User Group. A Closed User Group provides the means to limit

OVERVIEW OF CHAPS SECURITY

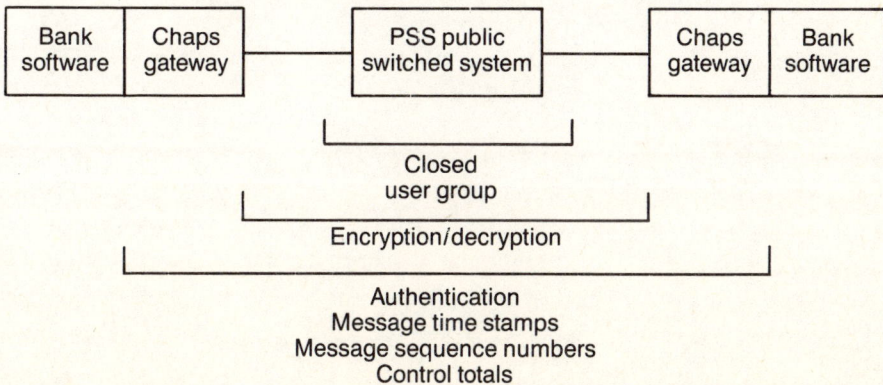

Bank software	Chaps gateway		PSS public switched system		Chaps gateway	Bank software

Closed
user group

Encryption/decryption

Authentication
Message time stamps
Message sequence numbers
Control totals

access to members of an exclusive club, allowing members to use a public facility as if it were a private network. Users of the PSS who are not members of the closed user group are prevented from communicating with those who are members. By adopting the closed user group approach, CHAPS settlement banks can ensure that they will only receive messages from each other and that they cannot send messages via CHAPS to anyone other than CHAPS members.

Appendix 13: BACS Security

The following is a summary of the security features provided by BACS, together with an indication of the control procedures which should be followed by users. Readers should refer to the *BACS User Guide* for further detail.

13.1 BACS Controls

1) BACS issue numbered identity labels which the customer attaches to each tape or diskette. The label number and the user identification are shown in clear and in bar code form. BACS will only accept a tape if a valid identity label is attached.
2) Security of access to BACSTEL is achieved by the use of passwords. A transmission will only be accepted after verification of the password against BACS records.
3) BACS will validate data at the input stage and during processing. Failure of a validation check could, depending on its gravity, result in:

- mandatory rejection;
- rejection unless processing is authorised by the customer's Sponsoring Bank;
- a report to the customer.

A complete file will be rejected if:

- all or some of the data is unreadable or suffers from major structural defects;
- it appears to be a duplicate;
- invalid transactions or nil amounts are included;
- record counts and totals cannot be reconciled with the control records provided by the customer;
- the processing dates given in the header label or the records are incorrect;
- the BACSTEL password is incorrect or non-existent.

Individual transactions will be:

- rejected if they are of a type which the user is not authorised to process;
- amended and returned if a destination sorting code is invalid.

4) A preset limit to the total value which can be processed in a specified period may be determined by each user and held by the system. If the limit is exceeded BACS will request permission to proceed from the account-holding bank, delaying processing until permission is received. The user can also set a maximum value per transaction, in which case any transaction exceeding that value will be reported to the user.

5) The File Authentication facility allows users to include in their file trailer labels a check total. This is calculated by the application of a standard algorithm to the Bank Sort Code, Bank Account Number and the transaction value of every record in the file. The calculation will be re-performed on receipt by BACS and, in the event of any discrepancy, the user will be advised via its sponsoring bank and the file rejected.

The mechanisms for reporting suspect transactions or files are:

- for BACSTEL files only, an on-line reporting procedure which enables a user to monitor and control submissions and obtain an immediate report of accepted and rejected files;
- for BACSTEL and non-BACSTEL files:
  - the Acceptance Report;
  - the Input Report.

13.2   BACS User Controls

In common with all 'bureau' and value-added services, BACS are only able to control data from the point at which the tape, disk or on-line transaction is received and the BACS security measures are directed to the provision of this assurance. The following basic precautions must be observed by the customer if this comfortable feeling is to be extended to all stages of the process.

Data Capture
1) Security procedures over the user's payment and collections processing system which restrict entry into BACS to data which is proved to be authorised, accurate and complete.

2) Procedures which ensure that all data is entered in the correct timescale.

3) Procedures which ensure that all errors are quickly identified and corrected.

4) Frequent reviews that the above controls still exist, operate effectively and (most important) are complied with.

Processing
1) Procedures to ensure that all programs and data used are the current and authorised versions.

2) Frequent (preferably irregular) checks to ensure that the system has correctly and completely carried out the payment and collection processing.

3) Procedures which ensure that the output from the computer system is checked sufficiently to detect errors prior to their affecting the preparation of BACS files.

4) Effective controls over the use of error-correction programs.

5) Password control, personal identification devices, PIDs or other comparable mechanisms used to control access to all operational data files and programs.

6) Independent review of all payments and collections software for unauthorised code.

7) Adequate control over the use and installation of utilities and other systems software.

8) Storage media containing payment and collections data and programs must be stored in a securely-locked area and adequately protected against unauthorised removal.

9) Personnel policies and procedures should contribute to the minimisation of fraud by employees.

10) All risks related to BACS processing must be covered by an appropriate insurance policy.

11) Frequent checks must be made to confirm the existence and effectiveness of, and compliance with, the above controls.

Preparation of BACS Files
1) Output from the BACS file creation program must be checked to detect errors prior to the transfer of the file to BACS.

2) If the above activity identifies errors, the complete run should be rejected for examination and correction.

3) The BACS submission file must be interrogated by a secure audit program under the control of an authorised person who was not involved in its production, to provide independent assurance that the contents of the file correspond to control reports and are authorised, accurate and complete.

4) Allocation of BACS data should aggregate transfers which relate to the same account number.

5) BACS data files must be safeguarded to prevent unauthorised access or substitution. The safeguards could include an effective maintenance routine or random checks of results.

6) Precautions should be taken to guard against media read failures.

7) If a proprietary software package is used for BACS data collection/conversion, it must be subjected to adequate testing and approved by management.

8) The above controls over collection of BACS transactions and their conversion to BACS format must be frequently reviewed and monitored.

Transfer of BACS Files

1) Controls are required over the original and duplicate identity labels issued by BACS.

2) Procedures must exist to ensure that input data will be received by BACS in time for the intended processing cycle.

3) Controls must exist to prevent data manipulation or substitution once the file is in transit.

4) There must be an effective system for monitoring the usage of BACS magnetic media.

5) Procedures must be in place which prevent accidental damage to media in transit.

6) Procedures must also ensure that a readable file reaches BACS.

7) Adequate controls must operate to maintain the integrity of passwords and PINs.

8) Appropriate measures must be taken to minimise the risks of fraud involving telecommunication links to BACS.

9) Each submission to BACS must be monitored and controlled.

10) Rejected or interrupted submissions must be corrected quickly and accurately.

Verification

Full use must be made of the facilities offered to users by BACS to help control submissions. These include:

- Encryption on dedicated telecommunications (BACSTEL);
- Checking of input and acceptance reports;
- Account Limits (£ values);
- Item Limits (£ values);
- Random audit samples listed on the input report;
- Authentication of key fields (physical media and BACSTEL).

Appendix 14: Security Aspects of Current UK Legislation

Applicability of Existing Laws to Computer Misuse

Before the passage of the *Computer Misuse Act* of 1990, attempts were made to apply existing laws to examples of computer misuse. In many cases these laws were held by the courts to be incapable of use in an EDP environment.

The Criminal Damage Act (1971) This can be interpreted to exclude destruction of data or software, which may not be seen by the courts to be tangible damage to property. However, an Appeal Court decision in 1991 (R v Whiteley) upheld the view that, if an alteration to the contents of a disk 'caused impairment of the value or usefulness of the disk to the legitimate operator,' the necessary damage was established.

Offences under the *Theft Act (1968)* cannot be applied to copying of confidential or sensitive information, since:

- the property involved is intangible;
- the owner is not deprived of anything;
- a machine cannot be deceived.

Despite this, the effects of unauthorised copying of data could be—and already have been—extremely damaging to UK commercial organisations and, by implication, to British industry. The effects of such activities in a Governmental context do not need further explanation.

The Forgery and Counterfeiting Act (1981) was held in the House of Lords ruling on R v Gold and Schifreen to be inappropriate when considering unauthorised use of a password to enter a computer system.

The Computer Misuse Act (1990)
This statute represents the first successful attempt in the United Kingdom to designate unauthorised access itself as a crime. There are three categories of crime:

- unauthorised access to computer programs or data (maximum penalty six months imprisonment and/or £2000 fine);
- unauthorised access with intent to commit or facilitate the commission of a serious offence (maximum penalty five years imprisonment and/or an unlimited fine);
- unauthorised modification of computer data or programs (maximum penalty five years imprisonment and/or an unlimited fine).

The Act, which was based on a report published by the England and Wales Law Commission (number 186) in October 1989, came into force on 29 August 1990. It applies to the whole of the United Kingdom, with adjustments to allow for differences between the legal systems of England and Wales, Scotland and Northern Ireland.

The offences can apply not only to external hackers, but also to employees who exceed their access authorisations.

The Act does not impose statutory duties on system owners, but in order to be assured of the full protection of the law they will need to take certain precautions, such as ensuring that:

- employees and other users fully understand the limits of their authority;
- all instances of misuse are detected and properly logged at an early stage.

In common with many other laws the Act has avoided defining the word 'computer'. The reason given is that this allows for greater flexibility. However, the uncertainty should provide a great source of debate (and income) within the legal profession.

The Act introduces new rules governing the jurisdiction of courts in the United Kingdom in dealing with international computer misuse. They follow other Law Commission recommendations dealing with fraud, and allow UK courts to prosecute cases of computer misuse directed at computers in the UK, wherever they originate. Similarly, a misuse originating from the UK which affects computers abroad can be prosecuted in the UK, provided it is an offence in the other country.

An adequate level of security will of course be essential, since defence lawyers will certainly seize on evidence of weak security measures as a possible defence or mitigation ploy.

The Data Protection Act (1984)

This Act given extensive publicity, and the Data Protection Registrar provided comprehensive assistance prior to, and after, the various requirements became mandatory. Nevertheless, prosecutions are occurring at a slow but regular rate, and the evidence from these suggests an alarming lack of knowledge about the implications of the Act (see Appendix 2).

The Data Protection Act has placed obligations on holders of personal data in a computer environment to provide an adequate level of security in order to prevent unauthorised access.

At the time of publication of this book, a draft Council Directive Proposal dealing with the harmonisation and extension of national laws on the subject had been issued by the Council of the European Communities. This document will, if agreed, expand the responsibilities of data users and considerably extend the definition of 'personal data'. It will provide the Data Protection Registrar with effective powers of investigation and intervention, the right of access to files covered by the directive, and the power to gather information. He will also have power to carry out, at the request of the data subject, the necessary checks on the files held for policing, national security, defence, public safety and other state-sensitive purposes.

The directive would empower the European Commission to:

- supervise the application of the directive by member states by establishing a working party on data protection to monitor events, to report directly on significant divergences between member states and produce an annual report;
- control the policy implications that arise from the transfer of data to countries not subject to the directive;
- exercise rule-making powers in order to enforce technical measures in certain sectors.

The draft also proposes that:

- data subject rights already established by the UK's Data Protection Act (the right to have inaccurate personal data corrected or erased; the right to claim compensation if damage is caused through the use of inaccurate personal data or if data is insecurely held) should be extended to personal information held in manual files;
- before the collection of personal information, individuals should be informed about: why the data is being collected; the obligatory or voluntary nature of any request for information; consequences if information is not provided; the identity of recipients of personal information; the right of access to, and correction of, personal data; and the name and address of the controller of the file;
- a right of opposition should apply in the private sector for legitimate reasons. If a data subject can object to the processing or disclosure of personal data, the processing or disclosure in question must stop;
- the right of data correction should be extended, providing in some circumstances the right to know who has obtained erroneous personal data;
- individuals should not be subject to an administrative or private action (such as credit refusal) involving an assessment of conduct which has as its sole basis the processing of personal data defining his profile or personality;
- erasure of personal data held for market research or advertising purposes should be free of charge;

- a prohibition, unless there is an overriding public interest, on holding sensitive data (religious beliefs, racial origin, political opinions, health, sex life, trade union membership) without the express and written consent, freely given, of the data subject;
- criminal conviction data should only be held in the public sector;
- where there is an exemption (such as subject access to personal data in certain sensitive areas), there are compensating supervisory powers for the Data Protection Registrar.

The draft directive significantly extends the scope of the UK Act in that it:

- includes manual files containing personal information within its scope, as the definition of processing includes all operations whether or not performed by automated means; but personal data files must be structured and accessible in an organised collection;
- covers all the activities that fall within the commission's remit (goods, services, transport, agriculture, economics and social policy) and makes suggestions in relation to those activities that do not fall within the scope of community law (such as national security);
- limits the use of personal data by the public sector to those functions supported by statutory powers; if public sector data is used by the private sector the controller must inform subjects of this fact;
- implies that the private sector should obtain prior consent of the subject for holding of personal data. (Consent is defined as providing the data subject with the reason why personal data is stored; the type of data; the identity of the recipients of the data, and the name and address of the file controller.) Consent can be withdrawn;
- allows an organisation to process personal data without the consent of the data subject only in accordance with the directive and if the processing (i) occurs within the framework of a contract with the data subject; or (ii) if the data originates from sources generally accessible to the public; or (iii) the controller of the file is pursuing a legitimate interest;
- defines the minimum detail to be registered with the Data Protection Registrar. (These details are: the name and address of the controller of the file; the creation of a personal data file; the reason why the file was created; a description of the types of data stored in the file; to whom the data might be disclosed; a description of the security measures taken to protect the personal data.)

Compliance with Business Requirements

Recent legislation has imposed stricter controls and stringent monitoring on businesses in the United Kingdom. Examples of these are given below. Although the business requirements have, in many cases, been understood and the necessary internal compliance mechanisms created, changes in IT requirements have not, in many cases, been fully implemented.

The Financial Services Act (1986)

This primarily regulates the ways in which organisations providing financial services perform their trade and deal with their clients. However, in order to ensure that these businesses will be conducted in accordance with the new rules, some significant changes to computer systems, data structures and practices have been needed.

In addition, requirements were outlined by the Self Regulatory Organisations (SROs) set up by the Act to monitor compliance. These have wide-ranging implications for the firms' IT operations and development. As an example, the regulations of the Securities Association—now part of The Securities and Futures Association—require that:

- member firms establish and maintain systems of internal controls;
- all records be maintained in sufficient detail and with sufficient cross-references to establish an adequate audit trail;
- the firm maintain procedures for the maintenance, security, privacy and preservation of its records.

The following, although not specific requirements, are highly desirable in order to achieve compliance with SRO rules:

- an organised systems development methodology;
- up-to-date documentation of systems;
- effective change control procedures;
- adequate testing of system changes.

For many reasons, including the need to maintain the 'Chinese Walls' between the different functions of each firm, access to computer-held records must be strictly controlled. This requires:

- effective access control software;
- procedures which ensure that passwords are issued, used and controlled in a secure manner;
- sensible password design.

The penalties for inability to trade, provide information or comply in the many other ways required are sufficiently stringent to send a chill up any corporate spine, and lead to the necessity for a disaster recovery plan which is:

- adequate;
- up to date;
- regularly tested;
- regularly reviewed.

More details of the implications of TSA regulations are provided in Chapter Seventeen.

The Banking Act (1987)
This has similar implications to the Financial Services Act. A Guidance Note was issued by the Banking Supervision Dept of the Bank of England in September 1987 to all institutions authorised to trade under the Banking Act. This Guidance Note—on *Accounting and Other Records and Internal Control Systems (AORICS)*—provided the Bank's interpretation of the Act's requirements on records and systems in order to assist:

- institutions to assess the adequacy of their own arrangements;
- reporting accountants appointed under the Act to assess compliance.

The Guidance Note covers a wide area, including the following topics:

- disaster recovery;
- systems development risks;
- data entry errors;
- business interruption;
- fraud;
- access to confidential information;
- organisation of a bank's computer department;
- PC-based applications;
- regular monitoring of internal control;
- the function of internal audit.

The Building Societies Act (1986)
This statute has similar provisions. A Prudential Note circulated by the Building Societies Commission expands on the implications for information systems of Section 71 of the Act, which extends the more general requirement of the earlier (1962) Act relating to the requirement for proper books of account and the need for a system of controls and inspection. The Prudential Note explains the need for a society to establish and maintain a 'system of control of its business' covering the totality of the business process. Security-related requirements identified in the Note are:

- identification and assessment of risks and the adequacy of controls;
- documented security policy and procedures;
- disaster recovery;
- adequate security measures;
- effective internal audit;
- assurance of accuracy of records;
- assurance of safeguarding of assets.

Companies Act (1985)
Section 722 of this Act requires that where a company's records are maintained by computer, there shall be adequate protection against falsification and provision of facilities to permit detection. In the event of a breach of this

section, the company—and every officer in default—is liable to a fine plus a daily fine in the event of continued contravention.

Admissible Evidence

Criminal Law
The law of evidence is vast. The standard work in the USA is Wigmore, which consists of ten volumes totalling more than 7600 pages. In England the shortest text is *Cross on Evidence*—a mere 700 pages.

In criminal cases a great deal of time is spent deciding whether evidence is admissible or not. Until 1984 the decisions were based on common law, refined by a number of—sometimes conflicting—judgements. The decisions required answers to the following questions.

- Is it real evidence or hearsay? (Was the evidence generated wholly by computer or with human involvement?)
- Is it reliable? Computer people may testify as experts, but this is only if their opinions are based on proper scientific analysis.
- Is it the 'best evidence'? This test has gradually been eroded in respect of business records. The rule rejects 'inferior' evidence such as a copy of a document or a witnesses description of an object if the original is obtainable. However, courts on both sides of the Atlantic are now happy to accept copies of original documents where they are not in dispute.

The *Police and Criminal Evidence Act (1984)* agreed for the first time, that computer output can be considered admissible unless it can be shown that the computer is faulty.

Section 69 of the Act governs all computer-generated evidence placed before the English and Welsh criminal courts. It states that such evidence will only be submitted if a certificate is provided by the system manager stating: that there are no reasonable grounds for believing that it is inaccurate because of improper use of the computer; and that at all material times, the computer was operating reliably, or, if not, that any respect in which it was not operating properly or out of operation could not have affected the production of the print-out document or the accuracy of its contents.

It should be noted that the phrase 'no reasonable grounds' features only in the first clause. Its omission from the second clause means that the system manager must be certain that the system could not have acted incorrectly during the period during which the relevant information was entered, stored and printed out or, at least, that any such malfunction would not have affected the integrity of that information. Anything less and the evidence will be excluded.

The recent case of R v Spilby made it clear that a section 69 certificate is only needed where there has been some human intervention in the computer process. A section 69 certificate would be needed to prove an entry in a bank statement relating to a withdrawal by cheque, since at some stage a human being has written the amount on it in magnetic ink. However, this section would not apply to an entry relating to a withdrawal through an ATM since there is no human input to the process. R v Spilby actually concerned printout showing the details of the telephone calls made from certain rooms at a hotel, captured by a Private Automated Branch Exchange in the building. The court ruled that, as there had been no human involvement, the printout was 'real' and not 'hearsay' evidence. The court could, therefore, invoke the legal presumption that the equipment was working properly and ignore section 69.

Civil Law

In civil cases, exceptions to the hearsay rule are codified in the *Civil Evidence Act (1968)*. Section 5 was drafted explicitly to cover the admissibility of computer evidence. However, the section is limited in its scope and reflects the state of technology at the time the Act was passed. The section refers to a computer as 'any device for storing and processing information', which covers the hardware but ignores the existence of software.

For a computer print-out to be accepted as admissible evidence in a civil case the following conditions must be satisfied:

* the printout must have been produced by the computer during a period over which the computer was used regularly to store and process information for the purpose of any activity regularly carried on over that period;
* over the period there was regularly supplied to the computer, in the ordinary course of those activities, information of the kind contained in the statement or of the kind from which the information so contained is derived;
* throughout the material part of that period, the computer must have been operating properly or, if not, the impairment must not have been such as to offset the correctness of the result;
* the information contained in the statement reproduces, or is derived from, information supplied to the computer in the ordinary course of those activities.

However, the provisions might exclude output which is not *regularly* generated (for example *ad hoc* reports produced for internal or external auditors, or a print of the system log).

General Regulations

The requirements of the Inland Revenue, Customs and Excise and the Health and Safety Executive can also have an impact on IT systems and installations.

Compliance officers have been appointed in most relevant organisations to confirm compliance with specific regulations. They can be seen as extra components of internal control and the security officer's terms of reference may include monitoring these activities to ensure that:

- the risks entailed in breaching these and other regulations are understood;
- the compliance activities are effective controls against occurrences of the risks.

Appendix 15: Security Aspects of Current US Legislation

In addition to the *Foreign Corrupt Practices Act* and SEC rules referred to in Chapter Sixteen, the following statutes are relevant.

The *Counterfeit Access Device and Computer Fraud and Abuse Act* of 1984 prohibits unauthorised access to and disclosure of:

- information protected or restricted from disclosure for national security reasons;
- financial records kept by financial institutions or consumer reporting agencies;
- information stored on any 'federal interest computer'.

The law provides for fines of up to US $10,000 or up to ten years imprisonment for first offenders. Although some computer crimes could be prosecuted under long-standing federal laws against wire fraud and interception of communications offences, this was the first federal law that specifically targeted computer crimes. Under the law, fraud associated with automated teller machines became a federal crime.

The Computer Fraud and Abuse Act (1986)
This statute extends federal jurisdiction to cover computer crimes which affect federal interest to major financial institutions and businesses involved in interstate commerce. It also sets a minimum of US $1000 per year on the loss of value a person or organisation must suffer to pursue an action; extends the 1984 Act's coverage to medical records, examinations, diagnoses, care and treatment; makes fraudulent or improper use of passwords illegal; and further defines the term 'financial institution'.

The Act makes it illegal for an unauthorised person to obtain classified information by a computer 'with the intent or reason to believe that such information so obtained is to be used to the injury of the United States or to the advantage of any foreign nation.' An unauthorised person is defined as one who 'knowingly and intentionally accesses a computer without authorisation or exceeds authorised access'.

At the time of writing, the US Department of Justice is suggesting that the words 'intent or reason to believe' should be dropped on the basis that the

Act as it stands is virtually unusable. However, since the suggested amendment would relieve the prosecution of the need to provide proof of actual or intended espionage, it would be a crime merely to use or cause the use of a computer to obtain classified information without authorisation. Since the maximum penalty for a first offence is ten years' imprisonment, with 20 years for any succeeding breaches, the fact that a culprit could be found guilty of espionage without proof of intent is causing some concern.

A more lurid aspect came to light in 1989, when the US Government House Banking Committee was told that drug barons, forced by federal law enforcement crackdowns in the United States to find new methods to launder illegal money, were using unregulated international wire funds transfers to move funds around.

The US Treasury Department proposed that all international wire funds transfer messages should contain information on the source and destination of the money. They also proposed that domestic financial institutions in the United States or clearing houses involved in such transactions should verify the nature of the customer's business, and that private individuals should not use DES over public lines.

It was suggested at the time that the *US Bank Secrecy Act* may have to be revised in the light of the committee's findings. The Act, passed in 1978 and subsequently amended in 1986 and 1988, was the first in a series of laws in the United States designed to stop unlawful money transactions being processed.

At present each US financial institution must file a special report with the Internal Revenue Service every time a customer deposits, withdraws, exchanges or transfers more than $10,000 in cash. Although more than six million reports are expected to be filed in 1991—six times the number in 1984—the Committee recommended that the $10,000 limit be lowered.

The Electronic Communications Privacy Act (1986)
This broadened the definitions of electronic communications provided by the original 1968 wiretap law, although it added specific exceptions for a variety of uses 'readily accessible to the public'. It allows prosecution of criminals who gain unauthorised access to computers across state lines via telecommunications networks, and encouraged communications service providers to take advantage of the Act's protection by scrambling and encrypting their signals. Equally important, the Act authorised, for the first time, recovery of civil damages as well as criminal penalties.

The Computer Security Act (1987)
This gave the National Institute of Standards and Technology (NIST) authority over computer security in non-classified federal interest computers. This covered non-classified government agencies and public databases; the responsibility for protection of classified data remained with the National Security Agency. All agencies are required to report on their plans to implement security features and develop security awareness training,

although at the time of writing staff shortages were severely reducing the Institute's ability to provide effective monitoring.

Credit Card Fraud Act
On a related subject, in 1984 the US Congress passed this statute, which used the term 'access device' to define credit, debit cards and ATM cards.
  The following activities were stated to be felonies:

- to produce, use, or traffic in counterfeit access devices;
- to possess 15 or more counterfeit or unauthorised access devices;
- to produce illicitly, traffic in, have control of or custody of, or to possess access device making equipment.

The Act also gave authority to the US Secret Service to investigate any activity that affects interstate or foreign commerce in regard to such fraudulent access devices. It also included the use of legitimate account numbers on illicit cards.

Forty-eight states have now passed computer crime or fraud and abuse laws. In many cases the state laws offer more protection than federal laws, and some allow civil litigation against the perpetrators not only for actual damages, but also for extra damages and costs. A Bureau of National Affairs review of state activity reported that 17 bills were passed in 1989, many of which dealt with viruses.

Appendix 16: A Summary of other Relevant International Laws

Introduction

The subject of data security has exercised the minds of members of many national legislative assemblies. The results are wide and varied, and in order to provide an indication of current thinking, a summary of some of these is provided below with descriptions of some legislation regulating national financial institutions. In addition to describing the prohibited activities and penalties, any definitions of relevant terms, such as 'data', 'computer' or 'access' are given. It will be noticed that in very few cases have any of these definitions been attempted. A reference is also made to any data protection laws in each country.

Australia

Amendment of 'Summary Offences Act' (1966) by Crimes (Computers) Act 1988 (Victoria)
Section 9a: 'A person must not gain access to, or enter, a computer system or part of a computer system without lawful authority to do so.'

Amendment made to 'Crimes Act' (1914) Following Proposals in 'Review of Commonwealth Criminal Law' (Nov 1988)
Section 3: '"Data" includes information, computer program or a part of a computer program.'

Section 87B(1): '(1) A person who, without authority, intentionally obtains access to:
  (a) data stored in a Commonwealth computer; or
  (b) data stored in a computer (not being a Commonwealth computer) on behalf of the Commonwealth or a public authority under the Commonwealth;
is guilty of an offence.'

Proposed Introduction of New Chapter to Tasmanian Criminal Code proposed by Law Reform Commission of Tasmania
Includes: 'Any person who, without authority, knowingly gains access to a computer, computer network or any part thereof, is guilty of a crime.'

'"Data" includes any information that is capable of being stored or being retrieved by a computer and includes computer programs.'

'"Data" means a representation that has been transcribed by methods, the accuracy of which is verifiable, into the form appropriate to the computer into which it is, or is to be, introduced.' (*Tasmanian Evidence Act*)

'"Access": includes to communicate with a computer.'

Canada

Canadian Criminal Law Amendment Act (1985)
Section 301.2 punishes 'everyone who fraudulently and without colour of right ...
  (b) by means of an electromagnetic, acoustic, mechanical, or other device intercepts or causes to be intercepted, directly or indirectly any functions of a computer system. . .'

In this section 'data' means 'representations of information or of concepts that are being prepared or have been prepared in a form suitable for use in a computer system.'

Denmark

Penal Code Amendment Act (June 1985)
Section 263(2): 'Anyone who gains unauthorised access to anyone's data or software intended for electronic data processing will be punished.' The penalty of up to six months' imprisonment rises to two years if the crime is committed for the purpose of stealing trade secrets.
  Section 279 punishes anyone guilty of 'Data Trespass', ie anyone who, with the intention of profiting, amends or deletes data or programs or attempts to disrupt computer processing.

The Danish Public Authorities Registers Act (1988) and Private Registers Act (1988) govern the use and registration of personal data in EDP systems. Supervision of compliance with the requirements is the responsibility of the Data Surveillance Authority (DSA), which has produced a set of standards (Recommended Security Measures) for the use of personal computers.

The Danish Supervisory Authority of Financial Affairs is responsible for the surveillance of banks, insurance companies and other financial institutions. It achieves this by:

- performing regular security reviews;
- issuing instructions to Certified Public Accountants on the audit of the financial sector.

The Bookkeeping Act (1959)

New instructions came into force in 1990 extending the rules of this statute to cover security and auditability of electronic vouchers. These include the following:

- The company should have all necessary updated documentation of systems, files, functions, etc concerning all applications and hardware in use in the last five years.
- The company should be able, irrespective of any changes in hardware or software, to print out all necessary vouchers, transactions, financial output which might be necessary in order to audit the last five years' bookkeeping.
- All transactions should be filed and be retrievable, including changes in basic files (parameters, variables, etc).
- All automatically-generated vouchers should be auditable through the system documentation.
- There should be a clear transaction trail (from the individual transaction to the financial statement) and a clear audit trail (including documentation, parameters and any algorithms used).

France

Law Relating to Information Fraud (1988)

Article 462–2: 'Whoever, fraudulently, accesses or remains within all or part of a data processing system will be punished.' The offence is punishable by:

- two to twelve months' imprisonment *and* a fine of 2000 to 50,000 francs; or
- two months' to two years' imprisonment with no fine; or
- a 10,000 to 100,000 francs fine.

Access or remaining in the system provides the offence—there is no need to prove intent to commit a further offence.

'Data' is defined as 'representation of a piece of information in an ordered form designed to facilitate its processing'.

Articles 462–3 and 462–5 impose sentences of:

- three months' to three years' imprisonment and fines of 10,000 to

100,000 francs for interfering with the operation of a data processing system;

- similar terms of imprisonment, with fines of between 2000 and 50,000 francs, for interfering with the authenticity and integrity of the data.

Under Articles 462–5 and 462–6 it is illegal to falsify a computerised document to the detriment of any person or to use such a forged document. The punishment for either offence is one to five years' imprisonment and a fine of between 20,000 and 2 million francs.

Germany

Second Law for the Prevention of Economic Crimes (1986)
Section 202a: '(1) Any person who obtains without authorisation, for himself or another, data which are not meant for him and which are specifically protected against unauthorised access, shall be liable to a penalty of three years' imprisonment or a fine.' (2) 'Data within the meaning of subsection (1) are only such as are stored or transmitted electronically or in any other form not directly visible'.

Section 263a prohibits—on pain of up to five years in prison or a fine—causing loss to another, with intent to gain, by influencing the result of a DP operation by the following means:

- incorrectly configuring a program;
- using incomplete, unauthorised or incorrect data;
- other unauthorised impact on computer operations.

Section 303a creates an offence—punishable by terms of up to two years' imprisonment or a fine—to unlawfully delete, suppress, alter data or otherwise render it unserviceable.

Section 303b punishes by imprisonment of up to five years or a fine, conduct which impairs a data processing operation which is of vital importance to an external plant or another enterprise, by any of the offences described in Section 303a. If the same result is achieved by destroying or rendering unserviceable a data processing plant or data carrier, the same penalty applies.

Kreditwesengesetz (KWG) 1985
The main purpose of KWG is to safeguard and support the functioning of the financial apparatus, strengthening the foundation of the financial system by regulating competition, publicity and bank supervision over loans and liquidity.

KWG subjects all financial institutions to federal bank supervision and also implements a complete licensing system.

The security of bank deposits is ensured by the legal requirement to publicise large loans as well as certain types of loans to agencies or authorities, an activity performed by an organisation called 'Evidenzzentrale'.

Bundesdatenschutzgesetz (BDSG) 1977
The legal basis of BDSG is to protect the public from misuse of 'personal-related' data. It applies to everybody who handles such data in their work.

The protection of personal data from misuse applies during the saving, transferring, changing and deleting processes of data handling. Access to personal data requires the permission of the affected person, or explicit permission given by laws requiring the release of such information. The affected person has a right to request information about what is being done to his personal data, and to request the protection as well as deletion of the data.

Greece

Greek Penal Code (as amended by Law n.1805/1988)
Article 370C states that 'Anyone who obtains access to data entered into a computer or peripheral computer memory or communicated by telecommunications systems, if these acts have been perpetrated without right, especially by breaching prohibitions or security measures taken by their lawful possessor, is punishable. If the perpetrator is in the service of the lawful possessor of the data, this act is punished only if it is explicitly prohibited by an internal regulation or a written decision of the possessor or a qualified employee of his.'

Netherlands

The Franken Commission Proposals (April 1987)
Data is described as 'representation of facts, concepts or instructions in an agreed manner, suitable for transfer, interpretation or processing by persons or by automated means.'

If Proposal 1 is implemented, anyone damaging or causing a malfunction of a security measure in a computer could be imprisoned for:

- up to six months, or fined if the 'common good' were hindered by the act; or
- up to 15 years if the act caused someone's death.

By Proposal 2, the above actions, if caused negligently, could render the perpetrator liable to up to a year's imprisonment.

Proposal 4 recommends that one who deletes data, or makes it useless or inaccessible, should be liable to up to two years' imprisonment or a fine.

Proposal 15 lays down that any person who unlawfully intrudes into a computerised device protected against such intrusion, used for the storage or processing of data, or into a protected part thereof, shall be liable to six months' imprisonment or a fine. If he then sells any information taken during the intrusion, the punishment could be increased under Proposal 16 to 3 years' imprisonment or a fine.

Norway

Although there are few laws and regulations which directly regulate computer security in general, some current laws apply to specific areas.

Losbladforskriftene (13 May 1977)
This sets up provisions for documentation of 'business control systems' (primarily relating to record handling in accounting systems) using any other media than bound ledgers. The regulation states that there should be a description of the accounting system and the accounting functions included in the system and documentation of the control system established to ensure complete, accurate and reliable bookkeeping.

There should also be detailed and easily understandable documentation making it possible to trace and control each transaction for processing and presentation (an audit trail).

The regulation also sets up certain requirements in relation to the auditability of the cashbook, debtors' and creditors' ledger and the general ledger.

Changes in master datafiles that may affect the transaction processing are to be documented separately.

Regulations Concerning the Use of Computers and Terminals in Commercial and Savings Banks
Introduced by the Banking Inspection Agency (Bankinspeksjonen) on 12 October 1983, updating the *Public Supervision of Banks and other Financial Institutions Act* of 7 December 1956.

The regulations are intended to ensure that the development, maintenance and operations of EDP systems are orderly and secure. They cover the following areas:

- *Standards*. There should at all times be standards relating to system development, maintenance, operations and documentation.
- *System*. For purchasing, development and maintenance of systems there must be routines or procedures which ensure correct system specifications and adequate documentation.
- *Operations*. There must be established routines or procedures to ensure completeness and correctness in electronic data processing.
- *Information Interchange*. Automated information transfers between banks, customers and clearing houses should be regulated by written agreement in order to ensure the availability of necessary functional and operations documentation.

Documentation should cover:

- standards, routines and procedures;
- description of technical aspects for development, maintenance and operations;

- description of manual routines relating to data collection, error recovery and handling of system output.

Documentation should be sufficiently detailed to enable parties other than the original developers to use, maintain, control and perform error recovery.

Personvernloven (Individual Protection Act of 9 June 1978, No. 48)
This Act regulates the storage and processing of individually-related information. It covers manual as well as automated systems in both the private and public sector and applies to information related to any single individual, organisation or foundation.

The information held should be reasonable with respect to the administration and operation of the organisation conducting the registering. Unless it can be shown to be necessary, information should not be held relating to:

- race, political or religious conviction;
- an individual who has been suspected of, charged with, or sentenced for a criminal offence;
- health or alcohol and drug abuse;
- sexual matters;
- family matters other than family relationship and status.

Establishing a 'register' with personal information relating to individuals requires a specific concession. Additional regulations have set up several general concessions serving as exceptions to this requirement, allowing the use of more trivial information without the need for a specific concession.

The law also provides for the establishment of Datatilsynet as an oversight agency. It is established to handle questions relating to individual protection and give concessions for establishing registers covered under the law. Datatilsynet will also advise on securing registered data.

The Act makes provisions for an individual to gain access to registered information relating to that individual. It also regulates the manner of correcting incorrect information and the transfer of individual-related information to other countries.

There are currently no general standards regulating data security related to the *Individual Protection Act*, although the Ministry of Justice is working on regulations, based on an outline presented on 5 November 1987. This draft provides a detailed set of rules regulating the storage and processing of sensitive information covered by the *Individual Protection Act*.

Proposed Changes to the Penal Code, 1922, Section 270
The changes are related to fraud, and make it a criminal offence for anyone inflicting a loss or a possible loss by introducing changes in data or computer programs or in any other illegal way affecting the outcome of electronic data processing.

The penalty may be fines or imprisonment for up to three years.

Sweden

Swedish Data Act (1973)
Section 21: 'Any person who unlawfully gains access to a recording for auto-matic data processing or unlawfully alters or obliterates or enters such a recording in a file shall be sentenced for data trespass.'

An addition to the Penal Code in 1985 designated as a fraud the act of altering a program or otherwise, without permission, affecting the results of 'automatic information processing' in a way which involves gain for the offender or loss for others.

Appendix 17: CEC Green Paper on Cross-Border Payment Systems

The rapidly-increasing quantity and variety of cross-border payments has generated a need to promote improvements in the efficiency of payment systems. At the time of writing, intense discussion on the subject was taking place in the international community, and the European Commission produced a discussion 'Green Paper' in September 1990. This dealt with methods of satisfying the major requirements for efficient cross-border payments, which were seen as:

- speedy payment;
- ensuring that costs for users are reasonable, known in advance and subject to competitive market forces;
- clear delineation of the legal obligations of the involved parties;
- regular monitoring and risk control;
- lack of unnecessary restrictions;
- being useable for all cross-border payments, including those outside the Community.

Possible areas for improvement were highlighted, covering all means of payment:

- cash;
- bank transfers;
- cheques;
- payment cards.

The authors advanced for discussion four alternative suggestions aimed at improving the situation:

- streamlining existing correspondent banking procedures;
- establishing entirely new inter-bank arrangements for cross-border transfers;
- allowing EC member country banks to join automated clearing houses (ACHs) in all the member countries;
- building electronic bridges between existing national ACHs.

Future progress will be monitored by a Payment Systems Co-ordinating Group to be set up in 1991, its objectives being to:

- analyse the Green Paper proposals and any subsequent proposals;
- indicate priorities;
- co-ordinate and sponsor feasibility studies and set out the necessary steps to implement them.

Glossary: The Language of Security

1GL. The first generation of programming languages—Machine Code. The only language a computer actually understands.

2GL. The second generation of languages—assembler. Slightly higher level than a 1GL.

3GL. The generation of languages used for the development of most systems over the past ten years. Examples include Cobol, Fortran and PL/1.

4GL. The latest generation of languages, which are much more user friendly. A 4GL allows you to say what the computer should do, rather than how to do it. Examples include Focus, Oracle and Ingres. 4GLs normally incorporate their own Database Management System (DBMS).

access control. Procedures designed to prevent or limit access to sensitive data. Access can be controlled by physical means (e.g. access cards) or logical methods (e.g. passwords).

ACF2. A security software product which controls logical access to systems using IBM mainframe computers.

acoustic coupler. A device for coupling data lines to the receiver of a telephone for data transmission over the public switched network.

AI. *See* ARTIFICIAL INTELLIGENCE.

ambush code. A special code for an access control system, or digital keypad entry, which provides a warning to a remote control point that the user is under duress by potential attackers.

American National Standards Institute (ANSI). A body which organises committees formed of computer users, manufacturers, etc, to develop and publish industry standards.

American Standard Code for Information Exchange (ASCII). An 8-bit code for alphanumeric characters commonly used for digital data transfers.

Annual Loss Expectancy. A measure of the potential annual cost of a threat to system security.

ANSI. *See* AMERICAN NATIONAL STANDARDS INSTITUTE.

application. The particular business need an IT system is solving.

application program. A program, usually written in-house, for a specific user application (e.g. payroll).

application programmer. A person responsible for design, development, testing, documentation and maintenance of programs for user applications.

armour. Code which attempts to foil debugging or anti-virus software.

artificial intelligence (AI). The simulation or duplication of intelligent behaviour or expertise in a computer system.

ASCII. *See* AMERICAN STANDARD CODE FOR INFORMATION INTERCHANGE.

assembler. The second generation of programming languages.

asymmetric cipher. An encryption system that uses separate keys for encryption and decryption, making it impossible to deduce one from the other.

asynchronous attack. A technique for accessing information before protection takes effect, based on asynchronous timing between when security checks are performed and when user activity begins.

ATM. *See* AUTOMATED TELLER MACHINE.

attack. A physical assault or an attempt to gain unauthorised access.

audit trail. A record of the activities of a system that enables a transaction, or a series of activities, to be traced through the system from start to finish.

authentication. (1) Ensuring that a message is genuine, has arrived exactly as it was sent and came from a legitimate source. (2) Verifying the identity of an individual, such as the sender of a message or a person at a remote terminal.

authentication code. A set of characters, derived from the text of a message, or parts thereof, which is sent with the message to enable the receiver to detect changes in it since it left the sender.

automated teller machine (ATM). Terminal used by banks and other financial institutions to accept and dispense cash and perform other transactions.

backing storage. An intermediate storage medium (e.g. magnetic tape, magnetic disk etc) onto which data is entered for later processing by the central computer.

backup. The taking of a security copy of data and programs in case anything goes wrong with the original.

bar codes. Machine-readable numbering code in the form of a strip of vertical bars.

BASIC. *See* BEGINNERS ALL-PURPOSE SYMBOLIC INSTRUCTION CODE.

batch. Transactions or tasks which are collected together and run as soon as there is capacity available. Its main characteristic is a delay in the submission and processing of computer tasks.

Beginners All-purpose Symbolic Instruction Code (BASIC). The most popular programming language used for training, and very popular on home computers. A more powerful and complex version is also supported as a 3GL on some minis and mainframe computers.

bespoke. Development of application systems without using existing packages. This could be done by a software house or the company's own DP department.

biometric sensor. A device for positive personal identification. The techniques include recognition of eye blood vessel patterns, finger prints, hand geometry, palm prints, and signature analysis.

biometrics. A security technique which involves measuring some unique feature of a human being. *See* BIOMETRIC SENSOR.

bridge. A device to interconnect two or more LANS.

browsing. Viewing and copying material contained in computer storage.

bug. (1) An electronic listening device. (2) An error in a program or system. The term is reputed to have originated in the days of an electromechanical computer using relays. An inexplicable error was traced to the wings of an insect lodged between the contacts of a relay.

bulletin board. A remote public access system for personal computer users. A bulletin board provides a variety of services geared to the requirements of the user population. The user needs a communications software package and a modem to establish dial-up connection to the system.

bureau. An organisation which provides access to, and processing on, its own computers to other organisations.

CASE. *See* COMPUTER-AIDED SOFTWARE ENGINEERING.

cathode ray tube (CRT). The standard technology for VDUs.

CCTV. *See* CLOSED-CIRCUIT TELEVISION.

cellular radio. A low-power transmission network for telephone access from stationary or mobile sites.

certification. A technical evaluation of a system's security features.

Chaos Club. A German club of experienced hackers who have claimed success in attacking computer systems in Europe. It was alleged that Chaos members broke into the NASA computer system.

checksum. A fixed length field produced as a function of every bit in a unit of software or data. The field is added to the data to permit recalculation, comparison and detection of unauthorised changes.

cipher. A cryptosystem using a keyed transformation to disguise information.

ciphertext. Unintelligible (encrypted) text or signals produced by the use of cipher systems on the original.

classified data. Data requiring the highest level of protection against unauthorised disclosure.

cleartext. Unencrypted text.

CLODO. A French underground organisation, whose objective is the destruction of computers.

closed-circuit television (CCTV). Typically used for security monitoring.

coaxial cable. Cable which contains a conductor surrounded by insulation and metallic shielding.

Cobol. A 3GL.

coding. Programming.

coin purse. A method of smart card operation in a bank by which the user charges up the card with credit and the corresponding amount is deducted from the user's bank account. The smart card may then be used to pay for goods or services; at each transaction the amount on the smart card is correspondingly reduced.

cold site. A disaster recovery contingency site into which computer systems can be moved and run when needed. The site would be basic, with or without computer hardware. *Compare* HOT SITE, where the computer hardware is established and copies of software may be maintained to achieve less disruption.

communication protocol. A formally-specified set of conventions governing the format and control of inputs and outputs between two communicating systems.

compiler. A program which converts source code (in Cobol, Fortran, etc) into machine language (known in this case as object code).

computer-aided software engineering (CASE). Use of software as an automated tool for the analysis, design and development of application systems. Most CASE software supports a specific structured development methodology.

computer crime. A computer crime involves manipulating a computer system for gain.

contingency planning. Formulating plans to respond to the conceivable range of incidents, accidents, and disasters that could occur.

CRC. *See* CYCLIC REDUNDANCY CHECK.

CRT. *See* CATHODE RAY TUBE.

Credit Reference Agency. An organisation which provides information on the financial standing of applicants for credit facilities to potential suppliers.

creeping functionality. Loss of control during system design and specification as the development team allows the initial requirements to spread.

cryptography. Generation of encrypted text.

cyclic redundancy check (CRC). A field used for error checking, derived through digital polynomial division.

data dictionary. Details of all fields (and their relationships) held within a database, including description, validation criteria, etc—used as an aid to systems development and documentation. Normally an integral part of a Database Management System.

Data Encryption Standard (DES). The most widely-used encryption algorithm in the commercial world. Published by the US National Bureau of Standards, DES is now the subject of an interna-

tional standard and mandatory for federal agencies.

data flow diagram (DFD). Diagram used to convey understanding of the information flows and processes required within a system to a user. A technique used within the analysis stage of systems development.

data signature. A method of authenticating a document which involves encoding the document or part of it using the public key encryption system.

database. A shared, centrally-controlled, collection of related data with software organisation enabling retrieval through data characteristics, and supporting multiple user views.

database management system (DBMS). A computer-based tool used to set up a database, make it available to users, and control the integrity of the data resources.

data circuit terminating equipment (DCE). The equipment at the outermost end of a communications line.

data terminal equipment (DTE). The equipment which is connected to a data communications network to enable communication.

DBase 3 and 4. PC-based 4GLs for setting up and running databases.

DBMS. *See* DATABASE MANAGEMENT SYSTEM.

DCE. *See* DATA CIRCUIT TERMINATING EQUIPMENT.

DECnet. DEC networking product for data communication among VAX and other DEC computers.

Degausser. A device that erases magnetic media by overwriting information with the alternating magnetic field generated.

derived PIN. A PIN which is generated from some information related to the customer's account number or identity. The PIN is derived by an algorithm involving a secret key. Such PINs may be verified at any location, with access to the secret key used in the algorithm, without requiring storage of the PIN on the customer's card.

DES. *See* DATA ENCRYPTION STANDARD.

DFD. *See* DATA FLOW DIAGRAM.

diagnostics. Information provided by an operating system which shows how the computer is performing.

dial-back. A procedure established for positively identifying a terminal dialling into a computer system by disconnecting the calling terminal and re-establishing the connection. This is achieved by the computer system dialling the telephone number of the calling terminal.

dial-back modem. A modem which is activated by the caller, then hangs up and dials the caller's number to establish communication.

dialup. Simple telecommunications access via a telephone line and a modem.

digital signature. A data block appended to a message, or a complete encrypted message, such that the recipient can authenticate the message contents and/or prove that it could only have originated from the purported sender. The digital signature is calculated from: (a) the message, transaction or document, to be signed; and (b) secret information known only to the sender; and (c) public information employed in the validation process.

disaster planning. A branch of computer security dealing with the protection of systems against accidents and the provision of back-up systems.

disaster recovery plan. The planned sequence of events that allows for the recovery of a computer facility and/or the applications processed there.

discretionary access control. A means of restricting access to objects, based on the identity of subjects and/or groups to which they belong. The controls are discretionary in the sense that a subject with a certain access permission is capable of passing on that permission (perhaps indirectly) to any other subject.

disk operating system (DOS). Operating system commonly used on IBM PCs and clones.

DTE. *See* DATA TERMINAL EQUIPMENT.

dumpster diving. Obtaining confidential information by examining the contents of legitimate users' waste paper baskets, rubbish bins, etc.

duplex. Bidirectional data transmission.

dynamic password. This method—effective against replay attacks—is based on the use of random numbers and uses a device, rather like a pocket calculator, with a protected DES key.

EDI. *See* ELECTRONIC DATA INTERCHANGE.

EFT. *See* ELECTRONIC FUNDS TRANSFER.

EFTPOS. *See* ELECTRONIC FUNDS TRANSFER POINT OF SALE.

electromagnetic pick-up. A method of eavesdropping on a computer screen which involves picking up its emissions and reproducing them on a second screen.

electronic data interchange (EDI). The exchange of structured data between computers (e.g. automation of orders from customer to supplier).

electronic eavesdropping. The interception of wireless transmissions, e.g. radio or microwave transmissions or information-bearing electro-magnetic energy from electronic devices.

electronic funds transfer (EFT). An automated system for transferring funds from one bank account to another using electronic equipment and data communications.

electronic funds transfer point of sale (EFTPOS). The use of a point-of-sale terminal connected by a communication line to a financial institution's computer. The terminal reads and transmits the information recorded on the magnetic strip of a credit card and provides for the input of transaction details via a keyboard.

electronic listening device. A device used to collect and transmit information to an eavesdropper. Such devices may be secreted in a room or connected to telephone equipment.

electronic mail. A facility enabling users to exchange information addressed to a particular individual or group using computer communication facilities.

electronic signature. Synonymous wth digital signature.

EMI. Electromagnetic interference.

encipher. Encrypt.

enciphering algorithm. In cryptography, a set of mathematically-expressed rules for rendering information unintelligible by effecting a series of transformations through the use of variable elements controlled by the application of a key to the normal representation of the information.

encryption. The process of transforming data into an unintelligible form in such a way that the original data either cannot be obtained (one-way encryption) or cannot be obtained without using the inverse decryption process (two-way encryption).

encrypter board. A hardware device that encrypts data before storage on magnetic disk and decrypts the data after retrieval from the disk.

end-to-end encryption. Encryption of information at input to a communications network, postponing decryption to the final destination point.

erasable programming read-only memory (EPROM). Non-volatile memory that can be changed using specific writing devices.

Ethernet. A 10 Mb/second baseband shielded coaxial cable LAN.

exhaustive attack. Using all possible values sequentially in an attempt to find an unknown value (encryption key or password).

facilities management (FM). A service offered by specialist companies who take responsibility for all aspects of the client's DP requirements, including hardware, staffing, etc.

facsimile. The transmission of images over communication links which have a lower bandwidth than that necessary for video signals. The image is scanned by a light beam and a signal representing the brightness of the section of the image under the scanning beam is transmitted over the link in the form of a modulated analogue or digital signal. At the receiving station the signal drives an energy source to reproduce the image by photographic, thermal, or xerographic techniques.

Faraday shield. A conductive enclosure intended to prevent escape or intrusion of electromagnetic energy.

Fiat Shamir. A technique in which users can prove their identity to a verifier by an exchange of information. The exchange of information continues until the verifier has a high probability of correctly authenticating the user. The important advantages of this technique are that a wiretapper cannot derive sufficient information to masquerade as the user on some future occasion, the verifier cannot masquerade as the user, and the user may remain anonymous.

fibre optics. Transparent transmission medium (usually glass) carrying information through oscillations at near-visual wavelengths.

field. An element of an electronic record (e.g. name, age, rate of pay in a salaries record).

file. An organised collection of data containing many records of like information (e.g. names and addresses of all employees in the company).

file server. A disk server which maintains a complete logical file system. Networked microcomputer users can access information in the same directory areas and the file server mechanisms will deal with the problems of unauthorised access, concurrent accesses etc. A heterogeneous mix of microcomputers can also be accommodated by software, which resides in the microcomputers and converts operating system requests into equivalent file server requests.

firmware. (1) Hardware memory containing essentially unalterable program steps. (2) Software stored on a ROM chip.

FM. *See* FACILITIES MANAGEMENT.

Focus. A 4GL.

FORTRAN. Formula Translator. The most widely-used program for scientific applications. A 3GL.

front-end processor. A small computer used to handle communication interfacing, e.g. polling, multiplexing, or detection for another computer.

full duplex. A channel capable of carrying information simultaneously in both directions.

gateway. Equipment used to interface networks so that a terminal can communicate with a terminal or computer on another network.

gigabyte. 1,000,000,000 bytes.

hacker. A person trying to gain unauthorised access to a computer system using a communications link.

half duplex. A channel having bidirectional but not simultaneous data transmission capabilities.

halon. A family of gases based on halogens (chlorine, bromine, fluorine, iodine) which is used in fighting fires.

handshaking. An interchange of information across a channel to establish synchronisation, authentication, etc.

hardware. Physical devices such as computers, peripherals and memory devices.

hierarchical database. Database design where duplication of data is minimised through recognising the parent/child relationships within the data (e.g. for each employee the name will only appear once, but they may have several records for qualifications, job and salary changes, etc).

home banking. The use of a domestic communications terminal to conduct transactions on the customer's bank account.

hot site. A backup recovery computer facility that can be used in the event of a disaster. A hot site will typically contain established computers, peripherals and (possibly) networks, and may also contain software to minimise disruption in processing.

identifier. A mode of identification for

an individual computer user (or sometimes for a group of users needing common access).

impersonation. Use of the password of another person or process to achieve unauthorised access.

information centre. An organisation within a data processing department which provides direct interface to end-user computing and supports services for it.

Ingres. A combined 4GL and DBMS.

interactive. Real-time dialogue between two devices over a communication link.

interpreter. All languages need to be converted to machine code before the computer will understand them. Some are compiled, others have statements interpreted as they are entered. The ideal is a language which is interpreted during development, but can be compiled for more efficient running once completed.

intruder. A person who seeks to make illegal use of a data communication or computer system.

irreversible encryption. A cryptographic transformation of plaintext such that there is no corresponding decryption operation. This technique can be employed, for example, to store passwords in a secure manner. Also referred to as 'one-way encryption'.

Integrated Services Digital Network (ISDN). A communications system that will carry all telecommunications services including voice, data, images and text.

International Standards Organisation (ISO). An international body tasked with establishing communications standards.

jamming. The insertion of signal or noise into a system (usually electro-magnetically) to prevent normal operation of the system.

KBS. *See* KNOWLEDGE-BASED SYSTEM.

kernel. A confined software module containing protected security functions.

key. (1) A physical entity to lock (or unlock). (2) An electronic signal for carrying out a logic function. (3) A combination of numbers or characters used in access control. (4) A parameter used in the encryption and/or decryption of information.

key management. The processes concerned with the generation, distribution, storage, and destruction of cryptographic keys and related information.

knowledge-based system (KBS). Computer system which makes use of judgmental knowledge.

LAN. *See* LOCAL AREA NETWORK.

leased line. A dedicated telecommunications link. Sometimes called a private circuit.

link encryption. The application of on-line crypto-operations to a link of a communications system so that all information passing over the link is encrypted.

local area network (LAN). A communications link between PCs, printers, minicomputers etc over a limited area, normally in the same building.

logic bomb. An unauthorised destructive routine which is executed based on some parameter such as circumstance, date or time.

logical access control. The use of procedures related to information and knowledge, e.g. passwords rather than physical security.

MAC. *See* MESSAGE AUTHENTICATION CODE.

magnetic ink character recognition (MICR). The identification of characters printed with ink that contains particles of a magnetic material. MICR is used in the banking industry to record transmitted codes and account numbers on cheques.

mailbox. An area of storage provided to receive and store electronic mail messages.

mainframe. Large machines providing systems for anything up to several thousand users at any time.

mandatory access control. A means of restricting access to information based on the sensitivity of the information and the formal authorisation of persons to access information of such sensitivity.

mandatory security. Requirement that a person accessing information must have clearance equal to or greater than the data classification.

masquerading. An attempt to gain access to a system by posing as an authorised user.

megabyte. A million characters.

megastream. A British Telecom service offering digital communications.

memory. The temporary storage area used to hold instructions and data currently being processed by the central processing unit of a computer.

Menu-based. An easy-to-use method of using either a computer language or an application system, in which facilities are selected from options displayed on a menu.

message authentication. The processes undertaken to ensure that: (a) the message originated from the purported sender (b) the message contents have not been accidentally or intentionally altered or rearranged and (c) the message has been received in the sequence in which it was sent.

message authentication code (MAC). (1) A code in a message between the sender and receiver used to validate the source and part or all of the text of the message. The code is the result of an agreed calculation. (2) A group of characters included with a message for the purpose of verifying that the message has not been fraudulently changed. The code is a cryptographic function of all data in the message generated under control of a transaction key, and is therefore statistically unique to that message.

message exhaustion. A form of attack in which all possible plaintext combinations are encrypted and the corresponding ciphertext stored for future reference.

methodology. A structured approach to a particular job, such as systems analysis and design (e.g. SSADM— Structured Systems Analysis and Design Methodology).

MICR. *See* MAGNETIC INK CHARACTER RECOGNITION.

microcomputer. A small—typically single-user—computer, usually known as a personal computer (PC).

minicomputer. An intermediate-sized computer with capabilities and price between those of mainframe computers and microcomputers. Examples include IBM AS/400 and DEC VAX.

MIPS. Measurement of computer power, in Millions of Instructions Per Second.

modem. The device which converts the digital signal from a computer into an analogue signal required for a telephone line, then back again (MOdulator-DEModulator).

MTBF. Mean Time Between Failures. Expected operational time before a failure occurs.

multilevel security. Provisions for

simultaneous processing at two or more levels of security.

multiplexer (concentrator). A device that controls information sequentially from several input lines to an output line.

Multiple Virtual Storage (MVS). An operating system for IBM mainframes.

Natural. A 4GL, linked to the ADABAS database.

NBS. The US National Bureau of Standards, now National Institute of Standards and Technology (NIST).

need to know. A policy that restricts access to classified information to personnel whose duties necessitate such access.

network security controller. A secure computer that mediates security functions for a network.

networks. Associated components interconnected for such functions as communications and resource sharing.

NIST. National Institute of Standards and Technology.

node. Equipment in a communications network at a point where two or more lines converge, or at a network termination point. The equipment may be a computer, terminal, switch or concentrator.

node encryption. A method of encryption of network data in which the data is decrypted within an intermediate node, and re-encrypted under a different key for onward transmission. The decryption and re-encryption is performed in secure modules, and thus plaintext is not transmitted through the node. *Compare* with END-TO-END ENCRYPTION.

noise. Extraneous and unwanted signal disturbances.

Nomad. A 4GL.

NSA. National Security Agency.

object code. The machine language generated by a compiled program.

OCR. *See* OPTICAL CHARACTER RECOGNITION.

off-line. Processing equipment which is not connected to a computer or network, or the operations performed on such equipment.

office automation. The use of IT to support office and clerical activities, such as word processing, telex and desktop publishing.

on-line. Data processing and communication equipment which is connected to a computer or communication channel.

Open Systems Interconnection (OSI). A set of standards to enable computers from different suppliers to inter-work. OSI has seven layers, ranging from the ability to transfer data to the ability for applications to work co-operatively on different machines.

operating system. The software resident within a computer's memory which controls all the activities of the computer. Examples include MVS/XA, VM/CMS, VMS, VME, DOS and UNIX.

optical character recognition (OCR). The ability of computers to read printed text (as used on cheques, gas bills, etc).

Optical disk. Very high density storage medium using laser data reading.

Oracle. A combined 4GL and DBMS.

OSI. *See* OPEN SYSTEMS INTERCONNECTION.

PABX. *See* PRIVATE AUTOMATIC BRANCH EXCHANGE.

Packet Switch Stream (PSS). A BT

service providing switched data communications.

packet switching. A logical network transmission strategy for routing short segments of information (packets) independently through a network to maximise efficiency. Reassembly of data packets is required at the receiving end.

PACX. *See* PRIVATE AUTOMATED COMPUTER EXCHANGE.

parallel processing. Concurrent execution of multiple processes.

parity. A single-bit-assignment controlled to make the total number of ones in a sequence even (even parity) or odd (odd parity).

Pascal. A compiler and language developed to support structural programming techniques.

password. Unique identifying name or number which gives its holder access to a computer system.

patch. A section of code added to object code and thus not affecting the source code. Such patches may therefore bypass normal control procedures and could be used for illegal program modification.

PBX. *See* PRIVATE BRANCH EXCHANGE.

PC. *See* PERSONAL COMPUTER.

peer entity authentication. The action of communicating parties seeking to verify each other's identities.

penetration. Unauthorised physical or logical access or seizure of control functions.

peripherals. Devices that supplement the main functions of a processor (e.g. printers).

personal computer (PC). Micro-

computer such as IBM PS/2, Compaq, etc.

personal identification code (PIC). A sequence of letters and numbers used to verify the identity of a user of an ATM or terminal.

personal identification number (PIN). A unique number which enables a user of an ATM or remote terminal to complete a transaction.

physical access control. Measures which control access to a physical area or device, such as computers, peripheral equipment, communication gear, and buildings housing such equipment.

physical security. The use of locks, guards, badges, CCTV and similar measures to control access to a computer, other equipment or buildings.

PIC. *See* PERSONAL IDENTIFICATION CODE.

piggybacking. A method of gaining access to a system that involves intercepting signals to a terminal and modifying them before passing them on to a genuine user.

PIN. *See* PERSONAL IDENTIFICATION NUMBER.

PL/1. A 3GL.

plaintext. Unencrypted text, synonymous with CLEARTEXT.

point of sale (PoS). A term that describes systems used to record transactions at the point where sales are made.

port. A gateway between the memory and other devices in the computer (disks, printers etc), sometimes known as a channel.

port protection device (PPD). A device connected to the communications port of a computer which authorises user access to the port.

private automated computer exchange (PACX). A network data contention and switching system.

private automatic branch exchange (PABX). A computerised switchboard capable of handling both voice and data.

private branch exchange (PBX). Secure data switch for asynchronous and synchronous network data services.

PoS. *See* POINT OF SALE.

Prolog. A 3GL used to develop Knowledge Based Systems.

prototype. An approach to designing systems which typically uses 4GLs to experiment with different possible designs rather than spend a long time developing the system on paper first.

PSS. *See* PACKET SWITCH STREAM.

PTT. Post, Telegraph and Telecommunication authorities, who control the use of voice and data transmission within their own country.

public key encryption. Encryption technique in which there are two keys: one public, one private. The public key is used for encipherment but is not usable for decipherment. Security of the system relies on keeping the private key secret.

RACF. *See* RESOURCE ACCESS CONTROL FACILITY.

random access memory (RAM). RAM can be given values to hold temporarily. A computer's memory is made up of RAM. *Compare* ROM (READ ONLY MEMORY).

read only memory (ROM). Memory which cannot be overwritten. Used typically to hold the initial instructions required to start up the system.

record. A single set of related data within a file (e.g. details of one employee in a payroll file).

recovery. Restoration of computing facilities and capabilities.

relational database. A database design which allows dynamic linking of records from different files.

replay. A form of attack in which the message sequence is changed or a stored data item is replaced with a previously stored value. This form of attack can succeed even if the message or stored data item is authenticated or encrypted. In its simplest form, an attacker can simply record a message, including its authenticator, and re-insert it into the communication link. Such a message could, for example, cause a financial transaction to be performed twice.

Resource Access Control Facility (RACF). A security software product which controls logical user access to systems using IBM equipment.

reverse engineering. A process by which the design of a product is determined by a detailed study of the product itself.

reversible encryption. Transformation of plaintext in such a way that the encrypted text can be decrypted back to the original plaintext.

ring. A LAN topology where the data path is a ring.

risk analysis. An analysis of system assets and vulnerabilities to establish an expected loss from certain events based on estimated probabilities of the occurrence of those events.

Risk management. A disciplined approach adopted to identify, measure, and control uncertain events in order to minimise loss and optimise the return on the money invested for security purposes. Risk management encompasses risk analysis, management decision-making, and implementation of security measures and reviews.

Rivest-Shamir-Adleman (RSA). An algorithm which uses a trapdoor one-way function based upon the computational difficulty of factoring the product of large prime numbers (i.e. integers with several hundred decimal digits).

ROM. *See* READ ONLY MEMORY.

RSA. *See* RIVEST-SHAMIR-ADLEMAN.

safeguard. A protective measure to mitigate against the effect of system vulnerability.

salami technique. A computer fraud in which a criminal takes a little at a time from a large number of transactions.

scavenging. A physical or electronic technique for scanning through data or residue for useful knowledge which is not legitimately available.

schema. In databases, a map of the overall structure of a database.

scrambling. Mixing up the order of a sequence in a prescribed and unvarying way. Sometimes used in low-security applications for hiding information.

security log. A log of security-significant events, e.g. log-on, accesses to protected files, number of attempts at password entry, etc.

security officer. The senior member of management responsible for the organisation's information security, or a person delegated by that person to undertake specific information security responsibilities.

separation of duties. Structuring tasks so that each person has the least practical security exposure. For execution of critical tasks, the involvement of more

than one person should be required. Within IT, for example, separation of duties between programmers and the security officer is essential. The opportunity for any one person to subvert or damage the system must be minimised.

Sequential Query Language (SQL). The emerging 'standard' 4GL for accessing databases. Access to relational databases such as Ingres and DB2 requires the use of SQL. SQL can be used as a language in its own right or be embedded in a 3GL.

smart card. A card containing a microprocessor, ROM and RAM, used for high-risk functions such as point of sale transactions.

software. Instructions which control the computer. System software controls the operation of the computer, applications software develops systems such as stock control, payroll and word processing.

source code. The program (in Cobol, Fortran, etc) which is to be compiled.

spoofing. Misleading the system into performing an operation that appears normal but results in unauthorised activities.

SQL. *See* SEQUENTIAL QUERY LANGUAGE.

star. A LAN topology where all stations are connected through a central point.

store and forward. A system that stores message packets at intermediate points before further transmission.

supersmart card. A proposed new form of smart card with a microprocessor and 64 kilobytes of memory, a calculator with touch keys, a display window, a synthesised magnetic stripe and a battery. This card will allow off-line verification, identification and authorisation. It will also be possible to use the card with conventional ATMs and terminals; the user can simulate the magnetic stripe of conventional cards by keying instructions on the keyboard. In addition to the functions of conventional smart cards the supersmart card will provide the user with off-line display of customer information, transactions, account balances, credit limits etc.

superzapping. Using a program which bypasses application security controls.

SWIFT. Society for Worldwide Interbank Financial Telecommunication.

symmetric cipher. In cryptography, a cipher in which the enciphering and deciphering keys are equal, or can easily be deduced from one another.

system log. Data concerning connections, access and use of a computer system or network.

system penetration. Violation or circumvention of operating system safeguards.

systems development life cycle (SDLC). The process of developing and running a new system.

tailgating. Making use of another person's access rights after they have been authenticated. (This term can apply to physical or electronic access.)

tamper-resistant module. A device in which sensitive information, such as a master cryptographic key, is stored and cryptographic functions are performed. The device has one or more sensors to detect physical attacks by an adversary trying to gain access to the stored information, in which case the data is immediately destroyed.

tape streamer. A magnetic tape transport designed primarily for reading or writing continuous streams of data, normally used for backup operations.

telecommunications. The use of various communications facilities (networks, telephone lines, satellites, etc) to transfer data between locations and from computer to computer.

teletext. A method of transmitting information, stored on a computer, to suitably adapted domestic television sets. In broadcast services the data signals are transmitted in conjunction with normal TV programmes.

telex. An automatic dial-up teletypewriter switching service provided by common carriers.

Tempest. A program to meet the threat of information leakage by unintended physical communication channels.

Tempest-proofing. The prevention of undesirable radiation emission from a computer system which might otherwise enable an eavesdropper to record confidential information. Electromagnetic emission can escape by a variety of routes; to eliminate this risk, source suppression and encapsulation are used, together with shielding of all cables.

tiger teams. Teams of experts who legitimately test robustness of security features by attempted penetration.

time bomb. A set of program instructions entered without trace into a computer system to perform some function at a later time. Also referred to as a logic bomb.

token ring. A design of local area network which avoids message collisions by allowing a communication node to transmit a message only when it possesses a network 'token'.

traffic padding. A technique used to disguise traffic flows; it includes padding out messages to standard lengths, generating spurious messages, and using spurious connections.

transaction key. A technique in which the cryptographic key, employed to protect a transaction, is derived at the terminal and host computer, using secret information available at each. Thus the key does not have to be transmitted.

transaction processing monitor (TP monitor). Software such as IBM's CICS, which provides a secure, easy-to-use environment within which large on-line applications can run successfully.

transparent. A process or procedure which is invoked by a user who is unaware of its existence.

trapdoor. An intentional or unintentional weakness in a system that can be exploited by an intruder to gain access to it.

Trojan Horse. The addition to a system of an apparently useful program that contains routines that collect, modify or destroy data.

trusted computing base (TCB). The totality of hardware and software security features in a computer system.

trusted software. Software that is depended upon to perform special security functions.

turnkey. A total system package, including hardware and software.

twisted pair. Twisted insulated conductors used for short-distance information transmission.

uninterruptible power supply (UPS). A device inserted between a power source and a system, to ensure that the system is guaranteed a precise, uninterrupted power supply, irrespective of variations in the power source voltage.

user-selected PIN. A PIN chosen by the user and conveyed to the bank where it is stored with the corresponding account numbers.

utilities. Special programs provided with operating systems (e.g. sort and merge, compilers, etc).

vaccine. A program for detecting and protecting against virus programs.

Virtual Memory System (VMS). Operating system for VAX computers.

virus. A program which infects other programs by modifying them to include a copy of itself.

VMS. *See* VIRTUAL MEMORY SYSTEM.

voice mail. A system in which spoken information is digitised and stored either in a network memory or in the appropriate apparatus at the destination for the message. The spoken message is later retrieved by the called party.

vulnerability. A weakness in control which could be exploited to gain unauthorised access to information or disrupt critical processing.

white card fraud. A form of credit card fraud using a counterfeit credit card.

wide area network (WAN). Telecommunications links over a wide area (nationally and internationally) using leased lines, satellites, etc.

wiretapping. Unauthorised interception of messages. The purpose of passive wiretapping is to disclose message contents without detection, while active wiretapping involves the deliberate modification of messages, sometimes for the purpose of injecting false messages, injecting replays of previous messages or deleting messages.

worm. Unauthorised coding which travels through a computer system or network, by copying itself, overwriting data and software in the process.

X.25. A standard for transmission of data using packet-switching techniques on public data networks (PDNs).

X.400. A standard for electronic mail interchange.

ZAP. (1) Unauthorised modification of a program to bypass its control mechanisms. (2) To destroy data or programming.

Index